Contents

INSULTING THE PUBLIC?
The British press and the European Union

Peter J. Anderson and Tony Weymouth

 LONGMAN

London and New York

Addison Wesley Longman Limited
Edinburgh Gate
Harlow
Essex CM20 2JE
England
and Associated Companies throughout the world

Published in the United States of America
by Addison Wesley Longman Inc., New York

Visit Addison Wesley Longman on the world wide web at:
http://www.awl-he.com

First published 1999

ISBN 0 582 31740 1

British Library Cataloguing-in-Publication Data

A catalogue record for this book is available from the British Library

Library of Congress Cataloging-in-Publication Data

Typeset by 43 in 10/11pt Palatino
Printed in Malaysia, PP

Anderson, Peter J.,   1954-
      Insulting the public? : the British press and the European Union /
   Peter J. Anderson and Tony Weymouth.
         p.   cm.
      Includes bibliographical references and index.
      ISBN 0-582-31740-1 (pbk.)
      1. Press--Great Britain.   2. European Union--Press coverage.
   3. European Union--Great Britain.   4. Press and politics--Great
   Britain.   I. Weymouth, Tony, 1938-   .   II. Title.
   PN5124.E87A53   1999
   072'.09'045--dc21   98-45964
                                                                          CIP

Preface

Britain's relationship with the European Union has rarely run smoothly and never has this turbulent liaison been more controversially depicted than in certain sectors of the British press.

In this book we have attempted an assessment of the performance of the British press, in relation to the EU, in the period immediately preceding the General Election of 1997, and during the British presidency of the Union from January to June 1998. But we do not confine our analysis to the task of assessing press performance alone. We also identify some of the possible key consequences of this performance for the interests of British citizens.

We have approached this study mainly from two disciplinary perspectives. The first has its origins in media/discourse analysis, and the second in political science. This is a powerful and fruitful alliance that has allowed us to identify some fundamental character-istics of media discourse, on the one hand, and to assess, on the other, the quality of its content by reference to the European debate that has taken place within the disciplines of political science and international studies during recent years. We have tried especially to make two complex areas of study accessible to the non-specialist reader and to demonstrate that they are indeed mutually enhancing in important ways.

Such an approach is not without problems. Discourse analysts may feel we have hardly touched the surface of what could have been said about the texts we have examined. Similarly, political scientists may also reflect that not all the European debate is included here. All true. But our objective is to offer a picture of Europe on a broad multi-disciplinary front to readers from a variety of different academic and professional backgrounds, and to show how the issues have, or have not, been represented in the press. We would particularly hope that our approach will make our findings and commentary of interest to press professionals and students of both the media and European politics/international relations.

For readers who may wish to become acquainted with the arts of discourse analysis, in a media context, Chapter 1 makes essential reading and Appendix I provides further help. Others more directly interested in the political aspects of the question, could, if they wished, read the conclusion of Chapter 1 and proceed directly to Chapter 2 and the other chapters.

Among the many organisations, political and commercial, which have helped us, we are particularly grateful for the cooperation of several national newspapers, the Press Complaints Commission and the Representation of the European Commission Office in London. Our special thanks are also due to the following whose help, encouragement and advice were crucial in the preparation of the manuscript: Norman Fairclough, Aileen McLeod, Keith Jenkinson, Charlotte Thomas, Claire Wieclawska, Gordon Parsons, Saleel Nurbhai, Phillippa Sherrington, and Sally Driscoll. If we have ignored their advice, we have done so at our peril.

Important note

Late in the preparation of this book we encountered unforeseen obstacles to its completion in its intended form. This was due to the refusal by some authors, or their agents, to grant permission to reproduce certain extracts from articles written for the News International publications *The Times* and the *Sun*.

As researchers and writers used to operating under the 'fair dealing' principle in matters of copyright, the limited quotation from articles, providing there is full acknowledgement, is for us the very stuff of free speech and open debate which we take for granted. Our experience in this connection with News International indicates that this assumption is unfounded and this is cause for concern, particularly as the material we wished to quote represented the opinions of some well known journalists and public figures in the Eurosceptic camp.

Rather than cut out all mention of these articles – they were after all selected for their importance, interest and relevance – we have decided to indicate in our text all instances where we have been prevented from printing a particular extract and to give a brief account of its content and noteworthiness. We also indicate how our readers may best gain access to these articles. Past copies of *The Times* are frequently held in libraries on CD-ROM or microfiche; past editions of the *Sun* may not be held but can be consulted if necessary on micro-film in the British Library. Where it is possible for readers to consult these texts we strongly recommend that they do so.

Acknowledgements

We are grateful to the following for permission to reproduce copyright material:

Steve Bell for a cartoon from the *Guardian* 19.3.97, © Steve Bell, all rights reserved; Demos Ltd for an extract from *The Search for European Identity* by Mark Leonard (1998); Express Newspapers plc for extracts from articles in editions of the *Daily Express* newspaper; Guardian and Observer News Service Ltd for extracts from articles in editions of the *Guardian* newspaper, © The Guardian; Independent Newspapers (UK) Ltd for extracts from articles in editions of the *Independent* newspaper; The Financial Times Limited for extracts from articles in editions of the *Financial Times* newspaper; Ewan MacNaughton Associates for extracts from articles in editions of the *Daily Telegraph* newspaper; The Mirror Group for extracts from articles in editions of the *Daily Mirror* newspaper; News International Syndication for extracts from articles in editions of the *Sun* newspaper; News International Syndication for extracts from articles in editions of *The Times* newspaper, © Times Newspapers Ltd and a cartoon from *The Times Magazine* 8.3.97; Oxford University Press for an extract from *The Economics of the European Union* edited by M.J. Artis and N. Lee (1995) and an extract from *Policy-making in the European Union* edited by H. Wallace and W. Wallace (1996) and Solo Syndication Ltd for extracts from articles in editions of the *Daily Mail*.

CHAPTER 1

The press, Europe and questions of cultural identity

Introduction

This book is specifically about the portrayal of the European Union in the British press in the year preceding the General Election of 1997 and during the British EU presidency of 1998. It embraces a study of two fundamental elements in our democracy: first, the organisation and role of the media in general, but particularly that of the written press, and second, and more importantly, the nature and quality of the process of mediation in respect of Britain's current and future role within the European Union.

To take the European issue first: in the year preceding the General Election of 1997, Britain's future role in the development of the European Union was thrust into the foreground of public debate by the right wing of the Conservative Party. Indeed, in one of the more dramatic moments of the election campaign itself (April 1997) the then Prime Minister, John Major, presented the nature of Britain's future engagement with the EU as the single most important issue upon which the fate of the government should turn. In the event, this insight into the most important issue occupying the minds of the electorate appears to have been clouded. What, in retrospect, now looks clear is that John Major's gamble served only to emphasise his party's deep divisions over Europe with what some observers have deemed to be fatal results.

It is probably true to say that the most articulate expression of 'Euroscepticism' is indeed located in the parliamentary Conservative Party. But it also found expression to the right of it in the Referendum Party, and to the left, among 'old' Labour parliamentarians such as Douglas Jay, Tony Benn and, most recently, the former speaker of the House of Commons, the late Lord Tonypandy. Euroscepticism, then, is a phenomenon which straddles the political divide, both inside and outside Westminster, although its most intense manifestation (and most pronounced consequences) has been mostly apparent on the right of British politics.

The new British government under the premiership of Tony Blair has a self-declared more unanimous and relaxed attitude towards Britain's role in the European Union. Nevertheless, it is clear that New Labour is proceeding in its approach to the issue of our future EU commitments in a manner which ranges from caution (employment, single currency, common foreign policy, fishing) on the one hand, to outright resistance (abolition of frontier controls, common defence force and foreign policy) on the other. The proposed move by the EU to the single currency means that the New Labour government (and indeed the British people, since they will be consulted by referendum) face a period of difficult decision making in respect of Britain's political, social and economic participation in Europe in the twenty-first century and beyond.

We come now to the second element, the part played by the media in this process of decision making about Europe. Political action in a western liberal democracy does not normally occur in an arbitrarily imposed and unannounced fashion. If it does then there are other names for the regime – autocratic, authoritarian, totalitarian – with which to qualify its character. The political process in Britain is the expression (however convoluted) of public opinion expressed regularly at the ballot-box and less formally through other means between elections. Public opinion, in turn, is constituted and shaped by information being presented to the public sphere (via parliament, official reports, on-the-spot investigative journalism) and its sub-sequent relaying to the people by the media. So, along with the rest, British policy towards further European integration is mostly repres-ented to the people by the media. We find our information, and form our opinions, by consulting, using and interacting with one of the most sophisticated systems of communications in the world.

In this study we set out to answer some important questions about the democratic process in Britain today which relate specifically to the origins of information about Europe, and to the manner in which this information is relayed to the public by the media in general and by the press in particular. To be more specific, these questions envelop complex and sensitive issues linked to perceptions of national identity, to our history, to political and economic contingencies, and to the role of the media in representing (or mediating) these issues to the public. As these themes suggest, we shall need to approach the subject via a series of questions which invite answers from a range of disciplines and sources. These questions, to which some answers will be sought in the course of this book, may be summarised as follows:

- How do the British perceive themselves? Is this perception justifi-able and in any case does it support or undermine further development in British participation inside the EU?
- How are British claims to identity and special interests represented to the public?
- What are the arguments for and against Britain's further integra-tion with the European Union?
- What is the quality of representation of European issues in the media in general and how does the public interact with this representation?
- Does the written press in particular offer an adequate representa-tion of these European issues to the public?

Specifically, in this chapter we shall examine aspects of what, for want of a more precise term, may be called British cultural identity, and the way in which this identity is expressed in media discourse. We shall point to a trend towards an alleged *conversationalisation* of public discourse, to the presence of media bias in both overt and covert forms, and comment upon the way in which these phenomena may influence or be used by the public. Finally, we shall propose an approach to the analysis of media texts – critical discourse analysis – which underlines and takes account of the essential socio-cultural factors which underpin, and bear upon, the diverse expressions of media discourse within a modern democracy such as Britain. This chapter, then, lays the foundations for a fuller understanding of our commentaries on the press coverage of Europe which we offer in Chapters 3, 4 and 5. We shall maintain the focus upon the representation of Europe by frequent illustrations of discourse taken from the press on this topic.

Let us begin this chapter then by examining certain contemporary issues which are linked to the concept of cultural identity in Britain and the manner in which this identity finds, or fails to find, its expression in the media.

Perceptions of identity

There are today diverse and widespread perceptions held by a variety of social and ethnic groups relating to an imagined community called Britain, and they partly account for ambiguous British attitudes towards continental Europe. In particular, there is one perception (to which we shall return a little later in this chapter) which is noteworthy at this point, if only to demonstrate how perceptions of ourselves may change in the course of a few decades.

There was a time, not so long ago, when a perceived British fondness for reticence, understatement and stiff upper-lipped authority was a longstanding and slightly baffling joke among people who lived beyond our national frontiers. It was, of course, a myth, or at least a very incomplete perception, and one furthermore which was half-encouraged (since it was a convenient and mostly benign caricature), possibly originating in our imperial past, and our geographical and linguistic isolation from the rest of Europe. One characteristic of a mythical, imagined identity is its tendency towards over-generalisation, sometimes to the point where the original grain of truth loses its force. It seems unlikely that the British *by nature* are or were any less outgoing than the French or the Italians, or any other peoples for that matter. This particular view of ourselves, as we have said, may derive from linguistic and geographical factors as well as from a limited contact abroad with a group of British colonial administrators, diplomats, soldiers, scholars, and well-heeled travellers who together constituted a small and mannered social elite. In the light of the current revival of interest in regional and national identity in Scotland, Wales and Ireland, this perception of cultural identity, extrapolated from a small elite of English language speakers and applied to the whole national community, has long outlived its uses. If we add to this revival of regionalism the presence of people who constitute significant ethnic minorities living in

3

Britain today, then the original perception described above becomes even less sustainable.

We shall return to the role that an imagined cultural identity plays in British attitudes towards Europe later in this section. For the moment we use the example quoted above to underline the difficulty in reconciling such a self-serving view of ourselves (self-serving, that is, for a particular minority at a particular time in history) with those now emerging from regional, ethnic and other social groupings (not the least of which was that which emerged from the explosion of a youth culture in the 1960s), which have apparently turned this particular myth on its head. In the latter case, the irreverence, raucousness and distinctly uncontrolled outburst of cultural determination which began thirty or so years ago, is the very antithesis of the earlier representation of restraint, understatement and authority fostered at a different time by a different social stratum of British society.

How, then, should the British be perceived or perceive themselves? The wise counsel must be 'with extreme caution'. Social theorists are at pains to point out the pitfalls that beset traditional views in matters relating to cultural identity. Perceptions based upon popular notions of historical 'essence' of the kind commonly expressed in some sectors of the media (see Chapter 3) are considered, at best, partial and, at worst, crude representations of cultural identification. Hall and others, offer a traditional view of cultural identification (in order to refute it) of the kind we have mentioned briefly above as follows:

> ... identification is constructed on the back of a recognition of some common origin or shared characteristic with another person or group, or with an ideal, and with a natural closure of solidarity and allegiance established on this foundation. (Hall, 1996:2)

It is worth briefly noting here that this traditional attitude towards cultural identity, which characterises some media representation (although no longer in quite the crude fashion as in our original example) in Britain, is not restricted to this country alone. Nor, it has to be said, is it completely without foundation: claims to group identity based upon ethnic characteristics and historical events can be valid but they are always incomplete and transitory. These kinds of traditional, historically rooted perceptions of identity are to be found in all western democracies. However, Hall and other contemporary social theorists disavow this traditional (or essentialist) view in favour of what may be called a process of *discursive practice*. In this light, cultural identification is not perceived in terms of a set of cohesive features – our essence – identifiable in our past as well as our present. It is seen instead as an ongoing process of construction which is never completed. For Hall identity is a phenomenon of *becoming* rather than being, of where we are going rather than of who we are. The concept of 'closure' mentioned above, and associated by social theorists with the essentialist view of group identity, designates the response made by a specific social group, at a specific place and time (usually at a time of uncertainty) which is intended to defend a perceived *status quo* from some external threat or 'the Other' as the latter is often referred to in the literature. This 'closure' around a perceived identity, according to Bauman, is 'a name given to the escape sought to that uncertainty' (Bauman, 1996:19). Thus (and relating to an important aspect of the subject matter of this book), according to contemporary social theory it could plausibly be argued that one element at least of recent expressions of Euroscepticism in Britain stems from the presence of and perceived threat from an external 'Other', namely continental Europe. To elaborate slightly: contemporary views in social theory support the explanation that traditional cultural identity, claimed for Britain in some sections of the mass media and elsewhere, is based on perceptions not only of what Britain *is* in terms of its historical essence, but also upon perceptions of what Britain is *not* in certain key domains of our national life, compared with the rest of Europe. In other words, in addition to its alleged 'essence', its identity is further constituted negatively in response to the (external) presence of the 'Other'. Let us support this proposal more fully by examples, taken from our data, which suggest that this kind of traditional perception of identity is inferred by a negative response and closure to Europe in certain key domains frequently represented in the media as follows:

Economic: the British pound is sound (as opposed to the currencies of several European countries which are weak or weakening). Joining the single currency will undermine basic, proven British freedoms to control and determine Britain's economic future. Britain's economy is strong but, if we join a single currency, it will be subsumed under the authority of a central bank directed by and located in Germany. The British taxpayer will subsidise the public expenditure of other governments whose economies are less efficient.

Political: Britain's historically proven record in parliamentary democracy is among the best in the world. Its authority is likely to be subsumed under that of a (non-elected) EU bureaucracy – the European Commission. In particular Britain historically has excelled in its own brand of foreign policy. Further involvement in Europe means loss of control in this crucial domain.

Ideological: Britain's traditional political groupings have their origins in a kind of non-doctrinaire pragmatism which has contributed significantly to the political stability of the nation. These current political groupings are in danger of being undermined by the strands of radical republicanism (republicanism moreover in which the residues of communism remain) still at large in contemporary European political thinking (whence the 'Social Chapter' of the Treaty of Maastricht).

Military: Britain is strong militarily. Its national security is at risk by any further military integration of its armed forces with those of the member states of the EU. A coordinated military presence under the aegis of NATO and comprising national rather than supranational contingents is the preferred alternative.

Health: Britain is a healthy nation and health standards are rising. Just as Europe was historically the origin of plague and disease, it still constitutes a health threat in the case, say, of rabies and other diseases which until recently were effectively excluded by a maritime frontier.

Religion: (Northern Ireland) Britain is historically a founder member of a community of protestant nation-states. Europe is the source of popery and the anti-Christ.

(This list can be considerably expanded to include other domains, such as industrial relations, industry, the legal system and so on.)

We have outlined above, somewhat simply, the way in which some groups may be said to lay claim to a particular cultural identity by means of the two processes of identification and closure. Both processes could be used in plausible, traditional terms by a journalist arguing from a particular socio-economic-historical-cultural perspective (although it is unlikely that either term 'essence' or 'closure' would be used to designate the line drawn around a set of identifying features). We would wish to argue, however, that these processes are more satisfactorily and usefully explained, as we have suggested above, as being constituted by the presence of a perceived external threat, in this case a supra-national 'Other' in the form of the European Union. We shall provide examples taken from the media which further illustrate the process of closure later in this chapter. At this point, let us add a new, historical perspective to national identity, to the view stemming from social theory outlined above.

Marquand, in a penetrating historical analysis of British (and sometimes English) self-perceptions, quotes Churchill's 'Humble Address to the Sovereign' in 1945 as a classic example of what he calls a 'Whig-imperialist' view of the past (and the then) British state:

> ...but it is kingship to which all the other governments of the Empire feel an equal allegiance ... It is the golden circle of the Crown which alone embraces the loyalties of so many states and races all over the world...
>
> ...we may certainly flatter ourselves. The wisdom of our ancestors has led us to an envied and enviable situation. We have the strongest parliament in the world. We have the oldest, the most famous, the most secure, the most serviceable monarchy in the world. King and parliament both rest safely and solidly upon the will of the people expressed by free and fair election on the basis of universal suffrage. Thus the system has long worked harmoniously both in peace and war. (Marquand, 1995:186)

According to Marquand, this Churchillian perception of British identity which had emerged from a uniquely successful political history, defined (or redefined) the nation as, in essence, 'imperial, oceanic, discoverers of the secrets of free government and gradual progress' (Marquand, 1995:186). He claims that this imperial attitude dominated post-war British thinking on both the left and right and that, despite the loss of empire and the unravelling of the imperial coat, it still exists as a significant perception today. It exists even though time and events have moved on. In an argument which supports the one we have already outlined above, Marquand points out that the United Kingdom (an apparent misnomer) is now the site of heterogeneous forces which find expression in a plurality of voices ranging from ethnic minority groups, which have settled here in the post-war period, to the more strident tones of the regionalists coming from Scotland, Ireland and, to a lesser extent, Wales and elsewhere. Marquand claims – significantly for this media-centred study – that the unravelling of the Whig-imperialist political underpinning of British society has left a *vacuum of language* reflecting a vacuum of feeling with regard to Europe (Marquand, 1995:189). Marquand's point of view is very persuasive. There is indeed an absence of widely accessible discourse which positively locates Britain economically, politically and socially as part of a greater Europe or indeed, for that matter, as an evolving site of socio-cultural plurality.

Discourse

If social identity is not God-given nor derives from other less divine forms of 'givenness' (e.g. history or ethnic origin) whence does it come? Contemporary thinking identifies language as the principal vector of self and other perceptions. Social theorists such as Foucault and Hall take the view that identity is determined not by 'essentialist' claims to being, but is *constructed* instead in what may be called a process of *discursive practice* or *discourse*. It is commonplace among social theorists, and discourse analysts to view language not merely as a system of meaning but as a mode of action which is historically and socially situated. Language is shaped by society and in turn socially shaping in its own right. It is this dynamic, changing process which is referred to as discourse. Discourse, through language, is the way in which we simultaneously represent our 'lifeworld', enact and negotiate social relations and create our social identity. According to Fairclough and others, this social use of language, or discourse, is simultaneously constitutive of three important interactive social phenomena: *social identity, social relations* and *systems of knowledge,* and discourse itself is seen as existing hierarchically in what he calls *orders of discourse*[1] (Fairclough, 1995:54–55). Orders of discourse, are further characterised by *discourse types* and *genres*. A discourse type, for example, could be the specific form and content of the interactive language that occurs between doctor and patient, teacher and pupil, rock singer and audience, journalist and reader. The genre of the discourse type refers to its organisational structure, that is, whether it is an interview, a speech, an advert, or whatever.

A further important distinction can be made within these orders of discourse and between discourse types by what is called *public* and *private* discourse. An example of a public discourse could be the Queen's Speech at the opening of parliament or the opening headlines on the 6 o'clock news (Radio 4), whilst a private discourse might be a telephone conversation between friends.

The importance of this kind of analytical approach to media discourse proposed by Fairclough can hardly be overstated. It is rooted in the multi-disciplinary domain of critical discourse analysis (CDA) and is inspired by a wide body of work from sociolinguistics and by contemporary social theory of the kind proposed by Foucault (1972), Bourdieu (1977) and others. Fairclough's work is significant because it draws our attention to a proposed systematic relationship between language and power. If the media do exert an influence over the public, and it is generally accepted that they do, then it is in this kind of approach that the nature of that power may be revealed.

At this stage we need to remind ourselves of two points. The first is that because discourse, or more precisely, discourse types, are perceived as forms of action as well as of knowledge, situated in time and social context, they are also perceived to be in a state of constant change (a) internally to the social group from which they spring (notice for example the stylistic change and the increasing numbers of discourse types occurring in radio broadcasting since 1945), and (b) in terms of their dominance or relative importance in the overall orders of discourse existing within a community at a particular point in time. The second is the claim that these discourse types are the most powerful expression of personal and group identity within a given culture. The turbulent socio-cultural transformations which British society has undergone since 1945, and which have accelerated in the last two decades of the twentieth century, find their respective identities in, and are shaped by, new types of constantly evolving discourse types. These partial, and often transitory identities (in the sense that they often outlive their relevance), embodied in a particular discourse type, are nevertheless resilient phenomena and appear never to efface themselves completely from our cultural/discursive recall. They recede rather than disappear altogether into a collective background, lie dormant in the wainscotting and upholstery of memory to be resuscitated in a time of perceived national need. We would argue that the residue of 'Whig-imperialist' attitudes is a good example of how a former perception, outdated in Marquand's sense, remains as an important influence within our contemporary discourse and still finds expression in various discourse types one of which, Churchill's speech, we have quoted above. We shall return to this theme later in this study when we discuss in greater detail British attitudes towards closer union with the rest of Europe.

The conversationalisation of media discourse: bias and ideology

Fairclough and Fowler and others have pointed to a trend in media discourse, related to socio-cultural change, which they call the *conversationalisation* of public language. This process is one which effectively serves to weaken the boundaries between private and public discourse with the adoption by the latter of colloquial speech patterns, non-specialised vocabulary and even 'taboo' words which a decade ago would not have found their way onto the airwaves or into newspaper columns. Readers may recall a *Today* presenter on Radio 4, in the spring of 1997, referring to a character in the *Archers* as 'a bit of a shit'. This succinctly illustrates the phenomenon which Fowler and others (see Fowler, 1991; Fairclough, 1995; Giddens, 1991; Featherstone, 1991) generally identify as 'conversationalisation', 'de-traditionalisation' or 'informalisation' of public discourse.

Below are three longer examples of different kinds of media texts. Texts 1.1 and 1.2 illustrate the manner in which the boundaries between private and public discourses have become blurred over the last half-century. Text 1.1 is a version of public discourse in use in the mid-twentieth century whilst Text 1.3 is a contemporary one. Text 1.2 exemplifies a strong version of a trend towards 'conversationalisation' in what was formerly deemed to be a domain of public discourse.

Text 1.1 Example of mid-twentieth century (predominantly) formal public discourse (*Daily Herald*, 18 September 1944)

Neutrality Myth

> Britain's sympathy for the low countries and her knowledge of their contribution to Europe dates far back into history.
> Belgians and the Dutch sought their safety in the illusion of neutrality.
> We can hardly blame their rulers. Purblind British statesmanship instructed the world in the impracticability of a collective system. We can hardly blame them if they took us at our word. Our interests and theirs have been interlocked for centuries.

Text 1.2 Example of late-twentieth century (predominantly) conversationalised public discourse (The *Sun*, 17 June 1997)

Stand by to spend a cent
(The Eurocrats have just banned the penny)

> Brits may soon be unable to spend a penny – because Eurocrats plan to kill off our favourite coin after more than 1,200 years . . .
> Brussels bosses intend to replace the penny – introduced by Anglo-Saxon king Offa around 750 AD – with the new Euro Cent.
> But the cash Brussels hopes we will use immediately came under fire. Shocked coin experts predicted that the new 'funny money' would be deeply unpopular . . .
> Britain and Germany ganged up to stop France cooking the books to qualify. But that may backfire on debt-ridden Germany.

Text 1.3 A contemporary version of a public discourse moving towards the conversational style (*Guardian*, 17 June 1997)

Bank official coins it with winning euro design

> A Belgian Bank official, Luc Luycx, has won a £17,000 design for the eight single currency coins, writes Stephen Bates.
> The coins depict the map of Europe with the other side reserved for a national symbol. The 1, 2 and 5 cent coins show Europe 'situated in the world' – a small globe against a backdrop of straight lines connecting six stars on one side with six on the other. The larger one and two euro coins show the European Union without borders – although Britain and Ireland remain separated from the rest by the channel . . .

Without embarking upon a detailed analysis of the three texts, a brief examination will reveal their essential differences. The public discourse of the *Daily Herald* text is predominantly formal in grammar, vocabulary and style. Indeed, some might argue that its style is more formal than that of the *Guardian* text even though the target readership for each paper is socially very widely separated. The inclusion of the archaic item 'purblind' (meaning dimsighted or obtuse) pushes the text very firmly in the direction of a formal, public discourse. It is worth noting two points at this stage: first the *Daily Herald* was a paper designed to be read by a largely working-class public; second, the text is direct, clear and comprehensible, but makes few concessions to working-class speech variation (even so, the meaning of 'purblind', despite its odd prefix, is easily worked out). Opinions as to the role of this type of public discourse, its merits (informative, educative and disarmingly 'spin-less'?), and demerits (top-down expression of class and possible gender domination?) vary considerably and will be discussed in more detail at a later stage in this book.

We referred above to the *Herald*'s discourse as being *predominantly* formal in style. We are choosing our words carefully here and should explain. For convenience – in order not to over-complicate what is a complex process – we have so far characterised discourse trends in terms of a shift away from formal public discourse types, on the one hand, towards those of informal discourse types, on the other. These trends are often realised by a phenomenon which discourse analysts refer to as *intertextuality*. The concept of intertexuality designates the presence of not one, but several discourse types within a single discourse genre (e.g. a newspaper article). Thus, in the *Herald* article in Text 1.1 above, we can distinguish between at least two discourse types occurring consecutively. The first is formal discourse type of which 'Belgians and Dutch sought their safety in the illusion of neutrality' is a good example. The second is a less formal discourse type which has the resonances of a more conversational style realised by the use of the personal pronouns 'we' and 'us', the possessive 'our' and the slightly colloquial phrase 'took us at our word' in 'we can hardly blame them if they took us at our word'. Discourse genres such as newspaper articles, by the frequent juxtaposition of different discourse types, exemplify this phenomenon of intertextuality often to express different degrees of formality (or informality). In the case of the *Herald*, the overall impression is still one of distinct formality. This is in sharp contrast to the discourse of its descendent the *Sun*, fifty years later, in a different socio-cultural context. Here, whilst we can still detect the residues of a more formal public discourse, the overall impression is one of distinct informality.

The *Sun* text is a good example of the way in which a type of public discourse has been predominantly conversationalised. The topic of the launch of the newly proposed Eurocurrency may be deemed to fall squarely into the public domain. Its representation however is both personalised and conversationalised (some may say 'trivialised') first by the lavatorial 'spin': the alleged importance for users of the new currency with regard to a colloquial euphemism, and second by the colloquial style overall, particularly at the end of the text where such items as 'ganged up on', 'cooking the books', and 'backfire' push the text firmly in the direction of an informal, conversational style. Like the *Herald* text, the *Sun* article is aimed at a reader who falls in the 'C' and 'D' category of social classification, that is to say those groups which in the mid-twentieth century were deemed to belong to the working class. The assumptions which can be inferred from the *Sun* and *Herald* texts about their readers could hardly appear more disparate.

The *Guardian* text, a contemporary version of public discourse, is closer in style to the *Herald* than it is to the *Sun* although, unlike the *Herald*, its readership is constituted firmly of social categories A and B – what used to be called the middle or professional classes. However, the temptation to pun in the title (albeit in a more relevant manner than in the *Sun* headline) and its simple, uncluttered structures are appropriate indications of the current trend, also apparent in the rest of the so-called quality press, towards a move in the direction of more informal, conversational discourse styles.

We stated with reference to the *Daily Herald* text above that it was 'direct, clear and comprehensible'. These are non-linguistic value judgements which could, and no doubt will, be challenged on the grounds of their subjectivity. We freely admit initially to having used our intuitions as first language English speakers in arriving at these conclusions. However, we can back them up with slightly more concrete notions of the underlying criteria for these judgements. By 'direct' we mean there is an absence of *obvious* 'spin'; the text appears to address the topic as worthy in its own right. This is not to suggest that the text is necessarily objective or neutral in its message[2] (also see the sub-section *Ideology* below). By 'clear and comprehensible' we mean that the text, although demanding of its target reader, is sufficiently accessible to enable the majority to understand the message. In contrast and by the same criteria, we would argue that the 'spin' placed on the *Sun* text obscures by trivialisation ('spending a penny/cent') the topic of the introduction of the Eurocurrency. Also, in contrast to the underlying assumptions to be inferred from the *Herald* – that its readership could be both challenged and informed – the *Sun* text appears to make no such assumptions. On the contrary, it meticulously avoids any structures or linguistic items which could be remotely construed as demanding of its target reader.[3] Why should this be so?

Before we attempt to answer that question, it is time to bring to the analysis of these two texts a more serious theoretical underpinning which goes beyond the intuitions we have offered so far. In the previous section we briefly mentioned three functions which Fairclough identifies as interacting simultaneously in discourse: *representations*,[4] *social identities* and *social relations*. In the case of the written press these functions can be defined and exemplified as follows:

- Representations designate, as the term suggests, the representing of a topic or communicable event, such as the introduction of the

Eurocurrency in the case of the *Sun* and *Guardian* texts, plus a point of view. This point of view occurs in both stated and in covert form (the covert aspect Fairclough calls *ideology*).

- Identities designate the presumed identity of writer and reader with regard to the event. This presumed identity may be, for example, that of a specialist reporter and a politically sympathising reader. The latter identity is illustrated by the *Herald* text, whereas in the *Sun* the writer assumes a non-specialist, humorous, emotional and hostile stance in relation to the event in question. The assumption here is that the reader is in sympathy with the writer's projected status and attitude, thereby endorsing their mutual identities.

- Relations designate a presumed relationship between writer and reader (e.g. formal or informal, close or distant). The *Sun* text implies a close, informal relationship whilst the *Herald* text suggests distance and formality.

We mentioned in an earlier section the state of change and regeneration which is a constant characteristic of discourse practice and which occurs in parallel with socio-cultural change. We offered as an example of this process of change the clear stylistic changes in the representation of the radio news over the last three decades. We also noted the progressive increase in the number of new discourse types establishing themselves currently within the order of media discourse. The most striking stylistic transformation, as we have already noted, is the trend towards the conversationalisation of information/news illustrated in this section by the *Sun* article (Text 1.2).

Using Fairclough's three inter-related and simultaneously operating discourse functions of representations, social identities and social relations, we can explain how a change in the relationship between these functions brings about the blurring of the boundaries between public and private discourse. We would argue that there has been a progressive weakening of the informational element of the representational function, and of its interaction with the other two, social identity and social relations, whose functions have become more dominant. There are several external socio-cultural factors which have influenced this change of emphasis within the internal structure of public discourse resulting in its progressive conversationalisation and it is to these that we can now turn.

The socio-cultural context

The principal socio-cultural factors which have influenced the trend towards conversationalisation of public discourse may be summarised as the following:

- A weakening of class boundaries which, it is claimed, has particularly affected former working-class people, as a consequence of changing work patterns.

- A clearer perception on the part of the public of their civil rights, social entitlements and privileges, encouraged by the introduction of the Welfare State and improved access to educational opportunities. These perceptions have been sharpened over the last decade or so by the emergence of a new source of 'consumer rights' stemming from the market.
- The post-war baby boom whose children grew into a social stratum in its own right with its own youth culture, associated economic power and specialised market.
- Advances in electronic technology which, from the transistor radio of the 1960s to the voyages in cyber space of the present, offer an exponential increase in communication outlets and in the demand for new discourse types on a scale unknown since the invention of the printing press.
- The dominant use of the image as the preferred mode of communication in Britain as in the rest of western democracies (conversational 'voice-over' and 'talking head').
- Finally, and perhaps most importantly, the advance of the global economy and, in the case of the mass media, the creation of a highly competitive market resulting in the commodification of information which is sold to the public (or 'consumers' as they are increasingly called) strictly on a profit basis.

Each one of these socio-cultural factors deserves a chapter to itself, but unfortunately they cannot be pursued here in greater detail since they are not the central focus of our study. We shall, however, return to some of them more fully a little later. For a comprehensive, engaging and clear account of post-1945 socio-cultural change in Britain see Hobsbawm (1994).

Let us now return to the mainstream of this discussion to examine a series of related issues relating to the nature of media representation itself.

Truth: a bouquet of thorns?

In a book with a title such as this one is, the question of the nature of media representation is unavoidable. It is generally agreed that terms with such philosophical connotations as 'truth' present media specialists with a bouquet of thorns which, if they are wise, is best left ungrasped. We too prefer not to enter this problematical domain. Nevertheless, there are truth-related issues such as the notions of impartiality, neutrality and objectivity which are constantly raised in a media context and which we must at least touch upon here. Within the wide range of media-related studies there is a matching spectrum of opinion which bears upon these elusive notions with varying degrees of persuasiveness. At one end of the continuum are located viewpoints founded upon democratic and ethical principles and their interaction with the pragmatic, day-to-day operations of the media. At the other are found a set of more complex, more theoretical propositions derived from social and cultural theory, and discourse analysis.

To take the pragmatic end first: McQuail, whilst acknowledging and rightly setting aside what he calls the 'naive notion of unambiguous truth' (McQuail, 1992:184) proposes a 'provisional version of objectivity' as follows:

- balance and even-handedness in presenting different sides of an issue;
- accuracy and realism of reporting;
- presentation of all main relevant points;
- separation of facts from opinion, but treating opinion as relevant;
- minimising the influence of the writer's own attitude, opinion or involvement;
- avoiding slant, rancour or devious purpose.

(Boyer, 1981, quoted in McQuail, 1992)

These guidelines represent a commonsensical view of media representation, and aspects of them frequently figure in discussions related to the constituent elements of media ethics. As another example of this 'ethical' approach, Lichtenberg points out that, unlike the press of the nineteenth century which made no claims to objectivity, the contemporary mass media do claim to describe the world 'as it is' and, in consequence, this assertion imposes upon them the obligation to perform in an objective and neutral manner in the processing and the relaying of information (Lichtenberg, 1990:124). Whilst attitudes such as Boyer's and Lichtenberg's are often expressed in media circles, not just by academics but by practitioners as well, they may indeed, by the standards of other theoreticians (see below), be judged to be naive in conception. Certainly they are little reflected in current journalistic practice in Britain today (apply Boyer's ethical criteria, for example, to the evaluation of the *Sun* text above). There can be few more partisan and biased newspapers in Europe than certain titles of the current British written press.

Bias

We have argued elsewhere (Weymouth and Lamizet, 1996) that bias in the media, and particularly in the written press, of the kind that takes account of the market (i.e. which accommodates the activity of advertisers), is a recurring and inevitable phenomenon. This is a cause for concern but not for total dismay. We would also wish to argue that in addition to this commercial bias, there are also political biases (overt and covert) of a sufficiently diverse nature to facilitate the critical debate in the public sphere (i.e. the existence of various newspapers of different political persuasions). This claim is subject to two conditions: first that these biases are understood by the public, and secondly, that the laws within which the press operates sustain a framework which promotes a pluralism of opinion (i.e. different titles) within the public sphere.

To some extent the first condition is satisfied in the British case. Few readers would mistake the right-wing rhetoric (the overt bias) of the *Daily Telegraph* or the *Spectator* for the left-of-centre opinions (again, overt bias) expressed in the *Guardian* or *New Statesman*. However, in some cases, events such as the spectacular political *volte-face* of the kind announced by the (now defunct) *Today* and in 1997 by the *Sun*, from supporting the right towards supporting the left must give rise to confusion on the part of readers and to scepticism on the part of critics who accuse Rupert Murdoch's News International of acting more out of market-driven opportunism than political conviction. Even so, where political bias is declared, and recognised as such by the public, it should be deemed to be a legitimate and necessary presence within the public sphere. Such declared political positions constitute the pluralism of representation (different voices) required to promote social cohesion through social group membership and the formation of public opinion. However, as we shall point out in greater detail below, whilst the political bias contained in the 'declared' rhetoric of the *Guardian* and the *Telegraph* may be readily perceived, it is less likely that their covert commercial and political bias is equally as well identified by the public. These covert forms of bias are referred to in the literature as *ideology* and we shall return to it shortly below.

With regard to the second of the two conditions mentioned above – the operational context of the British press and the extent to which it promotes a plurality of representation – there is equally a cause for concern. In Britain, in common with all other European countries, two trends dominate the written press: first, the overall decline in circulation over the last half-century and, second, the concentration of ownership of titles, in the same period, into the hands of a small number of powerful business groups. In Britain today, four large companies – News International, Mirror Group, United Newspapers, Daily Mail and General Trust plc – own between them over 90 per cent of the British national and Sunday press. Notwithstanding the wringing of hands by academics, journalists, press freedom campaigners and a few politicians, the trend of concentration of ownership continues. The argument which underlines and supports the presence of press bias, as we have already pointed out, is conditional upon a context of press pluralism. The current trend towards concentration of ownership must therefore be a significant issue in any examination of the quality of press performance in Britain today. We shall return to this issue in later chapters.

Truth as construct

If we accept the presence of bias in the media as both necessary and unavoidable, we arrive at the other more theoretical end of the spectrum relating to media representations. This approach to media representations of events assumes that they are realised, not impartially or objectively as Lichtenberg suggests they should be, but are projected instead into a known and understood political perspective from which they and their particular public present and make sense of the external world. This perception of the representation of events is therefore viewed as a process of opinion formation by discursive practice, the *construction* of a point of view, of the kind referred to earlier, rather than the expression of an impartial, eternal verity. If we can speak of truth at all with regard to the media, it is in the context of the simultaneous representation of different and often conflicting socio-political views culminating in an act of choice on the part of the public to belong or not to belong.

Two brief extracts from the press may help clarify what we mean. On 17 April 1997, Mr Major announced that Conservative MPs would be allowed a free vote on the issue of Britain joining a single European currency. This same event was represented respectively by *The Times* and the *Mirror* as follows:

Text 1.4   (*The Times*, 17 April 1997)

Major offers free vote on Europe

Text 1.5   (The *Mirror*, 17 April 1997)

Tories split on EU-turn

The single communicable event is represented by *The Times* as low-key procedural matter (a 'free' as opposed to 'whipped' vote), whereas in the *Mirror*, the same event is represented as doubly significant: a divisive reversal of policy. As can be seen, in each case a very different construct is placed upon the same communicable event. The particular 'truth' that is accepted here will be determined by the readers in their initial selection of a particular newspaper, and by the construct the latter places upon the event.

Commercial bias: the market

According to Habermas and others, the European written press has undergone a major structural transformation in the twentieth century which has been imposed largely by the influence of two related forces: the market on one hand, and the advertisers on the other. The result has been what he calls the 'homogenisation' of information, particularly at the editorial level within a newspaper, and the serious undermining of the 'rational–critical debate' relating to important issues in the public sphere. Habermas claims that the space occupied by the rational–critical debate has been usurped and replaced by a false agenda confected by the principal players in the media market – media groups, advertisers, individual press owners – who have privileged access to the media through wealth. This alleged manipulation of information in the public sphere has been given an additional impetus by the development of the corporate art of public relations. For Habermas the art of PR is a deception designed to exploit public opinion for political ends, or as he puts it: 'it mobilises for the firm an entire system of quasi-political credit, a respect that one displays towards a public authority' (Habermas, 1989:194). This point of view finds extensive support in media studies, particularly in the field of critical linguistics. Fowler unequivocally cites the economic interests in the press as forming a major influence upon the nature of its discourse styles:

> from the advertisers' point of view, the textual content of a newspaper must be broadly congruent with the products to be advertised, and this is a well-known constraint on what the paper can say. (Fowler, 1991:121)

This view is similarly expressed by Fairclough who, whilst acknowledging the plurality of voices in the press,[5] nevertheless insists that:

> ...these voices are so ordered that overwhelmingly the system, with respect to consumption and consumerism, is constantly endorsed and re-endorsed. (Fairclough, 1996:13)

Fairclough, in an engaging analysis of media discourse, advances the concept of covert bias in the media (ideology) to the point where he claims it is all-pervasive within their discourse styles, but with potentially varying degrees of effectiveness upon the public.

Ideology

For Fairclough, ideology comprises a set of assumptions and presuppositions (the 'given') within a particular discourse style which are realised linguistically and assumed to be held in common between writer and public relating to what Habermas has called a shared 'lifeworld'. The linguistic expression of these assumptions is implied in the discourse rather than overtly stated. According to Fairclough, and we have no reason to disagree, this ideological sub-text operates in the service of power, it impinges upon our decision making and produces 'unequal relations of power, relations of domination' (Fairclough, 1995:14). The role of the ideological content of the discourse is more significant in some texts than in others. Two examples will help illustrate the function of the ideological element within a particular discourse style or text.

The first is taken from the *Mail on Sunday*:

Text 1.6   (*Mail on Sunday*, December 1996)

Franco-German plot will hit Britain's wait-and-see policy
MAJOR OUT IN THE COLD

The first item of note is the omitted article 'the' or 'a' in the opening headline. It is a space saving and accepted journalistic style to omit the article, but the omission here of one or the other could be said to serve the ideological purpose of the discourse. The use of the definite article – *The* Franco-German Plot – may be deemed to be too strong since it suggests that both writer and reader know about it already, which is unlikely. On the other hand, the use of the indefinite article – *A* Franco-German Plot – could be deemed too weak since the existence of *the* plot is central to the discourse.[6] So the matter of whether the communicable event that has allegedly taken place between France and Germany is mutually shared is left in abeyance until we come to the second item, 'plot'. This latter item trades on a whole web of assumptions about foreigners, and in particular about German and French politicians, which appear in the British press at regular intervals. They have certainly appeared in one form or another in the *Daily Mail* in the last two years. They can be summarised (and anecdotally checked by the reader) as follows:

- There are a range of issues of specific interest to France and Germany from which Britain, either voluntarily or by design on the part of France and Germany, is excluded;
- The French and the Germans have the most to gain from joining a single currency;
- French and German politicians, particularly Jacques Delors, the late François Mitterrand and Chancellor Kohl are/were personally, passionately and possibly deviously committed to a single currency.

These assumptions, we suggest, have regularly appeared in the *Mail* over the last five years and in consequence form part of the assumptions or ideology which underpin its Eurosceptic discourse. It is important to understand that they are not events which are external to the discourse; they have all been 'said' before and, in their saying, entered into the shared knowledge between writer and reader. They stand, as it were, at the edge of the current discourse awaiting public recall and insertion into the current debate. Figure 1.1 shows in diagrammatic form how the utterance 'Franco-German Plot' draws upon assumptions made about shared knowledge and, by so doing, acquires an ideological force.

Communicable Event
(past discourses in smaller print)

Ideological Force
(paraphrased in italics)

French and Germans most to gain
from single currency

↓

Britain excluded voluntarily
or by design

↓

Franco-German Plot   =   *the* Franco-German plot
which we all know about
(*recall previous discourses*)

↑

German and French Politicians
passionately/deviously committed
to single currency

Figure 1.1 The 'given' ideology of a discourse type

The second example is taken from the spoken foreword by the former Speaker of the House of Commons, the late Lord Tonypandy, to the pre-election video put out by the Referendum Party in April 1997.

Text 1.7

> My support for Sir James Goldsmith's initiative is natural for me for I am in harmony with the sturdy defence of our British parliamentary system advanced by my predecessors in the Speaker's Chair of the House of Commons. For me to remain silent would be an act of treason, for such a cowardly act would betray the noble heritage handed on to me in the House of Commons. God bless you in your efforts as you battle for Britain. I wish you well.

This discourse is underpinned by an ideological content in which may be perceived clear references to other past discourses relating to the historical development of a parliamentary system in Britain (recall Marquand's arguments about Whig-imperialist attitudes mentioned above). 'The sturdy defence of our parliamentary system' is not in fact a direct reference to the one being conducted by the late Sir James Goldsmith, but to the one conducted in the past by 'my predecessors in the Speaker's Chair'. The 'given' here is the implied, historically rooted genius and superiority of the British parliamentary system which is threatened from without, by another 'given', the presence of the European Union. 'To remain silent' is synonymous with treason and cowardice, that is, the betrayal of a set of values enclosed within another historical 'given' – 'the noble heritage ... in the House of Commons'. The discourse ends with a benediction which implies a divine partiality for British-style democracy and includes the viewer, as sympathiser, in all the foregoing discourse(s): 'God bless you in your efforts as you battle for Britain', with even a passing reference to a former great British air victory in Europe in 1940.

Ideology, then – the implicit assumptions made about our 'lifeworld' and derived from previous discourses – is a universal characteristic of discourse itself. We accept Fairclough's opinion that it functions 'in the service of power' but the importance of its role is variable depending on the particular socio-cultural location of the particular discourse type. Thus in the classroom, for example, its influence is central to attitude formation among the young; equally its presence in the mass media contributes significantly to the formation of public opinion. The extent of this influence with regard to the media is disputed. On this issue it is worth noting that recent studies in media impact upon public opinion have laid considerable stress upon the manner in which the public *interprets*, *receives* and *consumes* media discourse rather than upon the alleged effects of the discourse itself independent of interpretation. Again, we shall return to this approach to the understanding of the effects of discourse later in this book.

So far we have touched upon a considerable range of important media-related issues as well as upon concepts which help us place them in an explanatory context.

In particular, we shall be making considerable claims for the effects of the conversational trend in press discourse, as well as for the importance of the ideological element, in Chapters 3, 4, 5 and 7.

It is for our readers to branch out at will into any of the fields of investigation we have introduced above in order to explore further the particular aspects of media discourse which are of special interest. This would appear to be an appropriate point to pause for a moment and establish what may be called a summary point of our own discourse in this chapter so far.

Summary and a new direction

The argument so far has made the following principal points:

- Perceptions of cultural identity in Britain are changing rapidly to reflect the emergence of new socio-economic, political and ethnic groupings.
- These new perceptions are frequently at odds with former, prevalent 'Whig-imperialist' attitudes towards identity, where, among other perceptions, 'British' was also often confused with 'English' and disregarded other regional and national claims to identity.
- Perceptions of cultural identity find their dominant expression in language, or more precisely, in discourse.
- Contemporary social theorists and discourse analysts favour the concept of knowledge – and, by extension, information – as a social construct, the product of discursive practice or discourse. Concepts such as 'truth' therefore, though not invalid, are problematic.
- Discourse is shaped by socio-cultural change but, in turn, discourse also influences and shapes society. Through discourse (also referred to as discursive practice) we represent our lifeworld, enact and negotiate social relations and establish our social identities.
- In media discourse there has been a widely perceived shift away from formal public discourse styles towards the more informal and conversationalised forms which both reflect and express the socio-cultural changes we have experienced in the second half of the twentieth century.
- One important, contributory reason for this shift of emphasis in favour of conversationalisation is undoubtedly the influence of market forces upon the producers of information in the written press sector.
- Viewed in a positive light this shift of emphasis towards the conversationalisation of media discourse is deemed to give the public greater access to the nature of complex ideas, ethical issues, political decisions and the activities of public figures and institutions.
- There is evidence to suggest that the balance between the three principal discourse functions has changed to prioritise social relations and social identities rather than the representational (informational) elements in media discourse.

- Critical discourse analysis proposes two kinds of bias in media discourse. The first is of the overt political or commercial kind: the openly persuasive. The second is covert rather than openly stated: that which is implied, or assumed to be part of the shared lifeworld in the discourse. This phenomenon is referred to as ideology.

The points mentioned in this summary underpin in a fundamental way the commentaries on the media coverage of the European Union in Chapters 3 to 5 and some important arguments contained in Chapters 7 and 8. The purpose, therefore, of this chapter as a whole is to provide a foundation for much of the media analysis which follows.

A new direction in the discourse of this book

The discourse of this chapter has focused predominantly on media-associated issues generally and upon the nature of media discourse in particular. The origin of this chapter's discourse is academic and located in the domain of critical discourse analysis (CDA). The following chapter marks a change in direction of the discussion by focusing on the arguments for and against Britain's further integration with the European Union. The origin of the discourse of the next chapter is *different* from that of Chapter 1 but clearly no less academic. It should be distinguished from the discourse relating to Europe appearing in the mass media with which it will subsequently be compared. The discourse of Chapter 2 emerges then from the examination and views of academics and other specialists of the events, implications and consequences for Britain of further integration with Europe *as seen from the perspective of political science*.

The juxtaposition of the two perspectives of critical discourse analysis and of political science may not be entirely new, but we know of no other work where their respective contributions have been so carefully delineated for a particular purpose. We do so here in order better to compare in Chapters 3, 4 and 5 the potential communicable events relating to the European question with those which are actually represented in the British press.

Notes

1. The term 'order of discourse' is used by Fairclough (1995) as the totality of discursive practices of an institution, and relations between them (p. 166). In the social domain of a school, for example, the discursive practices which surround classroom talk, written assignments, school assembly, staffroom talk and playground talk, form the elements which make up the 'order of discourse' for the school. In other words they are a set of recognisable and conventionalised practices. For discourse analysts, the process of examining the boundaries, first between the elements within an

order of discourse and then, between other distinct orders of discourse (e.g. the home, the neighbourhood, the church) highlights points of conflict and struggle and gives significant insight into important aspects of social structure and change.

2.   As Fowler (1991) points out, no text is or can be neutral. However some are less rhetorically or ideologically 'charged' than others.

3.   In fact in the full text the item 'numismatic' (of medals and coins) is used but the inclusion of such an arcane word is so rare that it confirms the rule.

4.   The use of the term 'representation' here refers to a theoretical function (one of three) of discourse. It should not be confused with the same word when used in a more general sense to refer to the way in which events are mediated or represented to the public by the press.

5.   For a full account of the concept of 'voice' see Bakhtin (1981).

6.   For a clear explanation of this phenomenon see Fiske's discussion of 'exnomination' (1987:290).

Chapter 2

European integration: the issues at stake

Introduction

The European Union has often been accused of leading with its chin as far as relations with the British press are concerned. Strange, culturally insensitive directives (the real as opposed to the purely mythical), relating to such things as nationally treasured foods, have been the gratefully received sources of many column inches of contrived indignation in the written press and in the tabloids in particular. It has also been the case that many people within the European Commission have felt, with some justification, that some British newspapers specialise in distortion, representing only the worst aspects of the news concerning the Union either for political reasons (recall the headline from the *Daily Mail* in the previous chapter) or for commercial ones – the need to sell as many copies as possible in a ferociously competitive market. Specialist European observers are frequently dismayed by what they see as the intentional distortion of events by the press for political purposes of the kind already discussed in the previous chapter. They are no less frustrated by what they perceive as the unintentional misrepresentation of the European Union as the result of over-concise or poorly researched reports.

The consequence of all this has been that at times during recent years a significant proportion of British press reporting concerning the EU has portrayed the latter as primarily a foreign-dominated forum for fish wars and sausage spats, and as a launching platform for those who wish to 'drag sovereignty away from the mother of parliaments' and to subject Britain to a 'mercilessly centralising' bombardment of rule by Euro-money and Euro-directive (recall Lord Tonypandy's speech and the *Sun*'s discourse presented in the previous chapter).

Does any of this matter? Is there a cause for concern if the dominant picture which many readers of the British press receive of the European Union is a negative one? After all, it should be remembered that there is longstanding evidence to suggest that not everyone believes what they read in the newspapers (see Chapter 4). Most people in Britain today place more faith in other forms of mass media than they do in the written press. Furthermore, these other forms exist in abundance: there is a variety of television and radio news and current affairs programmes which provide a significant counter-balance and corrective to any distortion or omissions on the part of the national press. However, this situation does not alter the fact that by its very presence the national press remains the provider of an important opinion-forming and opinion-reinforcing service that is readily accessible to the British electorate on matters concerning the European Union.

The analysis of the data which forms the basis for many of our conclusions relating to the coverage or representation of Europe in the British press reveals differences in quality ranging from the outrageously shallow and xenophobic through to the admirably objective, analytical and profound. In order to identify these opposing extremes of press performance more readily we propose to present in this chapter an evaluation of the 'European question' viewed not through the eyes of the media but from the perspective of the social sciences and of politics in particular. This will demonstrate the breadth and depth of the debate on the membership costs and benefits of the European Union and will provide a rough but nevertheless effective yardstick which will help readers appreciate the quality of press coverage of the EU presented in subsequent chapters. So what follows is a selection of the principal arguments, grouped under relevant areas of political, economic and social policies underpinning the EU, which support or oppose the further integration of Britain with its European partners. What we will also do at the end of this chapter is draw some conclusions as to whether some of those arguments might convincingly be said to be more compelling than others.

The EU as a security enhancer in Europe

War, especially in the nuclear age, is potentially the biggest killer of all. The spectacularly murderous use of force by Russia in the Chechen Republic and the genocidal activities of the Bosnian Serbs in the former Yugoslavia have demonstrated in the 1990s that the willingness to use brutal military force within Europe (and indeed elsewhere) does not appear to have declined. The fact that the conflicts mentioned above are classified by many analysts as 'only' civil wars does not in itself provide any proof that major inter-state wars cannot recur in Europe. Consequently, one of the most significant perceived benefits of membership of the EU – its capacity for reducing the likelihood of war in the region – merits first examination here. A selection of radically different competing arguments on European security is set out below.

The case for continuing integration as a means of substantially enhancing the security of the citizens of Europe[1]

There are some opportunities for improving the framework of a region's security that are likely to present themselves only once. The completion of European integration (to the point where the various EU member states have integrated most of their major economic functions, together with several of their central political functions) according to one of the models available, might be one such opportunity. (The

Eurosceptic nightmare of a centralising 'federal superstate' is only one such model; other, rather more likely models, would, using the principle of subsidiarity, leave a variety of key political functions in the hands of states in order to preserve cultural identities and avoid alienating core concerns of the EU's various ethnic groupings.) Such a project would reduce the chances of a European war in a manner which no mere alliance system could emulate. The Atlantic Alliance may have done Europe a great service in the past, but despite the strength of American NATO leadership in Bosnia since late August 1995, the post-Cold War US commitment to European security remains subject to uncertainty. The Clinton presidency has demonstrated clearly that American and European perceptions of security cannot always be expected to converge. Whether or not America's NATO allies can expect help from it is entirely dependent upon how a particular president or how Congress define US security interests at any one time together with the degree of agreement between the two, as well as upon the prevailing balance of power between them. Such a situation of uncertainty that surrounds American commitments to the security of Europe would seem to emphasise the need for further European movement towards integration. Yet, despite the progress that has been made on EMU, some leading European political groupings, such as the British Conservatives, remain resolutely opposed to it, as does much of the British press. For reasons which will be elaborated in later chapters, this latter factor has constrained the freedom of manoeuvre of the New Labour government on EMU. Equally, the common foreign policy so far has been only fitfully and very partially realised, and there is little sign that a common defence policy will get very far. All of these factors make it possible that European integration might not be achieved to the degree that would be necessary to ensure that war between the current member states could be virtually ruled out as a future possibility.

A pessimistic 'realist' reading of the consequences of European integration not being completed in the manner described at the beginning of this sub-section suggests that such a failure may create the conditions within which the old habit of major, highly destructive regional wars could recur in the twenty-first century, with the additional element of nuclear weaponry present in the equation. This claim can be further substantiated by the drawing up of a 'risk list' in an attempt to calculate the range and likelihood and importance of the potential adverse consequences for security of not proceeding quickly enough with further European integration, or of doing so in too partial a manner, or indeed, of making no further progress at all.

The risks involved in taking no or too few further steps towards European integration, or of moving too slowly

The current stage of European integration is such that the point has not yet been reached where the EU member states are so closely linked together that in all foreseeable circumstances the idea of leaving the Union and striking out on their own would seem completely impracticable. This possibility has been demonstrated, for example, by the speculation that was rife during various periods of 1993–94 that, should Chancellor Kohl not be re-elected in 1994, then the new generation of German leaders might be much less tied to the idea of European integration. For Germany, a declaration of independence from the EU might be seen as a serious policy option, should, for example, the already high cost burden of membership that it is expected to carry become simply too great. The German economy is of sufficient size and (until the EMU comes fully onstream) still independent enough from the economies of the other EU member states to permit such a consideration. Furthermore, the ending of the Cold War and the reunification of Germany have together given German governments much greater diplomatic flexibility than previously. Should a future German administration decide to leave the EU, then the impact of such a move on the remaining member states, in terms of its political, economic and psychological consequences could be so serious as to cause the rest of the Union gradually to disintegrate. (Among other things, one of the consequences would almost certainly be a severe loss of confidence in the European Union, in the absence of a country now deemed to be the hub of Western and Central Europe.) Such a possibility might be seen as suggesting that the EU should carry integration forwards to the point where Germany becomes irrevocably bound into the heart of the Union as quickly as possible, before there is any change in German politics in favour of EU withdrawal. Whether or not such a view should be agreed with, however, will significantly depend upon the answer to the question of how much of a possible threat to Europe's security might such a disintegration as that mentioned above present.

In order to answer this question we need to look at the record of Europe within the recent and less recent past. First, the historical record suggests that it is unwise to presume that a long period of peace between the major European states will last indefinitely. There have been such periods before and all have come to an end eventually. Second, while it has been suggested that the best route to the continent's security is not via a greatly more integrated Europe, but through finding a way of tying the American government into a close and continuing long-term alliance relationship,[2] the recent difficulties which the Europeans have experienced in doing precisely that suggest that it is questionable as to whether alliances alone are capable of keeping the long-term peace (as has been pointed out already, even the American Bosnian involvement cannot be taken as a statement of a long-term US commitment to intervene whenever needed in Europe). Arguably something more is needed, something that will bind states so closely together that war becomes impracticable. Third, in the long sweep of human history, it is still only a relatively short time since Germany and Italy, two of Europe's greatest civilisations, were ruled by political movements prepared to resort to murder, oppression and aggression on a massive scale. These movements have been defeated but not eliminated within those and other European societies, and are reappearing in mainstream politics in such revamped forms as the Italian MSI (which has restyled itself in order to be electorally more appealing). The wars between the Serbs and the Croats and the Bosnian civil war, together with a series of attacks upon and murders of foreigners in Germany, have exposed the extent to which the barbarism that was displayed in the Second World War still lurks beneath the surface of European civilisation. Fourth, it has been demonstrated by the situation in the former Yugoslavia that, where binding factors are removed, savage wars can result even between ethnic groups that have lived harmoniously together for many years, as in the case of Bosnia Herzogovenia. Fifth, the removal of the superpower-imposed iron discipline which has resulted from the end of the Cold War has reduced significantly the potential obstacles to the use of military force that were previously in place. Should the US interests in the New Pacific develop to the extent that Europe's economic importance to Washington declines greatly, then a further reduction of the American military presence in Europe may be anticipated. Such developments would further lessen those constraints. Sixth, while some, particularly on the right, argue that the EU has outlived its purpose because prosperous democratic states do not go to war with each other, there is little evidence to support this view. For example, prosperity within the contemporary global capitalist system is insecure. The Asian economic turmoil of 1998 gave a hint of just how quickly prosperity can be threatened in the global economy. There is also no iron law which states that, 'once a democratic society, always a democratic society'. As the twentieth century has demonstrated already, economic collapse can very rapidly pose a severe threat to democratic political systems.

All of the above considerations, it could be argued, make a Europe which does not pursue a policy of deeper integration with sufficient enthusiasm a potentially dangerous place. Indeed it could be argued that, given the scale of possible future security risks, the deepening process would need to continue to the point where both secession from the European Union or war between any of its member states becomes wholly impracticable. Even if this process did not involve full economic and monetary union, it would have to include something very nearly like it or of near equivalence in its binding capability. Without this capability, for the reasons already stated, there could be no confidence that in a Europe where one or more of the major western states left the Union, peace could be guaranteed over the long term. Given the nature of the weaponry that would be potentially available to seceding states, even the smallest possibility of them becoming aggressive towards others in the future is wholly unacceptable. Nuclear weapons are possessed only by France and Britain at the moment but, while there is no popular enthusiasm for such a move, it should be remembered that both Italy and Germany are well capable of developing small but highly destructive arsenals of their own. In addition, as was evident during the second Gulf War, modern conventional weapons can make even brief non-nuclear wars enormously destructive.

In short, it follows from all of this that European integration needs to continue to deepen at a pace which is rapid enough to pre-empt any major member state defections. If it is designed and implemented in a skilful enough manner, then the region's states can be bound so closely together as to diminish the small but wholly unacceptable risk of future military conflict between any of them. What is meant by 'skilful enough' here is of course crucial. Fundamentally, the requirement is for closer integration to take a form which satisfies at least the four western European states which are militarily the most powerful. This is because any future European conflict of potentially disastrous consequence would require their participation. Furthermore, should the economic and military strength of Russia be rebuilt in the early part of the twenty-first century, and future Russian governments show signs of possible hostile or expansionist intent, and should the American commitment to Europe decline, then it would be necessary for the EU states to be linked closely enough to form a counter-balance to Russian designs.

From all these points of view therefore, a continuing deepening of European integration is essential if the security of the states within the European Union is to be enhanced.

Risks: a counter argument focusing on NATO

Key figures on the right of the British Conservative Party argue that it is wrong to credit the European Union with a substantial present or future role in the enhancing of European security (the views of William Hague, the party's current leader, can be examined unabridged in Appendix III). They believe that the Atlantic framework of the NATO alliance continues to dwarf any contribution which the EU has made or can still make to that security. Is this a line of argument that can be credibly sustained? At first glance it would seem grossly to underestimate the EU's security importance. In his book *A Working Peace System* (Mitrany, 1966), David Mitrany argues that ever-increasing integration will eventually so enmesh societies within webs of interdependent, cooperative arrangements that war would effectively become impracticable. Indeed, it is precisely this process which, albeit in a rather different way than that envisaged by Mitrany, has been operating within the EU and which has prompted many observers to see it as a major contibutor to post-Second World War European security.

However, critics of a further deepening process of integration would argue that, in the first instance, this process had little relevance to countering the former Soviet threat, other than helping to provide the economic prosperity and stability which prevented the communist parties coming to power in France and Italy.

The reliance on NATO during the Cold War, it is argued, was partly the result of the western Europeans' own inability to create an effective

European defence organisation, as was demonstrated by the failure of the European Defence Community in 1954. Furthermore, the Soviet Union was so much more powerful than the European states that only the United States could effectively balance it. It follows from this that Western Europe would have been obliged to remain reliant upon the United States irrespective of whether or not it had managed to set up a defence community.

In the second instance, critics of further integration would argue that, in the context of the post-Cold War period, the nature and depth of the European Union's failure in the former Yugoslavia, and the need for American diplomatic and military leadership over the Bosnia question before the conflict could be ended, has demonstrated conclusively that the European idea, and the European Union as an organisation, remain simply too weak to facilitate an effective European security regime. Furthermore, the brutality of Russian action in the Chechen war has demonstrated the capacity for military aggression that remains within post-Soviet Russia. Should the latter eventually succeed in re-invigorating itself economically during the early part of the twenty-first century, then it is quite possible that it will become once more a security problem for Europe, east and west. Under present arrangements it is likely to remain a nuclear super-power in terms of the nuclear weaponry which it will continue to possess. In consequence, it could be argued that it will be necessary for the European Union to continue to rely on the United States as the only power with the capaciity to deter the Russians from the temptation to throw their weight around Europe in the twenty-first century.

In addition, it could be said that the potential economic and military power of Germany is such that, should it decide to strike out on its own, it would have no great problems in doing so. Indeed, even if the EU becomes more closely integrated via the EMU, Germany will remain the most powerful partner and will be strong enough to disengage from the Union in a manner not available to other member states. Should it choose to do so, and should it once again become a military threat to its neighbours, then it is likely that the Europeans would need the help of the United States in countering German power. Germany, as we have mentioned already, has the technology and the resources to develop nuclear weapons rapidly and this capacity would neutralise the current advantage of the small nuclear arsenals held by Britain and France.

Moreover, the EU has internal political problems not possessed by NATO. There is, for example, the presence of the neutral states such as Sweden, as well as the lack of a credible 'prime mover' in defence matters. It is unlikely that the member states and other neighbouring countries would be prepared to accept German leadership in the field of military security. It is also unlikely that either France, Britain or Italy would be strong enough to act as alternative candidates, despite the possession of small nuclear armouries by the first two. In any case, there are doubts within political and military circles in Britain and

France as to whether each would provide a reliable long-term military partner if defence leadership were to be thought of in a joint context. Italy's politics are simply too inwardly directed and unpredictable for it to figure in any such possible joint leadership role. Many of the supporters of the NATO alternative argue that it has been an effective organisation simply because of the preparedness of the United States at most (though not all) times in the post-1949 period to exercise strong leadership. For them, bearing in mind the above considerations, the European Union could not begin to emulate NATO's success without the presence of a state able to perform the same function.

Finally, it could be argued that the security of the states of the EU is not just a matter that can be defined in regional terms The seizure of Kuwait by Saddam Hussein and the consequent potential threat to western oil supplies demonstrated the need for the security of the EU to be defined on a global basis. At the moment, only the United States has the global force projection capability to be able to launch the kind of operation that was conducted during the 1991 Gulf War. While the Europeans made significant contributions, these were dwarfed by the size of the American effort.

From this point of view, therefore, the EU's actual and potential security role remains strictly limited, and to argue that the EU provides any substantial security benefits when compared to the record of NATO is simply to misunderstand the realities of the military and political situation within the region.

Further integration could undermine, not enhance, European security

From yet another perspective it could be argued that the commitment of the EU to continuing integration could itself threaten European security. Initially a case could be made out for claiming that the integration that has occurred so far has indeed added to European security in two major ways: first, by providing a framework for friendly trading and political relationships conducive to preventing old mistrusts and rivalries from reaching a point where they could become possible causes of war once the Cold-War straitjacket was removed; second, by helping provide the foundation for the necessary economic strength to fund a credible level of military commitment to the NATO alliance.

However, these crucial positive benefits could be threatened by further integration producing disharmonies which threaten the stability of the Union. The civil unrest that was caused in France during the latter part of 1995 can be offered as a potential warning in this respect since it appears to have been the result of public anger at the policies designed to prepare France for entry into the European Monetary Union. The cost of entering and sustaining a membership in EMU could be too great for any of a number of EU states both large and small, and the consequence could be an electoral backlash which would force them to withdraw. The failure of one of the key planks of European integration, should it occur, along with the accompanying electoral dissatisfaction with the EU in general which it would generate in the withdrawing states, could spell the beginning of the end of the EU as an organisation.

Further serious problems could arise as the result of attempts to create a common foreign and defence policy. The failures in EU policies towards the former Yugoslavia during the early 1990s severely dented the confidence of the governments of the member states and did little to enhance the image of the EU in the eyes of its various electorates. New failures on major issues in the common foreign policy area risk leading not only to more disillusionment but also to considerable acrimony. Such events would further undermine the European Union and help dislodge the thinning mortar which holds it together.

The same could be true of attempts to go too far with a common defence policy. Doubters within Britain, in particular, would point to the failure of the European Defence Community in 1954 and argue that a repetition of that kind of fiasco could again lead to both serious acrimony and disillusionment with the EU among the governments and electorates of its member states.

So, from this point of view, the European Union is a good idea as far as it goes, but it should not go significantly further. To do so would, according to this line of argument, risk damaging European security interests rather than benefiting them.

Further integration could increase the risk of global war

Another perspective might look at the implications of continuing European integration from a global angle. It could be argued that to build up anything that could become a new military superpower would be highly dangerous from the point of view of global security. This is especially true if the EU succeeded in creating a common defence policy with German participation and became a significant nuclear power as well. The world, it could be argued, is already a dangerous enough place with one military superpower and two other countries – Russia and China – aspiring to that status. To add one more major player to the equation would over-complicate an already complex situation and create the possible relational permutations within which a new global conflict could be provoked in the future. From this perspective the European Union would be better advised staying as it is, or at the very least, not greatly developing a common foreign and defence policy. If the efforts to establish common foreign and defence policies were halted then the EU could remain a junior partner to, rather than a military rival, of the United States. These would be the only viable ways in which the EU could help to protect global and European security, instead of threatening it through adding to the already dangerous complications of the international environment.

The European economy

The single market

A lot of the promise and razzamataz of the European Community's '1992' campaign for the completion of the single market in goods, people, capital and services has now been forgotten. By the time the appointed date of the end of 1992 arrived, the Community had been knocked somewhat off balance by a combination of factors which included an economic downturn that significantly affected member states such as Britain. Consequently, the '1992' celebrations were kept at a relatively low key. What is significant, however, is that a large part of the single market programme was in place as promised by the deadline. Moreover, many of the measures which could not be introduced in time continue to pass quietly through the EU's decision-making processes towards implementation and the member states remain committed to the idea of the single market. Whilst the completion of the single market is by no means the only initiative of the EU, it remains one of its most important, not least because of its role in providing one of the fundamental bases upon which the EMU is founded. From the point of view of the people of Europe it is important because one of the major justifications of its proponents is that it will improve living standards and create greater prosperity for all. It should be remembered also, when mention is made of improving living standards, that for some influential figures within Europe, a vital link was envisaged between the single market and social policy. We shall be examining this aspect of integration a little later below in the section on the EU's social and regional policies.

It might seem a little strange to include the single market in an investigation of the pros and cons for the UK public of further integration, given that its original deadline date of 1992 has long passed. However, it is analysed here for two main reasons. First, as pointed out above, one of the major grounds upon which EMU has been justified is that it is necessary if the full beneficial potential of the single market is to be realised. Before we can begin to look at the pros and cons of EMU adequately therefore, we need to have some idea of the arguments as to whether or not the single market actually has any significant beneficial consequences and potential from the point of view of EU, and, in particular, British citizens. If it doesn't, then a large part of the case for British entry into EMU is invalid. Secondly, given that, despite the passing of the 1992 deadline, the single market has still not been fully achieved, it is therefore a matter of continuing integration.

The single market: the arguments in favour

To avoid baffling readers not very familiar with economic theory, it is intended here to combine the arguments for the single market as a benefit to ordinary people into one cohesive case, and to do the same with the arguments against.

One need hardly be a Marxist to recognise that, despite the convenience of treating them separately, politics and economics are often inextricably intertwined. Thus in this section and the one which follows, political factors will be introduced where the dictates of speaking about the real world make this necessary. The first case then to be presented is the one representing the single market as a benefit for the citizens of Europe. Let us look initially at the economic logic underpinning the single market. The stated necessity for the '1992' single market programme, as it became known, was the fact that while the common market set up within the EEC had been successful in removing tariffs in trade within the community, by the mid-1980s it had still not dealt with many non-tariff barriers (NTBs) to trade. These included, for example, time-consuming bureaucratic practices at frontiers which slowed the movement of goods between the member states and made products more expensive; preferential treatment for 'home' companies of member states in the context of national procurement decisions; trade-impeding differences in safety, technical regulations and standards; national policies for providing state subsidies for industry, and so on. Individually and collectively, these barriers were believed to impede economic growth within the EU and therefore to keep the living standards of ordinary people lower than they would otherwise have been. Such barriers kept consumption at a lower level than it would have been in a community free of NTBs by making goods more expensive. As the result of consumption being at a lower level, fewer people were required for employment in the production of goods and services. The resulting level of unemployment was therefore higher than necessary. The fact that more people were receiving unemployment benefit further encouraged the trend of 'under-consumption' and this in turn meant that the economies of the member states could not operate at their optimum levels. This consequence was also a discouragement to investors. However, advocates of the free market argued that this situation could be reversed if NTBs were removed. Consumption would be encouraged by the consequent cheapness of goods, and increased consumption would create new jobs and spending power. Provided there was a sound economic management to support it, a free, single market would create a virtuous circle whereby each new increase in employment would stimulate consumption and in turn encourage investors to put new funds into the economy, thus creating new jobs and so on.

Another argument put forward in favour of the abolition of NTBs was that it would expose the less efficient European industries (which previously had been protected by NTBs) to a bracing new 'cold shower' of competition. This would leave them with no choice but to cut costs and prices, thereby contributing to the process of wealth creation and growth outlined above. The abolition of such protective 'feather-bedding' of inefficient firms by state subsidies would force them into a situation where the survival of the fittest would be the rule.

Without protection, firms that were too inefficient would go out of business, and production would become concentrated in the factories of the efficient.

Advocates of the single market also argued that economies of scale were important because of the advantages of large-scale production which accompanied them. Such advantages can be generated in several ways. For example, large-scale manufacturers can often negotiate much better price deals with suppliers of raw materials than their smaller counterparts simply because the larger business deals offered make suppliers anxious to secure contracts with them. Cheaper raw materials allow such firms to lower their costs and decide whether to increase their profits or pass on the benefit in the form of lower prices to their customers (some might decide that they are in a position to do both). Price reductions should again help stimulate an increase in economic growth in the way described above, providing that the product concerned is one for which the demand is sufficiently expandable or elastic. A further way in which the benefits of economies of scale are compounded arises from the manner in which a large-scale manufacturer, successfully marketing its own products, can pay off the high cost of production plant more quickly than the small-scale producer. This enables it to cut production costs much more quickly and thereby reduce the prices of its products more rapidly. By so doing, it will help benefit the European citizen by contributing to the stimulation of economic growth in the manner already described.

The 1992 programme was intended to help generate such economies of scale by the opening up of a truly enormous single market within which large-scale producers would be able to reap considerable benefits. For example, instead of having to engage in the extremely costly practice of manufacturing different versions of telecommunications equipment to comply with the varying standards of the various member states, as they were previously required to do, firms would now be able to cut costs by producing equipment to a single standard acceptable right across the Community. They would not need to use as many types of production plant and would now aim single products at much bigger markets. All of these benefits would translate into higher profits and lower prices.

Economies of scale such as those outlined above were seen as being desirable, not just because of their anticipated contributions to economic growth, but also because it was believed that they would enhance the Community's ability to stand up to competition from Japan and the other new Asian industrial powers as well as from the giant American multi-nationals. The theory was that the incentives that flowed from the economies of scale being opened up would encourage cross-border mergers or agreements of association between EU firms and that this would result in the emergence of new giant companies large enough to compete with the Japanese and American corporations. Prompted by the prospects of such economies of scale, for example, three hundred major mergers and acquisitions occurred during 1987 (Dinan, 1994:151).

Finally, another theoretical assumption was that the less efficient EC states would be forced to improve their performances by competition from the most efficient states once the single market was established. This would encourage economic convergence across the Community and thereby benefit the citizens of all the member states.

There are additional arguments which have been advanced from other quarters in favour of the single market (see, e.g., El-Agraa, 1994) and the preceding summary of a selection of key points omits some important considerations with regard to both the movement of capital and of labour. However, the above points are aguably the most important ones with regard to the promotion of the economic well-being of the citizens of the UK and of Europe as a whole. While it is a laudable aspiration to try to include everything that has been argued or asserted with regard to the benefits of the single market, there is regrettably no room to do so in a book of this kind, not primarily concerned with economics.

In summary then, the most important arguments that have been advanced in favour of the single market claim that ultimately it will boost economic growth, reduce prices for consumers and increase employment, thereby significantly raising the standard of living throughout the Community. It is of course not claimed that this will happen overnight. It could take well into the twenty-first century (i.e. the medium term) before some of the jobs which have been lost as the result of the less efficient producers dropping out of the market are replaced by new ones generated by the economic growth that the market is supposed to stimulate. It is also widely recognised that the extent to which any projected benefits can be attained will be crucially affected by such important considerations as the extent to which the various member states implement single market legislation over the next few years.

The single market: the arguments against

Having outlined some of the most crucial benefits of the single market programme, we come now to the case against. Critics of the single market argue that the first problem is the assertion that the weaker economies will be forced to become more efficient. That this would come about as the result of competition from countries with more efficient economies is viewed by opponents of the single market as a seriously flawed assumption. They argue that the head start in crucial areas (such as research and development) which the more efficient larger firms in the most successful states have, and the relatively huge resources which a number of them can draw on, will sooner or later simply overwhelm the smaller and more backward competition in states such as Greece and Portugal. During the next several years the weaker economies of some member states will be subjected to a further weakening as the result of the abolition of tariff barriers which previously provided them with some degree of protection. Such critics argue that even the significant expansion of the EU's regional and social funds, that has occurred in recent years, will not be enough to save them from the consequences.

Furthermore, even some of the 'Big Four' could find themselves in serious difficulties. Both Italy and Britain for example, have regions which have been for some time, or have more recently become, industrial wastelands. The distance of such areas from the most profitable markets, in combination with a range of other factors,[3] has left them without much in the way of manufacturing activity. In addition, much of the service industry which has developed in areas such as the north east of Britain is relatively unimportant in terms of general wealth creation because of the poor wages that it pays to the majority of its employees. Should the manufacturing industry which does operate from such regions prove unequal to the increased competition over the next few years, then their destruction as areas where decent living wages are available will be complete.

Doubts have been voiced too concerning the claim that, even if some states or regions suffer, the overall result of the implementation of the single market programme will be an enhanced rate of growth for the European Union. Returning for a moment to the concept of the virtuous circle explained in the previous section, some critics have pointed to the role of robotisation, new technology in general, and recent obsessions with such organisational concepts as 'flat management' as the potential causes of a decreasing demand for labour in the service and manufacturing industries as well as in management itself.[4] Others have argued that the non-interventionist emphasis of the single market programme will mean that many multi-nationals operating in the EU will feel free to continue moving jobs to low wage economies in Asia and Eastern Europe. The implication of all this is that new jobs will not necessarily be created on any substantial scale within the EU as was argued in the previous section. This could mean that unless significant levels of the new profits are transferred to the unemployed by taxation and the social welfare systems, then firms that rely predominantly upon the single market will come up against an inbuilt ceiling on both consumption and economic growth within the EU. Equally, the benefits of economic growth might be distributed much less widely than the supporters of the single market programme have anticipated.

Doubts have also been raised concerning the suggestion that the economies of scale resulting from the rush of cross-border mergers, initially precipitated by the single market process, will reduce prices and promote efficiency and growth over the next few years. Although the EU has a coherent policy in place aimed at controlling monopolies and restrictive practices,[5] it has little power to cope directly with situations where companies join together to create new super-large enterprises which are not quite monopolies but nevertheless reduce competition within their markets.

When mergers and other joint ventures are as widespread as they have become, it can be argued that the consequence is a significant overall reduction of the level of competition within the EU which may negate key benefits of the scale economies involved, and cause a lowering of efficiency compared with the pre-existing situation. Just as it can be argued that more competition stimulates efficiency, then it can be equally contended that less reduces it.

However, some contend that such criticisms miss a crucial point, that one of the main problems challenging the European Union is competition from the United States and the new Asian economic powers, and that European companies need to be bigger in order to match the resources of the Japanese and American corporations. Providing the EU does not simply turn into Fortress Europe at some stage and shut out such strong non-European rivals through high tariff barriers, their presence as competitors within the European economy will be more than enough to keep the newly merged EU companies on their toes.[6] So, those following this line of argument contend that the single market, with its encouragement of cross-border mergers, should enhance both the chances of the survival of the EU's key industries and their wealth creation capability. By so doing it should ultimately help make the idea of European integration something that has, and retains, popular support.

One of the most serious problems that has been raised with regard to the single market concerns the tradition of providing high levels of subsidies to industry in several states. There is a belief among a number of economists and critics of the single market that member states with a strong tradition of subsidising and protecting key industries will continue to do so despite claiming to be implementing the spirit as well as the letter of the programme. It is argued that they will find it almost impossible electorally to dismantle their subsidy systems completely, although they might well devise more subtle means of their application to give them reduced visibility.

The worst of all worlds for the EU would be one in which not only do subsidies continue in visible or invisible forms, but where they are surreptitiously increased as a means of compensating for the removal of other forms of protection. The effects of such practices obviously would be to leave such states as Britain (which under the recent Conservative government vigorously reduced state financial aid to industry), at a considerable disadvantage in the market place. The consequences of this in terms of lost production and jobs within those states who play by the rules, ultimately could generate bitterness and disillusion. In any case, as has been noted already, if during the first decade of its existence, the programme works as it is supposed to do and results in the inefficient, high cost producers being taken over or pushed out of business, then there is likely to be considerable unemployment in some parts of the EU. This is unwelcome enough but doubly damaging because it would be a consequence which could be directly attributed to the economic restructuring process itself as opposed to other possible causes. There is the added risk too that, if psychological factors such as a general lack of confidence in the economic future on the part of consumers led to a situation of continuing global or European recession at the time when such unemployment was occurring, then the likelihood of new jobs being created within an acceptable time scale would be even further diminished. In more politically explosive states than Britain, such a situation could lead not only to disillusion with the EU, but to a level of political unrest which could force their governments to consider partial or total withdrawal from the Union. It could also create the conditions for the rise to power of the neo-fascists in Italy or of other right wing nationalist groups across Europe, an eventuality which might in itself lead to the demise of the EU. Thus, economic stagnation would have triggered a substantial level of popular disillusionment, which in turn would have triggered a switch in ideological allegiance, provoking a higly negative impact on the prospects for change in the form of further European integration.

On the other hand, should the EU be lucky and the regional and global economy head into a period of sustained economic growth during the rest of the 1990s and through 2000 and beyond, then the single market programme could well benefit by association in the eyes of the electorate and its various elites and thereby help cement the European commitment to integration.

The activities of powerful interest groups in the form of some trade unions and lobbies led by members of the business elite of the EU, might also be important. Should some national industries feel themselves to be under unacceptable levels of pressure from the single market (the fishing industry, for example), then governments might well find themselves being heavily lobbied for some form of protection or partial suspension of their adherence to the offending parts of the single market programme.

The single currency: the arguments in favour

In addition to the debate surrounding the single market, there is the unknown quantity of EMU (see, e.g. Dyson, 1994:333–61). The case for such a union can be made on several grounds. First and most obviously, those who look to the United States as a model for a single market emphasise what they see as the American illustration of the all-important value of having a single currency. For them an EU single market without a corresponding single currency will never operate with full effectiveness.

So what precisely are the benefits which a single currency is supposed to produce? First, there is the simple fact that it eliminates the costs that arise for business, governments and individuals as the result of the exchange from one currency to another. Second, the introduction of a single EU currency should increase business confidence and promote investment which should, in turn, boost employment levels. This is due to the risks of investment in a single currency, backed by a powerful central bank, being less than those in currencies backed by the smaller economies of the EU states. An extension of this theme is the argument that the risks arising from exchange rate variation tempt multi-nationals to spread their new plant investment across several EU economies in order to hedge against such risks. A single currency, on the other hand would remove the need for such hedging, and allow investors to locate new plants according to economies of scale. This would lead to the creation of more plants of optimum size, and this in turn, would reduce unit costs of production and bring about a significant increase in efficiency (Artis, 1995:349).

Another argument in favour of the eradication of exchange rate uncertainty is that it would bring about a reduction in the risk premium in real interest rates. If this is correct, it should stimulate more capital accumulation and investment, which in turn should increase output per head (Artis, 1995:349). From a consumer's point of view, it should also be more difficult to sell goods such as 'same model, same specifications' motor vehicles more expensively in one EU member state than another, if the prices of such vehicles are in future listed using the same single currency (Artis, 1995:350).

An EU single currency would also permit the making of economies in the holding of non-European currencies. This is because the European Central Bank would not need to keep as large holdings of foreign reserves as the individual national central banks would need to maintain if the member states were to retain their national currencies (Artis, 1995:349–50).

The final argument in favour of a single currency and an EMU is the one which asserts that the EMU is necessary if the longer term security and safety of the European economy is to be protected. The contention is that the EMU is vital in so far as it will tie the economies of the member states so closely together that future military conflicts between them will be impractical. Given the huge economic costs of past wars – the Second World War cost Britain alone one quarter of its national wealth, for example – then this is a vital economic consideration that needs to be taken into account irrespective of whether there are other economic costs and benefits attached to the EMU.

The single currency: the arguments against

For many opponents of the EMU the major economic disadvantage is the loss of flexibility resulting from giving up exchange rate variability. Classical economic thinking contends that the justification for allowing exchange rates to change is their function as shock-absorbers for disturbances that impact upon different economies in different ways (Artis, 1995:350). Artis contends that exchange rate depreciations can, at the very least, provide a valuable breathing space while other policies are put into place in order to bolster the shock-absorber effect (Artis, 1995:352–53). However, he acknowledges that there is a range of alternative absorber mechanisms which can be used with varying degrees of effectiveness as substitutes if exchange rates are no longer available. These include EU regional policy, budgetary policy, national fiscal policies, factor migration (for example, the migration in recent years of unemployed British building workers to Germany where work was available) and wage-price flexibility (see also Dyson, 1994:242–7).

Whilst identifying these possible alternative shock-absorber mechanisms, Artis is cautious about the extent of their effectiveness within the EU of the present and immediate future (Artis, 1995:346–55).

Tsoukalis argues that the majority view among professional economists is even more pessimistic. With regard to the last but one of possible alternatives mentioned by Artis – the migration of labour – Tsoukalis states that most economists reason that:

> Economic integration in Europe has not yet reached the level where capital and especially labour mobility can act as near substitutes for changes in the exchange rate (labour mobility within the EU is at the moment extremely limited and in no way comparable to that in the USA, for example). (Tsoukalis, 1996:290)

He goes on to argue also that the European economy is not yet sufficiently homogeneous to protect different states and regions from frequently assymetric shocks.

This last point is highly important, for if it is correct, and if the pessimistic viewpoint about the likely effectiveness of alternative shock-absorber mechanisms to exchange rates is also correct, then the EMU could do considerable economic damage to the economies of some member states. According to Tsoukalis, labour market flexibility is a dubious potential shock absorber. He is even more pessimistic about the possibility of inter-regional budgetary transfers functioning as shock-absorbers (by reducing economic disparities) between states and regions. He maintains that, despite the recent considerable increases in their size, the structural and cohesion funds will remain simply too small in proportion to the problems confronting them (Tsoukalis, 1996:290). Tsoukalis goes on to argue that rather than the EMU, many economists would prefer a system of fixed but adjustable exchange rates for the EU, providing, that is, governments were not allowed to forget the adjustable aspect of the arrangement (Tsoukalis, 1996:291).

Tsoukalis also is concerned about the way in which the Maastricht convergence criteria for the EMU are likely further to split the member states into different tiers with some states left in the waiting room because of their failure to meet the criteria, and about the effects that this might have on the overall integration process (Tsoukalis, 1996:298).

Finally, given all of these problems surrounding the likely effectiveness of alternative shock-absorbers, some British Eurosceptics argue that whilst full monetary independence for most EU states is probably out of the question, a useful degree of independent manipulation still would be possible outside of the EMU. This might provide valuable help, which would not be available within EMU, in cushioning economies such as Britain's during periods of weakness. Thus, this line of argument contends that, far from benefiting from progressing towards monetary union, states such as the UK could find themselves saddled with problems which they otherwise could have avoided. The economic benefits which Britain obtained as a consequence of having to flee the exchange rate mechanism of the EMS during September 1992 are frequently cited in this respect (Jamieson, 1993:113).

An overall Eurosceptic economic perspective

In his book *Britain Beyond Europe*, Bill Jamieson, aided by prominent members of the anti-European Bruges Group, sets out a hostile perspective upon further European integration which, it can be safely assumed, emerges from the heart of the Eurosceptic camp. Much of the major thrust of Jamieson's argument turns on four alleged points:

- The logic of Britain's trade patterns;
- The high economic cost of Britain's membership of the EU;
- The negative economic effects of the EU's social policy and of the social welfare structures of leading EU member states;
- The argument that Britain's membership of the EU has prevented British policy makers from dealing with a whole raft of deep-seated economic problems that need resolving in order properly to rebuild Britain economically.

It would seem sensible to look at each of these criticisms in turn.

As far as the logic of Britain's trade patterns is concerned, Jamieson points out that during 1993, the year when Britain signed up to the Maastricht Treaty, the total of British portfolio investment in states outside the EC exceeded that for those within it, and was at a higher level than at any previous time in history (Jamieson, 1993:12). Using his particular means of calculating the distribution of Britain's overseas investment, Jamieson concludes that while UK earnings in, and interest from the EC are important, 80 per cent of British foreign investment by asset (and more by earnings) is concentrated in non-EC states in fast-growing economies (Jamieson, 1993:17). He disputes the claim that more than half of Britain's trade is with the EC. On the basis of his interpretation of the available figures, he asserts that this is true only of Britain's visible trade, and that when the EC visibles and invisibles are added together this gives a total of only 45 per cent of the UK's current account (Jamieson, 1993:18). He states that ever since the signing of the Maastricht Treaty, UK investors have been voting funds away from the EU. While the US remains the recipient of large British corporate and institutional investments, British trade and investment in South East Asia are also sharply increasing. His interpretation of relevant data leads him to assert that, while more than 50 per cent of the UK's top 100 quoted companies earn nearly one third of their profits from abroad, only 14 make more than one third of their income in Europe (by which, we presume, he means the EU). He claims that UK investments in the EU have declined from 29 per cent of total British foreign investment in the 1980s to 20 per cent today (Jamieson, 1993:22) and summarises his case as follows:

Britain's companies and financial institutions, by virtue of a cast of mind shaped over generations, and by voluntary allocations of billions of pounds, assert that Britain has other areas, and more promising areas, to do business with and to invest in. It would be reckless to discount this, and it would be foolhardy in any acknowledgement, to suggest that in an inventory of Britain's economic interests, it somehow counts for nothing. (Jamieson, 1993:22)

On the second point, the consideration of Britain's economic costs of membership of the EU, Jamieson claims that these have been 'ferocious', and that they have severely damaged the UK's balance of payments position. He sees the brief period of Britain's membership of the ERM as having been directly responsible for the bankruptcies of thousands of companies. He states that EU membership has exacerbated unemployment levels and increasingly confined Britain's options within a high cost, non-competitive, regionally minded economic bloc which is characterised by a falling share of world trade. He sees the UK's membership of the Common Agricultural Policy (CAP) as having threatened what he claims is Britain's historical role as a global trading nation. Jamieson views the EMU as offering the prospect of British institutions being stripped of sovereignty in such crucial domains of economic control as interest rates and monetary policy. He assesses the overall direct cost of EC/EU membership as being £108 billion. This comprises a cumulative UK visible balance of payments deficit of £87 billion since 1973 and a net British contribution to the EU budget of £21 billion (Jamieson, 1993:100–1).

Jamieson also sees Britain's manufacturing industry as having been seriously damaged by EC membership. He observes that the enhanced propensity to import finished manufactured goods from the EC states that resulted from the swing towards EC trade, exacerbated an already weak UK balance of trade situation. He also cites the increased tendency of the multinational motor vehicle manufacturers to import from the EC during the 1980s and 1990s as being mainly responsible for the UK's £6.5 billion record trade deficit in motor vehicles in 1990. He ascribes also the UK iron and steel industry's relative decline between 1975 and 1990 to the EC's production quota and minimum prices arrangements (Jamieson, 1993:103). He also sees membership as having brought with it a deluge of what he considers to be petty Euro-regulations which, he contends, have been a costly interference affecting all sectors of British industry. The plight of the fishing industry is seen to be the result of EU policy more than anything else (Jamieson, 1993:108). The single market and its promised benefits, for Jamieson, has not provided the expected compensations.

Moving on to the EU social and employment policy, Jamieson aligns himself with the criticisms of the CBI. At the time when he was writing, the latter centred on the Social Chapter and the Social Action Programme, arguing that the detailed regulation of employment practices, the hiring and firing of labour, working hours and benefits would seriously increase production costs and lead to growing unemployment as well as the worsening of EU uncompetiveness in world markets. He mentions also the CBI's criticism of the Commission's alleged tendency to 'harmonise upwards' with regard to social and employment regulations without any reference to the competitiveness of affected enterprises. Jamieson describes this as a sure recipe for pricing people out of jobs (Jamieson, 1993:89–90). He concludes by stating that, for British business, the most appealing aspects of the Treaty on the European Union were the opt-outs, including that on the Social Chapter.

Finally, it is necessary to set out the argument behind the claim made by Jamieson that British membership of the EU has distracted policy makers from the need to undertake crucial domestic economic reforms. He believes that

> The rhetoric of Europe has masked the realities of Britain's economic interdependence with the rest of the world and the need for a transformation in attitudes to industry. Britain's need to transform her productive base, to build on its attractions relative to the continent and to continue to attract foreign direct investment critically depends on offering opportunities and conditions that are different from and better than those of her competitors. It requires a low tax and social wage-cost regime. (Jamieson, 1993:164)

What is interesting here is the wide range of domestic economic factors which Jamieson blames for British economic failure in Chapters 10 and 12 of his book, ranging from serious weaknesses in national investment structures to the failure to secure price stability, the failure to control public expenditure, domestically fuelled overruns in UK consumer demand, inappropriate taxation policies, government disregard for the importance of manufacturing industry during the 1980s, and so on. When all these are viewed together, the reader might be forgiven for wondering whether many of the economic costs of the EU would still have been costs had the domestic factors weakening the UK economy been dealt with, and whether a stronger economy would have enabled them to become benefits. Similarly, the validity of blaming the EC/EU for distracting the policy makers from the need to introduce economic reforms seems to be undermined by Jamieson making it clear that UK governments were being seriously distracted long before Britain joined the EC. However, these are matters which await a fuller discussion in the next section.

An overall Europhile economic perspective

A typical Europhile case is unsurprisingly the converse of the kind of Eurosceptic view which we have just examined above. With regard to the continuing debate on just how much of Britain's trade is and is not conducted with its EU partners, and what the precise patterns of current British overseas investment are, the argument is a little more complicated however. Europhiles argue that even if people sharing Jamieson's views are right about Britain's trade being much more focused on the non-European world than currently is officially acknowledged, this still does not make the case for Britain removing itself from the EU. One of the key Europhile economic arguments for Britain's continuing membership of the EU is that whether or not the UK economy is ever properly resurrected outside the EU, post-imperial Britain would remain a relatively small political and economic unit in a world dominated by such current giants as the US, Japan, the European Union itself, and new emerging superpowers such as China. While the presence of 14 other member states means that Britain will frequently have to accept less than optimum EU negotiating stances on external economic matters, it at least has a vote proportionate to its size on such matters which it would not possess outside of the EU. This is particularly important given Britain's heavy dependency on world trade. For those who criticise the EU as being protectionist, or its policies as provoking protectionism in other powerful economic actors, then it is surely better to be in a position where Britain can have an opportunity at least of reducing these alleged protectionist practices.

As far as the economic costs of British membership of the EU are concerned, then there are few who would deny that some of these are or have been significantly high. There is no doubt, for example, that even though its costs have now been greatly reduced, the CAP has made food more expensive for British consumers than it would have been had world market prices been allowed to operate freely in the UK. Furthermore, in relation to the favourite 'bête noire' of the Eurosceptics, membership of the ERM in the early 1990s, it is generally accepted that this period was a costly episode for the British economy. However, as hinted at in the previous section, any evaluation of the costs and benefits of the EU membership to Britain must take account of the policies of previous British governments towards the Community/ Union. Had Britain not rejected the idea of Common Market member-ship in the 1950s, then the CAP would almost certainly have been shaped in a manner which adequately represented British interests, given the much greater economic and political clout that Britain had at that time. The fact that the policy was shaped according to German and French interests, and subsequently became such a cost to Britain, was the result of fatal self-exclusion. It therefore makes no sense to make such capital out of its negative aspects as the Eurosceptics have tried to do.

In addition, Europhiles have blamed much of the ERM debacle on the Conservative government's politically motivated decision to go in at a rate that was unsustainably high for reasons of prestige. The disastrous series of bankruptcies and the recession that followed from this were largely self-inflicted rather than Euro-inflicted. Furthermore, having laid so much of the blame for the recession of the early 1990s on the ERM, Jamieson throws doubt upon his own argument by sub-sequently stressing how much of that recession was home grown. He states quite clearly, for example, that by the time John Major took the UK into the ERM in October 1990, the British economy was heading for a recession that was the direct consequence of the consumer boom, fuelled by lending which pushed up inflation to nearly 10 per cent and interest rates up to 15 per cent (Jamieson, 1993:135). This view, together with the previously mentioned array of other home-grown factors mentioned by Jamieson, must lead logically to the conclusion that the ERM did not work for Britain because of domestic, economic weaknesses. The economy was simply not strong enough to sustain the central rate that the government had proclaimed as its goal.

Some of the other criticisms that Jamieson makes against the EU equally evoke counter-arguments from the Europhile camp. His previously mentioned point that the switch towards EC trade, which membership brought, weakened the British economy through increased imports, ignores the influence of the other key domestic factors which he lists in Chapters 10 and 12 of his book. In these he lays great emphasis on the way in which deficiencies in domestic investment structures and patterns have undermined the capacity of British industry to compete. He also stresses the negative effect of the downgrading of industry by the Conservatives in the 1980s and their emphasis on the supposed countervailing importance of services. In short, in referring to the importance of changing trade patterns towards the EU in hastening British industrial decline, he could be accused of mistaking a symptom for a cause.

The most credible reasons for Britain's limited abilities to compete with European firms would seem to lie at home rather than with Europe. Jamieson's argument that European Union membership has also damaged the British motor industry, by encouraging multi-national motor manufacturers to substitute British-made products for imports from Europe, is also a little curious. A more likely explanation for this happening over the last twenty years lies in the economic reality of other parts of Europe having a cost or quality advantage over Britain. Multi-national business corporations, after all, are hardly renowned for locating production on the basis of charity.

None of this would be to deny that there are clear economic costs to British membership of the EU. The costs of the CAP have been mentioned already and Britain is effectively penalised on the proportion of trade which it conducts outside the EU as a result of the Union's budgetary contributions arrangements. But what is crucial here is the extent to which the UK is in a position to counterbalance the costs by taking advantage of European market opportunities. If, as the arguments of Jamieson suggest, Britain is not in such a position because of deep-rooted internal economic and political weaknesses, then it seems somewhat perverse to suggest that the costs of EU membership have been more the fault of Brussels than of the British themselves. Equally, as pointed out above, it seems strange to blame the ERM for so much of the recession within the UK in the early 1990s when the evidence presented by Eurosceptics such as Jamieson suggests clearly that the reason why Britain was not in a position to turn ERM membership into benefit rather than cost was previous and continuing domestic economic failure.

All of this of course leads to the overall argument of critics such as Jamieson that whatever the costs of specific aspects of EU membership, the biggest disaster stemming from Britain's decision to join and stay in the EC/EU has been the way in which this has distracted British policy makers from the need to sort out the UK's internal economic problems. As pointed out previously, the long-term nature of many of the factors which Jamieson identifies as having weakened the British economy leads to the conclusion that UK policy makers were distracted from the need to sort out the economy and its governing institutions long before our EC/EU membership. The question is, therefore, why should the EU be blamed any more than the purely domestic factors which previously had provided such distractions? Indeed, Europhiles might go further and ask, where is the evidence from the Eurosceptic camp that the pre-existing distracting domestic factors suddenly became less important (as obstacles to an efficient economy) than the EC factors when Britain joined the Community? But perhaps the simplest criticism of this view derives from the original 1971 White Paper produced prior to British entry, which stresses the likely beneficial effects on manufacturing industry of the 'cold shower' of competition which the government anticipated would flow from our EC membership. It could be observed that the government of the day (and subsequent governments) failed to realise that EC membership would only be really beneficial economically if they perceived that the cold shower would necessitate the putting of their own house in order economically just as much as industry was required to sharpen its act.

In summary then, rather than the EC/EU being blamed for distracting British governments from the need for a proper sorting out of their own economic affairs, British governments and key domestic institutions should be held responsible for failing to see that increased competition from the EU made it imperative to reform the economy root and branch in order to be able to benefit from that competition. When the matter is looked at in detail, in other words, Jamieson's arguments appear to be seriously flawed.

The social dimension

The thinking behind the EU social and regional policies

For many critics, EU social policy has turned out to be the lion that mewed. While there has been real progress made in the construction of common social and regional policies over the years, the overall budget allocations for each remain woefully indequate given the scale of the social and regional problems across the Union. In addition, they are still kept relatively in the shade by the 50 per cent or so of the EU budget which continues to go to the CAP. Prior to New Labour's 1997 election victory, neither the Social Charter of the late 1980s nor the Social Chapter attached to the Maastricht Treaty was adopted by Britain. Even where progress has been made, such as in Britain's turn-around on the Social Chapter under New Labour, it has been less than the advocates of European social policy have desired.

However, others see the picture rather differently. They point out that EU social policy has been rather more substantial than many realise and by 1999 the various structural funds of the EU will account for 35 per cent of its overall budget (Liebfried and Pierson, 1996:194; Allen, 1996:210).

It is perhaps useful to consider briefly what the main purposes of EU social and regional policies are supposed to be. First, under both the single market programme of the 1980s and the push for the EMU of the early 1990s, both categories of policy were seen as being important aids to the process of economic convergence. Expenditure on both types of policy was increased as a result. The intention was that they should provide the infrastructure, skills and opportunites for training necessary to attract industry and services to deprived areas. For example, in 1989 five common objectives were set for the structural funds. The first of these was the development of the most disadvant-aged of the EC's problem areas, particularly the Mediterranean South and the Irish Republic. The second objective was the conversion of the regions in industrial decline via help from social and regional funds, the European Investment Bank and the ECSC where appropriate. The third concern was the combating of long-term unemployment, mainly via the social fund. The fourth objective was to increase employment opportunities for young people. The final objective was designed to attack problems in agricultural communities and included the promo-tion of the development of rural areas (Armstrong et al., 1995:193–5). In line with the completion of much of the single market, EC assistance to the various regions affected by the above objectives was doubled in real terms between 1988 and 1993. Furthermore, measures were put in place to try to ensure that the funding was concentrated on those areas most in need (Armstrong et al., 1995:195). While in 1989 only a small proportion of the available regional fund money for the most disadvantaged areas was thought likely to go to Britain during the period up to 1993, it was anticipated that Britain would receive 38.3 per cent of the available funds for regions in industrial decline (Armstrong et al., 1995:196). Subsequently, further reforms of the structural funds were announced during 1992–93 by which they would account for 35 per cent of the overall EU budget by 1999. At 1992 prices this meant that by then 30 billion ecus would become available for structural spending (Allen, 1996:210).

There are several reasons why it has been argued that there is a need for social and regional policy at an EU rather than at a national level. Two are particularly important. First, if the economic convergence necessary for EMU to work properly is to be in any way realisable, then it must be accepted that some EU states are simply too poor on their own to help develop their most economically unproductive regions. They need help from the other member states. Second, whilst the provision of this aid could be on a state-by-state basis, with the richer members agreeing to help the poorer ones, a coordinating body is necessary to ensure that the assistance provided is used both efficiently and cost effectively (Armstrong *et al.*, 1995:192). Otherwise unproductive duplication of effort or friction between the providers of incompatible projects could easily develop.

As far as Germany and several other states are concerned, a common social policy has been one way of trying to ensure that economic competition within the EU takes place on something resembling a level playing field. The aspiration to common key goals and obligations in social policy has been seen as a means of trying to ensure that Germany's major competitors do not engage in unfair competition by cutting back on social policies and taxation in order to become more attractive to foreign investors. In short, a common policy of social intervention has been seen as a means of trying to prevent businesses in competitor states from undercutting German firms as a result of lower costs resulting from tax reductions made possible by reductions in social expenditure.

But there have been less materialist considerations at work as well. For example, one of the early concerns of the common social policy was the provision of assistance to the physically disabled and young people who for various reasons might find skills training difficult to obtain. The Social Charter was particularly notable for its focus on improving the lives of ordinary people, with such things as better health and safety in the workplace, a minimum wage and greater consultation between employers and employees. However, such bene-volence has a more hard-headed, realist side as well. Jacques Delors pushed for the Social Charter particularly on the grounds that it was necessary to offer the ordinary citizens of Europe something within the 1992 programme which touched their daily lives positively and directly if they were to support it and not regard it simply as a jamboree for business. Furthermore, as Purdy and Devine note, some supporters of the social dimension saw it as an important step towards the creation of a people's Europe which would eventually rival the concept of the nation state as a focus of social identity.

> From this standpoint, the Social Charter was less a statement of legislative intent than the proclamation of a social ideal to stand alongside the market economy and parliamentary democracy as an emblem of European civilisa-tion. (Purdy and Devine, 1995:284).

Equally, the provision of assistance to the deprived regions of the EU can be seen as one means of trying to preserve social stability. Ultimately, however, the social policy of the EU, along with its regional policy has been caught between several conflicting demands. On the one hand, states such as Italy have viewed the two policies as useful means of obtaining assistance in dealing with substantial regional problems. On the other, Britain has traditionally seen the social and regional funds as a means of recovering some of its contributions to the EU, particularly since, having a relatively small farming sector, it is not entitled to a great deal of agricultural assistance when compared with other states such as France. In addition, under the Conservatives, Britain tended often to see EU social and regional funding as a means of substituting for its own expenditure. This has obviously displeased the Commission since one of the purposes, as we have already noted, of social and regional expenditure is that it should be presented to the people as evidence of the practical usefulness and proximity of the European Union (see Chapter 7 for further discussion). Even where the member states have been prepared to pay lip service to the declared objectives of the EU social and regional policies, there are problems. The most common is the reluctance on the part of national governments to incur the full expenditure that would be necessary to implement these policies in a way that really engages with the most serious regional economic disparities. Ideological factors have also played a role in restricting the possibilities for the development of a truly common EU social policy. The British Conservatives in particular have rejected the Social Charter and the Social Chapter on the grounds that they both interfere with what they see as central areas of national sovereignty and represent socialist ways of thinking which they consider outdated and costly. David Allen goes so far as to claim that the objective of securing economic and social cohesion serves more as a rationalisation than an explanation for the creation of the various structural funds. He sees the decisions to boost the funds as being predominantly a series of side payments intended to facilitate general packages concerned with the advancement of the EC/EU (Allen, 1996:210). Indeed, he argues that if the structural funds were run down, it might be possible for economic and social cohesion to be pursued via the operation of the market alone, with the aid of competition policy. On the other hand, he observes that, if it is the case that the structural funds are essential as facilitators and legitimisers of the basic deals by which the EU goes forward, then it might be difficult for such deals to be brokered in future if the funding no longer existed (Allen, 1996:231).

Given the many problems that have been outlined in this section, it might seem miraculous that real, albeit limited, progress has been made in the domains of social and regional policy. The extent to which this progress can be viewed either as costs or as benefits will be assessed in the next section. In addition to giving us a perspective on the extent to which the measures that have been introduced so far have or have not been beneficial, our analysis obviously will illuminate the overall question as to whether or not EU social and regional policies *per se* are a 'good thing' from the point of view of UK and other EU citizens. Given that calls for the expansion of such policies continually recur whenever further economic integration is discussed, this will in turn partially enable the reader to make a judgement as to whether or not such expansions are likely to be beneficial to Britain. (Equally, and importantly from the point of view of our project, readers of the British press would need to be given similar information in order to make their own judgements on EU social and regional policies.) From a British point of view, of course, a key part of that judgement will also be dependent on the extent to which such expansions are made in Britain's favour. Given that that is always a matter of competitive negotiation, we cannot make any precise judgements here as to the extent that that is likely to happen, other than to note that enlargement to the east will increase the demands for such assistance considerably and thereby reduce the likely funding that is available for Britain. It is to the above issues we now turn.

The arguments against the EU social policy

As noted in the section on economics, EU social policy has attracted severe criticism from many quarters. In 1993, for example, the CBI stated that most Commission initiatives in the labour and social affairs field during the preceding ten years or so had been detrimental to UK business interests (Jamieson, 1993:89). They were seen simply as potentially added burdens to industry, the effects of which would be to decrease its competitiveness in world markets. Jamieson's comments on the Social Charter and Social Chapter have already been noted in this regard. Purdy and Devine contend that the main objection to these initiatives was the philosophy of social regulation that underpinned them (Purdy and Devine, 1995:290–91). According to the opponents of this philosophy, the social policy of the EU was a bad idea because their own version of liberal capitalist ideology suggested that labour markets, like other markets, only worked efficiently if left largely to the invisible hand of free market economics. Government or EU intervention on any significant scale merely impedes this invisible hand and efficiency, and therefore has a negative effect upon economic growth. This view led to specific opposition to any interventionist policy which might add to employers' costs or restrict their freedom of manoeuvre within the labour market (Purdy and Devine, 1995:290). From this perspective, EU social policy is largely an economic cost on prosperity which goes against the spirit of the common market and it should be, in consequence, vigorously resisted. The former British Prime Minister, John Major, has frequently described the Social Chapter as a 'European tax on jobs' (for example, Conservative party political broadcast, 18 April 1996). When in power, he argued that its implementation would wreck the aims of his party of making Britain the 'enterprise centre of Europe', able to compete with the economies of the states of the Pacific Basin.[7]

The arguments against EU regional policy

Right wing free marketeers of a decidedly Eurosceptic disposition are highly dubious about the value of EU regional policy. They see it as only having a minimal effect in improving the economic performance of the poorer regions. On the other hand, they view this policy as having enormous propaganda value for the EU in so far as it is a highly visible symbol of the 'European ideal' in action (Jamieson, 1993:183). For some, the continuing growth of these regional funds is a crucial factor in the 'Euro-ratchet' effect which they perceive as forcing Britain down the road towards a federal superstate. As the funds grow ever larger, it is argued, parallel demands will grow for increased representation in the central institutions to influence the disbursement process. This, in turn, will lead to the increasing influence of the European Parliament and the Commission. The prospect of the continuing expansion of structural funds (under the guise of promoting economic convergence) is seen as diverting the EU away from the old ideal of the common market towards a Euro-federal goal which for the Eurosceptics is totally unacceptable (Jamieson, 1993:183–87).

Many on the right of free-market economics see regional development policies as a tax on the profitable areas of economic activity in support of the unprofitable. Attempts to create or to regenerate economic activity in areas which are geographically far from major markets or where the workforce is inflexible are ill-judged in the eyes of such people. The overall result, it is argued, is often a decrease in economic growth because the resources diverted to the poorer regions could be used far more productively in the richer ones. The best solution, therefore, is to leave matters to the market. The workforce within the European Union should start to behave more like that of the United States and move to areas where jobs are being created rather than wait for the jobs to come to them. Many Irish and Southern Italian nationals, for example, have in the past solved their problems of local unemployment by being prepared to move to the United States, so why should not the same process occur within the EU? The role of the EU should be restricted to ensuring that the labour market is allowed to act freely and to facilitate and encourage such a movement. Such a free-market process as this would, of course, require the most efficient working of the EU economy and one of the preconditions of such efficiency is that the workforce must accept rates of pay which favour rather than threaten job creation. Free marketeers claim to have at their disposition a range of strategies in order to facilitate this ideal.

The arguments in favour of the EU social policy

There are many on the left and centre left who believe that a strong EU social dimension is necessary in order to protect the interests of ordinary employees in Europe against the possible harmful designs of some employers. Right from the beginning of the 1992 process their concern has been to prevent what has been called 'social dumping', the levelling down of established wages, standards and rights, which it was feared would result from the removal of barriers to pan-European competition (Purdy and Devine, 1995:289). Such supporters of social policy include people who see closer economic integration as having negative consequences for some regions and social groups whatever the attitudes of employers. For them a strong social dimension is needed to compensate for such alleged negative effects as these. Such views are motivated by left/centre concerns for social justice as well as by a belief that markets cannot simply be left to their own devices without causing damage to certain groups of European citizenry and regions. From within this perspective, it can also be argued that the encouragement of a low wage, low welfare economy of the kind envisaged by the last British Conservative government simply depresses overall domestic demand because too few wage earners have the financial resources to boost consumer spending. This, it is argued, restricts domestic economic growth because those manufacturers relying primarily on the home market find little scope for any expansion of their sales. Such an economy, it could be argued, also encourages crime (for many the supplement of a low income). Moreover, to extend this argument, the need experienced by many people caught in this poverty trap to hold down several poorly paid and insecure part-time jobs, together with the pressures to work longer and anti-social hours, helps break down the social fabric of a state or region. This process most commonly expresses itself in the breakdown of family relationships, and a rise in the crime rate with all its attendant costs to society. In short, the failure to implement an adequate social dimension, both nationally and within the EU overall, could be argued to carry heavy costs in other respects.

Among the most committed social welfarists, within this perspective, there is a fundamental belief in the importance of maximising the well-being of all EU citizens, within what they see as the mainstream European tradition of *widely defined* social progress. Hence the concern, within the Social Charter, not just with straightforward salary matters, but with employee rights across the spectrum, from trade union representation to worker consultation, to the right to decent pensions, to the right to a safe working environment. For critics viewing it from within this perspective, precisely the extent to which EU social policy is believed to have been, and to be a benefit to the people of Europe, depends upon where such critics sit in ideological terms. Obviously those with the most far-reaching ambitions for EU intervention will be greatly disappointed, whereas this disappointment will decrease the further one moves away from such ambitions. Equally, those who take an incrementalist approach to the achievability of social change will be less pessimistic about the progress made so far than those inclined more towards the 'big bang' way of doing things. However, by any reasonable interpretation of social policy measures that have been made into EU law, the achievement so far, while having been of undoubted value from the point of view of many of their beneficiaries, has been extremely modest. Indeed, it is probably fair to say that most people within the EU would be hard pressed to name more than a very few aspects of the EU's social dimension that might affect them in a manner they considered beneficial. As with regional policy, one of the main limiting factors that restricts the amount of funds which might be made available for more far-reaching policy programmes remains the huge amount of EU resources still eaten up by the Common Agricultural Policy.

The arguments in favour of the EU regional policy

People holding many of the views referred to immediately above tend to be favourable towards the idea of an EU regional policy on the grounds that, without the coordinated and substantial assistance from the EU's richer states which a truly effective regional policy would provide, the poorest states of the EU will remain permanently poor. For them, not only is an EU regional policy necessary on social grounds, but the successes resulting from the American recovery programmes for Japan and Western Europe after the Second World War demonstrate powerfully that interventionist economics can be highly successful if handled in the right way. The reason, they argue, why so far the EU regional policy has not been dramatically successful (when compared to the scale of the need across the EU as a whole) is that it has not been adequately funded nor correctly shaped. There was also, in the case of Britain, the previously mentioned tendency of the Conservatives (during the Thatcher governments) to use EC structural funds to substitute their own spending, instead of adding to it, as was intended by the Commission.

From this point of view, therefore, what is necessary is for regional aid funds to be administered through channels and institutions that are designed to maximise the efficiency of their usage and the effectiveness of their targeting. Also, their size should be sufficiently proportional to the problems faced so as to enable substantial progress to be made towards the resolution of the latter. Should such requirements be met, then regional policy could begin to make the impact that inadequacies in each of the above respects have so far prevented. As far as Britain is concerned, the money that it has received for regional and social fund projects, has, at the very least, helped to compensate for the money which British governments have had to pay into the EU budget as a whole, and into the CAP in particular. Given the penchant for public spending cuts of the Conservative governments of the 1980s and 1990s, it has also, quite possibly, provided resources for those in need within eligible regions that otherwise would not have been made available.

The broader advantages of the social and regional policy

Some see EU social and regional policy in considerably more far-reaching terms than simply their basic economic and social dimensions. They see them as important building blocks towards much wider and more fundamental goals. Some of those who believe that the degree of European integration that has been achieved so far, or a continuing deepening of the integration process, is vital to future peace and security, in a continent that has long been prone to destructive wars, see social and regional policy as being an essential means of helping to secure long-term support of the EU citizens for the Union. Without such support, obviously, the EU could easily start to fall apart whenever the political going (on EU issues) got even only temporarily rough for some of its key member governments. Should the Americans decide to retire from Europe in the future, potentially catastrophic wars could become a real possibility, once more, in a politically fragmented continent lacking in the kind of unique close cooperation/ stability-inducing organisations that the European communities have represented for so much of the post-Second World War period. To the extent that regional and social policy can help build such support, therefore, they are highly important and should be promoted whether or not they make perfect economic sense.

The Euro-federalist view

Finally, there is the perspective of the out-and-out Euro-federalists who see old style European states in all their variety as being simply too small to represent the interests of the people of the continent adequately in an age of actual and emerging superstates such as the USA, Japan and the People's Republic of China. This moreover, in an age also characterised by the phenomenon of globalisation.[8] For them it is necessary to build a new federal Europe which is large enough to stand up to the world's giant powers and the newly emerging global economic forces, using all the available support mechanisms that can be mustered. In this context, regional and social policies, designed to appeal to the people of Europe, and thereby enhance the image of the EU, are a valuable part of the support building process. Equally, as Jamieson and others point out (see above), promoting the growth of such funds can be one way of increasing the powers and competence of EU institutions, thereby further advancing the integration process.

Conclusion

It would be possible to go on in this vein, citing arguments for and against the effects of further integration with the European Union for the British public, almost *ad infinitum*. For reasons of space however, we have to draw matters to a close here. The arguments on which we have focused are those that seem to us to be some of the most important and influential, and which best serve to illustrate the breadth and depth of the debate on the costs and benefits of EU integration. The readers' response to them will be mostly determined by their differing ideological convictions which will encourage them to accept some of the arguments we present whilst rejecting others.

However, we also stated at the beginning of this chapter that we would offer some thoughts on the relative potency of the various arguments. One insight which could be convincingly offered is that all other costs and benefits of the EU are subordinate to the issues of security and stability. Without these latter conditions, war and the use of bullying and violence short of war become once more viable policy instruments for those with the necessary power. We would wish to argue that, in this respect, the value of the EU to the British and other European publics cannot reasonably be doubted. Those who argue that NATO has been the main guarantor of post-1945 western European security do so with some credibility, given the huge and largely American supplied nuclear arsenal that Europe has at its disposal. Nor can it be denied that in the post-Cold-War world NATO retains a key role in the security architecture of Europe as a whole. But it is the European Community/Union that has provided the forum within which the old enemies of Germany and France have become close European collaborators. This is especially remarkable, given the partial withdrawal of France from NATO in the mid-1960s.

It is the European Community/Union working alongside NATO which provided a crucial part of the overall framework within which it was possible to reunify Germany in a way which allayed the fears of its neighbours, and of the United States and the then Soviet Union. It is also the European Union that has provided the stabilising core and motivating focus around which both its existing western members, and the former Warsaw Pact states can construct key economic and political ambitions in a cooperative manner.

The values of these stabilising roles played by the EU is easily overlooked by those who can only recall the comparatively war-free period that Europe has experienced since 1945. Those with a longer-term historical perspective will be aware of the instabilities that lie uneasily beneath the surface of European society and politics. Indeed, their continuing presence has been only too well emphasised by the bitter conflicts which raged in former Yugoslavia during the first half of the 1990s. Yugoslavia, as a state outside the EU system, demonstrated graphically how easily the hatreds that simplistic analysis might suggest are no longer a threat within European society can surface when the political framework of a European state is seriously destabilised.

It is true that there are arguments put forward in opposition to this view which assert that the war in former Yugoslavia does not in itself demonstrate that another trans-European war, as opposed to 'relatively minor and containable' civil wars, is a likely future scenario, if only because the larger European states are now too firmly democratic and stable for such a thing to be a realistic possibility.[9] Therefore, it is argued, the perceived stabilising role of the EU is no longer crucial within the wider framework of European politics. In order to oppose this view fully we should have to refer to a wide-ranging debate on the causes of war, crossing over the fields of political science, history, economics, psychology and sociology.[10] Again, space and the need to maintain our focus on the main topics of this book dictate brevity, and thus we propose here simply to list the range of conditions which would have to be in place before a 'no major war in Europe' claim could be made. They are as follows:

> Either the first two conditions set out below or, if these cannot be attained, all of those that follow them:

1. *It would be necessary permanently to remove the temptation to resort to violence in all forms of political behaviour at all levels of society.* Only then would it be possible to guarantee, for example, that in potentially destabilising circumstances of economic and social crisis, no ruthless persons or groups (with expansionist ambitions vis-à-vis other states) within one of the major European states would bully their way into power with the aid of street thugs, the collusion of the police and the tacit approval of the people, as happened with both Mussolini and Hitler.

2. It would be necessary for aggressive governments, should they achieve power in major European states in the future, to be effectively constrained in their ambitions by the fear that the nuclear weapons present in Europe might be used against them if they were to initiate a major war. Now that the head-to-head superpower confrontation is ended, it might be possible for such governments to doubt the resolve of the nations disposing of·the deterrent to use it. After all, one of the lessons of Chernobyl, that will not have gone unnoticed, is that radiation is just as likely to travel back towards the initiators of nuclear strikes as it is to poison the attacked. Equally, it would be necessary for small and medium-sized European powers, which may be tempted to initiate wars that could escalate into wider conflicts, to be constrained by *credible* conventional deterrents.

3. It would be necessary to remove the much documented tendency of many ordinary people to look the other way and 'look after number one' when faced with the rise of potentially aggressive leaders prepared to use tactics of bullying and intimidation to achieve power.[11]

4. *It would be necessary to remove forever the destructive phenomenon of racism from European society* which has so frequently led to some ethnic groups being dehumanised in the eyes of others and thereby transformed into 'legitimate' targets for violence. The killing of the Jews that continued in Poland after the Second World War, the burning to death of whole families of Muslims in the former Yugoslavia and of Turks in Germany in the 1990s, all suggest that there is a long way to go before such goals are attained.

5. It would be necessary for European democratic states to be able *to guarantee* that they would remain *permanently* free of extreme economic recessions and the accompanying social and political unrest that historically have provided the conditions in which aggressive leaders can rise to power. Liberal capitalism has yet to demonstrate that such a level of economic stability can be attained. Indeed, the combination of modern technologies, which allow huge capital movements from one economy to another in seconds, and the freeing of controls on such movements, has meant that the potential instabilities within the capitalist system have been enormously increased. This is one of the reasons why an effective EMU within the EU is argued to be necessary.

6. But this alone would not be enough. It would be necessary to find a way to prevent aggressive leaders from achieving power by any means or within any context, in all significant European states, on a permanent basis.
7. *It would be necessary to ensure that all potential future sources of serious grievance and misunderstanding, such as territorial disputes between European states, are removed.* The drawing and the re-drawing of European boundaries that has occurred after the major conflicts of the twentieth century provides latent sources of tension which could be reactivated immediately within favourable circumstances.

Unless either of the first two of the above conditions, or all of the rest, can be attained then it is not possible to claim with any confidence that a future European war is unlikely. Until they can be realised, therefore, it can be argued convincingly that the EU remains of great importance as a tried and trusted stabilising force in its own right, and with NATO, a vital part of the overarching European security frame-work. A joint concern of NATO and the EU states is to try to create the conditions within and between their members, and between the latter and non-NATO European powers, which will minimise the chances of instabilities of the kind mentioned earlier in the chapter developing. These objectives are aimed at the foreseeable future in which the United States remains a major and committed military force on European soil, and at the much longer term in which a future US President and Congress might decide to take their troops home and focus more on the Pacific or even on an isolationist position. This has been one of the declared, key concerns of Chancellor Kohl in tying the united Germany so firmly into both organisations.

What becomes crucial once this aim is accepted as fundamental to European security is how the European Union sets about trying to fulfil its half of this ambition. The questions of whether or not EMU will help or hinder this aspiration, for example, and of whether there are some ways of achieving EMU that are likely to realise it better than others, are perfectly legitimate areas for informed debate within the newsprint media and elsewhere. But if that debate is to be sincerely directed towards the best interests of the British people it needs to be free of simple business or nationalistic agendas on the part of proprietors and their editorial staffs and directed towards the wider interests of the public who partially rely on their newspapers for the supply of opinion-forming information and analysis. What needs to be hunted for is an answer to the EMU question which will best serve the security interests of the UK and the wider European public as the first priority and their broader economic and social interests as its second. Most crucially, if it is to be a useful debate it needs to be one that is informed by an adequate understanding of the issues by the journalists who partake in it on behalf of the media. Our subsequent chapters will address the question of the quality of media coverage of the EU.

This fundamental security function of the EU is something that needs to inform the broader coverage of EU issues within the media. The unprincipled proliferation of stories that focus on and exaggerate the EU's weaknesses purely for the sake of selling papers or to satisfy the prejudices of a proprietor or editor can be a serious threat to public support for the basic principle of EU membership, and in the light of this analysis, a device which undermines part of the framework upon which the security of present and future generations rests.

But, if the case upon which one of the key premises of this book is built can be constructed so centrally around security matters, this does not imply that they are the only grounds upon which it can rest. It was pointed out at the beginning of this section that many aspects of the economic and social debate over the EU are difficult to prove convincingly to all parties because of their dependence upon particular ideological perspectives and whether or not these are held by the individuals at which the debate is directed. However, obviously this does not preclude particular economic and social arguments from being important to those whose ideological perspective makes them appear so. They can be crucial reasons for supporting the EU for such people.

Finally, the sections of this chapter that cover economic and social issues are not only useful in showing something of the true range of arguments that is on offer concerning the EU, *but by so doing* provide a useful yardstick against which the quality of press coverage of the EU debate and of EU issues in general can be measured. As pointed out at the beginning, this is a crucial function of the chapter with regard to the later chapters concerned with analysing newspaper content on Europe. In addition. the very breadth of the debate that has been presented here emphasises that there is no open and shut negative case that can be advanced on economic and social aspects of EU membership as would often seem to be suggested by the overall perspectives presented within Eurosceptic tabloid coverage of the EU.

In the three chapters that follow, we shall closely examine the representation of Europe in the British press in the light of the discussions we have offered in Chapters 1 and 2. This, then, makes it the appropriate point in our book to cross a new discourse frontier in order to explore that turbulent media realm of the newspapers, and to find out more precisely what they have to say about Britain's future relationship with the European Union.

Notes

1. The various security scenarios outlined here represent only part of what is a wide-ranging debate. For additional perspectives see, for example, Park and Wyn Rees (1998) and Wyllie (1997).
2. This was the line of argument that was being publicly advanced by Malcolm Rifkind as part of the great squabble over Europe within the British Conservative Cabinet during February 1995.

3. For example, the disincentive for industrial investment created by political corruption and Mafia activity in southern Italy, or the inability of some traditional UK firms concentrated in the northern part of the country to adjust adequately to economic change.
4. For a slightly more sceptical view of the impact of developments such as robotisation see P. Kennedy (1993:94).
5. See Nugent (1993:251–3).
6. This is a line of argument that has been advanced within the *Economist* newspaper at various times, for example.
7. His social policy views echoed those of Mrs Thatcher. See, for example, Swann (1992:222).
8. For a useful introduction to the globalisation debate see Hirst and Thompson (1996), Bretherton and Ponton (1996) and Anderson (1996).
9. This is a view that has been advanced by some former Conservative MPs, for example.
10. A broad overview of key ideas within this debate can be obtained by reading, for example, Waltz (1959), Blainey (1988) and Anderson (1996).
11. See, for example, Grunberger (1971), and the well-documented preparedness of many people in the former Yugoslavia to tolerate brutal behaviour towards others on the part of their leaders when promised access to the property and goods of some of the brutalised.

Chapter 3

Euroscepticism in the British press

Introduction

Euroscepticism in the pre-election period

Euroscepticism is a phenomenon affecting both the left and the right in British politics. However, in the dying days of the last Conservative government it became almost entirely an issue for the right. Given the size of New Labour's victory, it is clear that Europe was not the deciding factor in the campaign, but it can be safely said that, if there were doubts about the fitness of the Tories to continue in government, then the schism opened up by the very public, emotional and un-disciplined debate within the Conservative Party did nothing to dispel them. So, when we speak of Euroscepticism as expressed in the press during the run-up to the 1997 election, we are talking mostly about the right-of-centre version represented in the Tory press, although as we shall see later, a more dilute form was to surface occasionally elsewhere.

The language of the hustings in British elections is no place for the faint-hearted. Their discourse is characterised neither by moderation nor by appeals to rational thinking. Europe, in the event, seems to have been wrongly identified as a major preoccupation of the electorate, but was certainly represented in the Eurosceptic press with all the fire, passion and antipathy of a perceived defining moment in the politics of the right. So, perhaps the press representation of the Eurosceptics' case in March and April 1997 turned out in retrospect to be a debate more about the future leadership of the Conservative Party than it was about which party was to govern the country. It was, as we have said, a passionate and emotional discourse, impressive for the force of its anti-European rhetoric but with some disturbing elements in it too. More of this later.

The British press sector

The British press sector is weighted very heavily towards the right-of-centre. Eleven of the total nineteen dailies and Sunday titles are unequivocally voices of the right and account between them for 21 of the total 26 million overall circulation (Peak and Fisher, 1997:45). Comparatively speaking, Britain has one of the most commercially successful press sectors in Europe. Its success is due in part to the financial advantages that flow from economies of scale which, in this case, translate themselves into high levels of concentration of owner-ship and in part to the distinctly commercial objectives of the sector which affects both the content and style of newspaper journalism.

In terms of Euroscepticism there are two main consequences which flow from this situation. The first is that, due to the concentration of ownership, and the dominance of the right in this media sector, Eurosceptic voices are in the majority. The second is that the inexorable commercial drive of the press sector to sustain itself at all costs has influenced the quality of the discourse. The discourse of some titles has become highly conversationalised, emotive and often strongly xenophobic. It frequently leaves much to be desired.

Approaches to the analysis and the commentary

Our approach to the analysis of what may be called the 'European discourse' of the written press was on a broad front and over a relatively short (but significant) period of time. It included the reading and the analysis of a range of discourse which appeared in the broadsheets and the tabloids in the eight-week period preceding the General Election of 1997 (March–April 1997). In addition, in order to include as much up-to-date material and comment into our work as possible, it also contains a second, follow-up commentary on the discourse of the press at four key points in the later post-election period when Britain, headed by a new government, presided over the Council of Ministers of the EU (January–June 1998).

We consider that our analysis of the discourse for the periods mentioned reveals the characteristic features of the voices, Europhile as well as Eurosceptic, which have *significantly* pre-dated and will post-date the time of our analysis within a particular newspaper. In other words, these voices are not 'one off' occurrences. They are not isolated nor localised in time, not least because, by our definition of discourse, their features derive from previously 'spoken' events at some un-specified time in the past, as we described them in Chapter 1 (see Figure 1.1) and, importantly, they will recur in a discourse yet to be generated in the future.

In the course of our commentary we shall refer to some of the concepts that we outlined in Chapter 1 relating to processes of cultural identification, to history and, importantly, to the nature and quality of the discourse itself. In order to make specific comments upon the European content of the discourse, we shall refer back to the arguments both for and against that we presented in the last chapter. In Chapter 2 we outlined the essential arguments for and against the further integration of Britain, at a deeper level, in the European Union. Whilst the set of arguments we include is fairly representative, it is nevertheless incomplete. Even so, we suspect that for many readers, the points and counterpoints made in this chapter were complicated enough (not to say byzantine in parts) to be deemed a sufficient and substantial working basis of information on the issues surrounding European integration. If, incidentally, the reader detects in our own discourse an overt as well as ideological pro-European underpinning, we should not protest. We should point out, though, that this pro-European leaning is related more to the manner in which Europe is represented in the media than it is to an entrenched position on the issue of integration itself. In short, we favour a more open-minded discourse on the issues relating to integration, particularly in some sectors of the written press.

So, bearing these points in mind, we propose in the next three chapters to examine the discourse of the Eurosceptic and the pro-European press, first by theme, then by newspaper title and finally in Chapter 5 by events. We shall need to quote from specific articles, although space dictates that these quotations must be selective and brief. In many cases, therefore, material deemed to be irrelevant will be omitted. This practice is not without problems which we shall mention more fully below.

The commentary based on our analysis which follows in this and the next chapter is undertaken with a broad brush. We wish to convey as big a picture as possible of the main themes of the anti- and pro-European arguments across the range of the British daily press. For this reason we have resisted the temptation to focus narrowly upon a micro-analysis of a small number of texts, preferring instead to illustrate the themes with as many examples as possible. Evidently, one of the disadvantages of this approach is the loss therefore of detailed analysis. But there are advantages too which we hope outweigh the others. This book is intended for use by a multi-disciplinary readership and one objective at least is to show how salient aspects of critical discourse theory can be used by non-specialist analysts to analyse media data in order to make meaningful judge-ments of (in this case) press performance. In Chapter 5 we adopt a slightly different approach with the focus of the analysis on just four events occurring during the British presidency, one which permits more depth of treatment and is weighted more towards the political aspects of the discourse.

At appropriate points in the commentary in this chapter and the next, we shall pause at an evaluation and summary sub-section in order that our overall assessment of the newspaper's performance can be made. Finally, at the practical level of the conventions surrounding the quoting of texts, we shall indicate an omitted section by the use of a three-point ellipsis ' ... Chancellor Kohl ... insisted that the criteria will be met in full ... '. Where the referent of the discourse is unclear due to editing of this kind, we shall insert the referent, and use square brackets to indicate our intervention in the text, as in, ' ... he [Chancellor Kohl] described the EMU as vital to the further deepening of the integration process'. At the end of the excerpt, we shall indicate the date, page and the name of the journalist, if known.

So, the time has come to invite the reader to accompany us on a journey through the sites of European discourse of both camps. Along the way, we shall encounter a variety of voices, some distanced and rational, others much less so. Indeed, there are yet others which are plainly disturbing for the extremity of the views they represent. Whatever the reader's reactions to the discourse are, we think that the journey will not be a dull one.

The discourse of Euroscepticism

Although the discourse of the Eurosceptics was to be found in every title examined, it was most consistently in evidence in the *Mail*, the *Sun*, the *Express*, *The Times* and the *Daily Telegraph*, as well as in their Sunday stablemates. The quality of the discourse ranged from the closely argued case opposing all moves towards further integration, drawing on many of the arguments outlined in Chapter 2, to the unveiled, if not naked xenophobic discoursal assault upon EU officials, upon other members of the European Union, as well as upon its underlying political, social and other objectives. The reasons for the opposition to further European integration fall into three unexceptional main categories – economic (with socio-political undertones), political (mainly sovereignty and defence issues) and the historico-cultural, including at its most extreme, a palpable dislike of foreigners, and of Germany in particular. These thematic categories sometimes overlap but nevertheless constitute a convenient way of structuring the commentary on the data. Using these categories, we can list under each the major issues which were the focus of the Eurosceptic discourse overall. These were as follows:

Economic (with socio-political associations)
- The economic consequences of the single currency for Britain were we to enter the EMU;
- The consequences for British industry were we to sign the Social Chapter;
- The evidence of faltering economies of our major partners as the consequence of their governments' attempts to meet the Maastricht criteria for EMU membership;
- The evidence of increased socio-political unrest in member states relating to issues raised by the requirements of future EMU membership.

Political (mainly issues of sovereignty and defence)
- The political implications for British sovereignty once we joined the EMU;
- The effects of current EU intervention in the governance of Britain (as a projection of things to come);
- The effectiveness of the institutions of the EU at the level of inter-governmental cooperation, including foreign policy and defence;
- The European Union as a political system and the effectiveness of its officials.

Historico-cultural
- The consequences of the activities of other EU member states and of the perceived expansionist ambitions of Germany in particular; in the light of the recent past.

- The effects of the intervention of the EU upon the traditional freedom of Britain to act independently on a range of issues now, and at critical moments in the future.

These, then, were the major themes of the Eurosceptic discourse. Before moving to the analysis proper, we need to point out three separate but oddly associated features of journalistic practice expressed in media discourse which are noteworthy since we shall be referring to them later in the unfolding of the commentary. When attempting to plot the dominant direction of a paper's discourse, we noted frequent recourse by journalists to verbatim quotations of politicians and others in respect of European issues, for example:

> Mr Evans, MP for Welwyn and Hatfield, said, 'don't trust the French and the Belgians to be there when it matters. Twice this century they haven't been there', he said. (*The Times*, 6.3.97:2)

This practice, it can be argued, amounts to the faithful, unvarnished relaying of information from source to reader without the apparent intervention of the journalist, and is by definition therefore desirable. On reflection, however, it will be seen that this practice, whilst it assumes a quality of impartiality by suggesting distance and objectivity, can be deceptive. Its potential for deception derives of course from the fact that it is selective – presumably for reasons of space, the integral text of the discourse cannot be repeated in the newspaper – but selection is often partial, serving to advance the bias of the wider discourse in which the selected quotes are embedded at a secondary level. Having drawn this practice to the reader's attention, we need to point out that we use selection extensively ourselves because we too cannot countenance the inclusion of full length texts in this book. We would wish to argue that our attitudes towards the selection of the data – edited excerpts from the papers – are more objective than those of some of the journalists who choose to quote from the speeches of the Eurosceptics or Europhiles, but, as we have already suggested, there is no absolute proof of the truth of this assertion. In this regard, just as it is a good principle to check out the whole speech of individuals quoted for their views in the press where necessary, so it may be a good idea not to accept our view of the texts we select at face value, but to trace them in the original, or at least to check the current editions of the paper concerned in order to confirm that our commentaries, in their general direction, are well judged.

The second feature of note is the practice common in all the British press of extending column space to major public figures, movements or parties either directly or in the form of an interview, as a platform for promoting their particular cause. This was the case with *The Times* which invited the Eurosceptic and defector to the Referendum Party, Sir George Gardiner, as well as another colourful Referendum candidate, David Bellamy, to write articles, in order to allow them to express their particular brand of Euroscepticism directly to the reader.

Finally, as well as providing a platform for public figures to express their views which are deemed to move distinctly with the flow of the paper's own discourse, newspapers occasionally offer column space to voices whose discourse actually runs in the opposite direction to the general flow. Such was the case when *The Times* published an article by Peter Riddell arguing strongly for the deepening of the integration process (see Text 3.5 below). Another was when the *Daily Telegraph* gave the German foreign secretary, Klaus Kinkel, a platform to present the Europhile case from a German/European perspective (see Text 3.25 below). The possible significance of these three practices will all be discussed again later in this book.

Let us now turn to the voices of particular newspapers starting with the Eurosceptic broadsheets, *The Times* and the *Daily Telegraph*.

The Eurosceptic broadsheets

The Times

The economic implications

One focus of *The Times* discourse in March 1997 is the economic and social anxieties which our European partners are experiencing in their attempts to meet the Maastricht criteria for entry to EMU. This focus is illustrated in Texts 3.1–3.4. below, and since it is an important issue, it will recur at later periods in 1998 as well as here. Moreover, it is not restricted to the Eurosceptic press, and, as we shall point out again in Chapter 5, the intentions to be inferred from the representations of this social and economic turbulence in Europe vary according to their press origins: in the case of the Eurosceptics they are in service of rejection of the single currency whereas with the pro-European they appear to support the voices of caution. Note in 3.1 below the extreme representation of German unemployment and, in 3.2 the way in which the closure of the Belgian Renault factory is elevated to a dispute between Belgium and France (instead of between the sacked workers and the manufacturer).

Text 3.1   (Roger Boyes, 3.3.97:10)

German jobless record batters Euro entry hopes

... but with unemployment running out of control ... and it [Germany] is thus set to fail the monetary union entry test on two counts ...

Text 3.2   *The Times* (Permission withheld)

Relates to Renault workers' protest march in Belgium.
See comments above. Access via CD-ROM or micro-fiche (4.3.97:12, ll. 2–9).

Text 3.3   (Roger Boyes, 7.3.97:15)

German unions urge brake on euro as unemployment rises

... It came as Germany announced it was still failing to bring down unemployment.

This discourse as we have said, focuses on a well-known and justifiable fear – unemployment – of the Eurosceptics which is not restricted to Britain. We shall encounter it frequently in this chapter as well as at a later stage in our commentary.

In addition to the above, *The Times* also gives wide coverage to the alleged 'gaffes' of the then Conservative MP for Welwyn, David Evans, for reasons which may be considered less justifiable. Note here the use of *secondary discourse* in the form of direct quotations.

Text 3.4   (Phillip Webster and Joanne Bale, 6.3.97:2)

... On the single European currency he said: 'We didn't have two world wars to give it up for the deutschmark. They've had two shots at us on the battle field and I happen to believe this is the third...'

In contrast to the distinctly Eurosceptic tone which dominates the discourse of *The Times*, Peter Riddell's is a lone voice of dissent:

Text 3.5   (Peter Riddell, 12.3.97:12)

Once the real alternatives and benefits of the EU are highlighted, I have little doubt that the people would again support our membership in a referendum ... So the Tories would be unelectable if they became openly hostile to British membership.

Riddell's regular and articulate voice is conspicuous for the opposing direction of its discourse to that of the dominant economic scepticism in *The Times*. Overall, as we have pointed out, the paper's stand on EMU is hostile.

The political implications

In this category of Euroscepticism, *The Times* focuses on several alleged weaknesses of the integration process of which a recurring note is the indecision and ineffectiveness of the EU in matters relating to foreign policy and to the enlargement question. Charles Bremner, in Text 3.6, raising the rare criticism relating to the worthiness of the then current presidency of the Council of Ministers (Holland) and the presidency of the Commission (Luxembourg), makes the point that Europe is led by politicians from the small, Benelux countries. Whilst this discourse is not wholly sceptical about European achievements in foreign policy, its tone is nevertheless critical, particularly where it sees federalism and common foreign and security issues on the agenda.

Text 3.6   (Charles Bremner, 3.3.97:10)

> ... Five years ago, at Maastricht, the Federal dreamers set about equipping
> the new Union with bigger clout abroad, to be backed up eventually with
> the military muscle that you need for serious diplomacy. But little has
> changed as America prepares to lead NATO into the old Soviet bloc while
> the Union finds excuses to delay its own move eastwards. Since the debacle
> of EU diplomacy in former Yugoslavia ...

Bremner, in Text 3.7 below, continues in the same vein, implying
that the political activities of EU politicians are usually cramped,
lacking in both cohesion and vision. Note the passing reference to the
'eastern front', in this case the applications for admission to the EU of
countries such as Rumania and Turkey, but which also mischievously
links with its older historical antecedent (and older ideological rami-
fication) which ended Germany's expansionist dreams of 1942.

Text 3.7   (Charles Bremner, 10.3.97:13)

> **Brussels pushed to settle conflict on eastern front**
>
> ... a gathering of statesmen in the drab Dutch *dorp* this week ... For once
> the 15 are to eschew domestic preoccupations ... they are to do something
> rare: think big [Turkish application to join the EU] ...

In addition to this sceptic voice on foreign policy, *The Times* also
published in this period three articles on European defence, one of
which discusses the issue almost entirely in the context of NATO,
dismissing by implication the possibility of a European defence
policy (3.3.97:6), and the second by the then Minister for Defence,
Malcolm Rifkind, in which the proposed European Defence Force is
explicitly dismissed (10.3.97:10). The third alludes to the EU defence
policy project as a 'blueprint' originating in Paris and Bonn (12.3.97:14).

On the issue of the political implications of joining the single
currency, Text 3.8 is a good example of the orthodox scepticism of
The Times on the constitutional implications and British sovereignty.
The comparison is with the development of a single currency in the
United States.

Text 3.8   *The Times* (Permission withheld)

> Contains interesting comparison between the euro and dollar in
> which it is argued that joining the single currency will strike at the
> core of British sovereignty by gradually moving Britain and all
> member states towards political integration.
> Access via CD-ROM and micro-fiche (Gary L. McDowell, 5.3.97:18,
> ll. 98–103, 131–34).

History and culture

In Chapter 2 we devoted a considerable space, albeit in passing,
to presenting the issue of European integration from a German
perspective. As might be anticipated, the scepticism of *The Times*

includes strong elements of Germanophobia which stresses the alleged unfinished nature of Germany's historic expansionist ambitions. It can be argued that the views of David Evans are significantly quoted in Text 3.9 below, evoking an old, but still active ideological reference to the Second World War for those who care to hear it in the same manner as in Text 3.7 above (see also Text 3.11 below).

Text 3.9   (Peter Webster and Joanna Bale, 6.3.97:2)

> Mr Evans said France and Belgium would be unfit to defend Europe and compared the creation of a single currency to Germany's wartime aggression ... 'I don't trust the French or the Belgians to be there when it matters.' ...

Chancellor Kohl, for some voices of *The Times*, personifies the Germanic qualities of historical aggression and military expansionism:

Text 3.10   *The Times* (Permission withheld)

> Contains colourful and strong Eurosceptic arguments. Europe is likened to the giant in the fairy tale *Jack and the Beanstalk* – i.e. 'Fee, Fi, Fo, Fum, I smell the blood of an Englishman'.
> Access via CD-ROM and micro-fiche (William Rees-Mogg, 3.3.97:20, ll. 196–202).

At a later date, in an extraordinary representation in the *The Times Magazine* section, this caricature of Kohl as an aggressive German voraciously pursuing German ambitions is repeated and, even though it is dismissed as a caricature, one wonders why it was reiterated here in the first place, if not to reinforce the image and its underlying ideological implication.

Text 3.11   (Roger Boyes 8.3.97:12)

> **Sad King Kohl**
>
> The British in particular regard Kohl's appetite as an unhealthy metaphor for the nation's ambition. The man guzzles two dinners, the nation eats up East Germany and, having barely digested the ex-communist state, turns its gaze on Europe. But this cartoon version of current events has always been too rough on Germany, too neglectful of 50 years of democratic rule ... His eating habits may upset those with frailer stomachs, but they do not reflect deep seated ambitions ...

In an insert embedded in this article, extolling the refusal of Margaret Thatcher to be impressed with Kohl, there is an interesting, associative cultural reference to the anatomy of a pig. The associative force of this reference is loose but distinctly unflattering and anti-German:

Text 3.12   *The Times Magazine* (Permission withheld)

> Extract relates how Margater Thatcher, as a dinner guest of Chancellor Helmut Kohl in Germany, was served with a dish containing morsel's of a pig's stomach. Mrs Thatcher subsequently

Figure 3.1   *Source: The Times Magazine*, 8 March 1997

comments upon Kohl's German (rather than European) qualities. It
is both pro-Thatcher and anti-German in tone.
Access via CD-ROM and micro-fiche (George Brock, 8.3.97:16,
col. 4, ll. 37 and col. 5, ll. 11–16).

Finally in this section featuring scepticism rooted in the comparative
histories and cultures of Britain and Europe, *The Times* publishes in this
period articles protesting about the damage caused to traditional British
freedoms in areas which include, among others, the destruction of our
countryside (2.3.97:7), the raising of pedigree animals (4.3.97:4), pensions
(6.3.97:19), corporal punishment (8.3.97:1), and ageism (12.3.97:6).

Summary and evaluation

The discourse of *The Times*, with one or two exceptions, is unequivocal in its opposition to further integration. The discourse, in the main, overtly opposes the integration process. Quantitatively the discourse is plentiful and in terms of the three theoretical discourse functions (representations, identities and relations) the referential or informational element of the representational function is strong with a well-developed ideological dimension (see below). As regards the identities function, there is a general presumption in the discourse of professional, often specialised journalists writing for informed readers. As far as the relations function is concerned, the discourse, in the main, projects a sense of formality and distance between journalist and writer. The only exception to this balance between the three discourse functions is the modification to both the identities (less specialised knowledge) and relations functions (less distance) introduced by the inclusion of secondary discourse – the direct quotations from the speeches of David Evans.

On a covert level of representation, we can detect the principal underlying ideological dimensions of Euroscepticism which we shall encounter repeatedly elsewhere in the course of our analysis reported in this chapter. This ideological underpinning can be summarised as follows:

- The single currency is potentially a source of social and political unrest.
- The single currency is a threat to sovereignty because it leads to federalism.
- A common foreign and defence policy is a federalist ambition.
- Germany still retains its historic ambitions for expansionism.
- The EU is interventionist by inclination and should be kept at arm's length.

Having looked at the discourse of *The Times*, we can now turn to examine that of its arch rival the *Daily Telegraph*.

The Daily Telegraph

Rival it may be, but this paper shares at least one thing with *The Times* – a profound mistrust of further moves by Britain in the direction of integration with the EU. Using the same categories of scepticism as we used for *The Times* we would draw attention to the discourse as follows:

The economic implications

When the *Daily Telegraph* addresses directly the question of possible British membership of the single currency, its discourse is unequivocal:

Text 3.13   (leader, 18.3.97:21)

Six weeks to look before you leap

...we have argued ... that a single currency and all that goes with it, should be eschewed...

Like *The Times*, the *Daily Telegraph* focuses extensively on the economic disquiet which our European partners are experiencing as they contemplate the need to meet the Maastricht entry criteria for the EMU (see Texts 3.14–17 below).

Text 3.14   (18.3.97:13)

We'll miss euro debt target, say Germans

...new rumours of a delay swept Europe's financial markets...

Text 3.15   (28.3.97:37)

European protesters in march for jobs

Workers across the continent are growing increasingly fearful as austerity measures to bring their economies into line with the Maastricht criteria for economic union begin to take their toll in terms of jobs...

Text 3.16   (Alan Gimson, 31.3.97:10)

Germany says no to euro tax

Germans are overwhelmingly opposed to tax rises to meet the Maastricht criteria for European currency...

Text 3.17   (Bruce Johnston, 31.3.97:10)

Rome's secret hope is outside rescue from EMU hook

Italy's resolve to meet the demands of Maastricht is beginning to buckle under the strain...

Anne Segall, writing in the Business Section of the paper, commenting on a letter signed by 23 businesspeople supporting Britain's entry to EMU and sent to the *Financial Times*, has no hesitation in condemning their views out of hand. Notice, in passing, the overt dismissal as well as the covert *implication* that pro-single currency arguments and their supporters are somehow unworthy, as suggested by the items 'flimsiness' and 'peddled'.

Text 3.18   (Anne Segall, 17.3.97:27)

Single currency supporters undermine their own case

[The FT letter] ... will help galvanise opinion against the idea of a single currency by showing up the flimsiness of the arguments peddled by its supporters...

When the *Telegraph* addresses the issue of Britain's possible signing of the social chapter, its discourse is strongly opposed:

Text 3.19   (leader, 23.3.97:32)

Chapter of Accidents

...The social chapter is a deceitful way of [New Labour] imposing social legislation ... [the Social Chapter] spawned only three measures...

Notice how in Text 3.19 above the Social Chapter is described as having 'spawned' three measures, the use of this term, we suspect, refers to a deeply held ideological view relating to the alleged plethora of bureaucratic 'diktats' which accompany European legislation and impact upon and hamper the British manufacturing sector. In Text 3.20 below notice the use of the item 'sclerotic' in reference to the impact of the social chapter which also taps into the same ideological vein.

Text 3.20   (Philip Johnston, 20.3.97:11)

Thatcher's surgery injected new life into Britain

...the Tories do not want to join the social chapter, which they believe, will introduce the sclerotic working practices of continental Europe and a minimum wage...

The political implications

As we have pointed out when discussing the discourse of *The Times* above, one of the features of its political scepticism was the emphasising of the alleged disarray of the EU member states in agreeing on crucial aspects of a common foreign and security policy. We encountered the same focus in the *Daily Telegraph* as illustrated in the following texts (3.21–3.23 below).

Text 3.21   (Toby Helm, 17.3.97:11)

Ministers run into stumbling blocks on the road to enlargement

...But rather than giving the process [enlargement] momentum, yesterday's discussions did the reverse. They provided a foretaste of the thorny diplomatic, financial and institutional battles that will need to be fought before membership of between 25 and 30 countries can be achieved ... How can new countries be admitted without either bankrupting the community or radically reforming the CAP?

On the issue of foreign policy the discourse is equally pessimistic. In Text 3.22, Christopher Lockwood underlines the perceived weaknesses in the EU's approach to the Bosnian civil war.

Text 3.22   (Christopher Lockwood, 18.3.97:13)

EU adopts hands-off approach to crisis

When the Bosnian crisis first developed ... Luxembourg's foreign minister declared it to be 'the hour of Europe' ... Instead the EU has opted for the bare minimum ... it deals a further blow to the aspiration of Europe's 'common foreign and security' which in the past has involved doing little or nothing...

The theme of disarray among the member states is not limited to foreign policy however. In Text 3.23 below it is extended to the single currency as well.

Text 3.23   (Toby Helm, 23.3.97:29)

Europe faces a mid life crisis at 40

...no amount of champagne can cure the problems it now faces ... but these problems are only part of the crisis it now faces. There is growing suspicion that the project [EMU] may be doomed...

On the burning issue of further deepening of the integration process, as we have said, the *Telegraph*'s political position is clearly one of downright scepticism, if not total opposition. But in one of those odd (but worthy) reversals of the general Eurosceptical sweep of its discourse, it publishes on 25 March 1997, an apparently unedited article written by Klaus Kinkel, the German foreign minister, which gives a pro-integration and German perspective on future European development:

Text 3.24   (Klaus Kinkel, 25.3.97:24)

You mustn't slow down Europe's Integration...

Kinkel's article makes a strong case for integration, much of which runs wholly counter to the dominant discourse of the *Telegraph*, and, since we are dealing in this chapter with the discourse of Euroscepticism, we shall not dwell on it here. It is worth noting however, the implication of the headline itself, which is conspicuous for the fact that it originates in the ideology of the pro-European camp. The use of the possessive apostrophe suggests that the process of integration itself *belongs* to Europe as if by historical, socio-economic and political right. This ideological assumption goes right to the heart of the pro-European discourse and its expression here in a headline of the *Telegraph* strikes a bizarre note. If only for that reason, we are not surprised to find that it does not go unremarked. In its leader column on the adjacent page, Kinkel's views are soundly rebuffed in the orthodox Eurosceptical manner (i.e. Britain was deceived).

Text 3.25   (leader, 25.3.97:25)

Europe 40 years on

And what of Britain? ... it is difficult to sustain the charge that the United Kingdom was stand-offish in its attitude after 1945. ... This did not mean however that Britain was prepared to become part of a European federation. Having come through the war undefeated, the British did not feel, as many Europeans did, that their national institutions had failed them...

The discourse of this leader article, which we have listed under the 'political' theme could have figured equally in the *History and culture* subsection below and this serves to underline the fact that our categories are far from discrete. This is principally because the issues we are discussing are multi-faceted so that, for example, the discussion of the single currency may in one text be presented purely from an economic perspective, whereas in another, it may be dealt with mostly as a political issue. They do form, however, a loose but convenient structure upon which to discuss the data.

History and culture

In a similar discourse to that of *The Times*, the *Telegraph* represents Germany, in particular as expansionist and ambitious in its European vision. It is also suspicious of the intentions of the French. Susannah Herbert in Text 3.26, on the alleged failing enthusiasm for EMU of the well-known neo-Gaullist, Charles Pasqua, gives sceptical vent to both the alleged German and French agendas.

Text 3.26 (Susannah Herbert, 19.3.97:14)

The sceptic who puts France first

The German-inspired march towards monetary union has prompted Charles Pasqua to call for his nation to speak for itself. ... M. Pasqua wants France to take advantage of its neighbour's struggles and create a Europe à la française...

In Text 3.27, the discourse focuses first upon the German finance minister, Theo Waigel, in order to discredit his professional competence, and subsequently upon Chancellor Kohl to imply a failing grasp over policy and his willingness to 'fudge' on EMU (the Eurosceptic term for a member state not meeting the Maastricht criteria for entry to the EMU yet presenting itself by means of devious accounting).

Text 3.27 (Andrew Gimsom, 20.3.97:21)

Economic reality breaks in on Waigel's flights of fancy over EMU

Theo Waigel, the Bavarian optimist who has been Chancellor Kohl's finance minister since when East and West Germany were still divided has always been fonder of fiction than of fact ... He [Kohl] knows the growing pressure of events could soon show him up as an out of breath old codger who has failed the German people ... If Mr Kohl decides he is too weak to fudge the criteria...

Depending on the journalist, it would seem that Germany is criticised either for wanting to fudge its entry to EMU, on one hand, or for insisting that the criteria are rigorously upheld, on the other. Susannah Herbert in sceptical voice on the ambitions of Jacques Delors and his alleged dissatisfaction with Germany, represents in Text 3.28 below the diametrically opposed view to that expressed by Andrew Gimson above:

Text 3.28 (Susannah Herbert, 21.3.97:15)

Delors ready to disown EU over euro

... The sub-text ... is critical of the German's obsession with the enforcement of the Maastricht criteria. The Germans have long believed that their vision of Europe can be achieved if the criteria governing candidates' national debt and deficits are strictly enforced...

The Eurosceptic discourse of the *Telegraph* during this period, of course, was associated with, and in the service of, the wider discourse relating to the imminent General Election of 1997. We have argued, persuasively we hope, that the anti-Germanic theme is an integral element of Euroscepticism. In Text 3.29 below, the discourse focus is Tony Blair's personality, but it neatly taps into the anti-Germanic discourse for no apparent reason other than the negative response the German item *Führerprinzip* (particularly the prefix 'führer') will evoke from any reader who has read a little history.

Text 3.29 (9.4.97:23)

Do you trust Tony Blair?

The election, says Mr Blair, is about trust. He is enthusiastic for what the Germans call Führerprinzip, the cult of the leader...

Finally, in addition to these overt or implied criticisms of our major partner states of the EU, the discourse of the *Telegraph* focuses on the threat which comes from the persistent interventionist policies of the EU that impinge upon the traditional freedoms of the United Kingdom. Among others, this Eurosceptic focus falls upon such areas of our cultural life as food safety. Notice in Text 3.30 below the relatively rare use in the *Telegraph* of the Eurosceptic ideological shorthand 'bureaucrat' (meaning unelected, unaccountable EU official) as well as the choice of the item 'police' instead of, say, 'monitor' or 'guarantee':

Text 3.30 (21.3.97:15)

EU creates team to police food safety

A team of European bureaucrats is being created to police food safety throughout the EU.

Other interventions reported in the *Telegraph* which allegedly threaten British freedoms include the impending EU ban on the independent manufacturing of spare parts for cars (17.3.97:29), border controls (22.3.97:2), the banning of English words in certain ingredients (23.3.97:8), and fishing (15.3.97:23).

Summary and evaluation

The discourse on Europe examined in the *Daily Telegraph* for this period, like that of *The Times* is both plentiful and distributed evenly across the three thematic areas that we identified at the beginning of this chapter. The balance of the discourse functions remain very similar too, with strong informational/representational and ideological elements and a comparable balance between the latter and identities and relations. It will be recalled that *The Times* allowed a wholly pro-European article (see Text 3.5 above) in a rare but welcome contrast to its dominant Eurosceptic discourse. The *Daily Telegraph* also allows the occasional pro-European voice to be heard. In this period it printed a substantial article by Klaus Kinkel, the German foreign minister, but is quick to refute his views in the leader, on an adjacent page, on the same day (see Texts 3.24 and 3.25 above). Nevertheless, as with *The Times*, the fact that this dissenting voice is heard at all must be deemed to go part of the way towards acknowledging the existence at least of other views in favour of the European integration. Such a gesture, however limited, is almost entirely restricted to the two Eurosceptic broadsheets and does not occur in their Eurosceptic tabloid companions who, as we shall see later, take no prisoners.

The ideological content of the *Telegraph* expressed in the period studied may be summarised as follows (it compares interestingly with that of *The Times* already mentioned):

- The single currency is potentially a source of social unrest.
- The single currency is a threat to sovereignty.
- The Social Chapter will hamper British manufacturing.
- The EU is more disunited than united on matters of foreign policy and security.
- Britain needs the EU less than the EU needs Britain.
- Germany is the driving force behind the single currency and this is linked to its historical attachment to its dreams of expansion in Europe.
- Germany and France remain rivals rather than partners in Europe.
- The pro-Europeans [New Labour] are to be associated with 'treason' and will *abandon* the veto, *surrender* the pound, *sign away* traditional British rights.

The Eurosceptic tabloids

Unsurprisingly the discourse of the three Eurosceptic tabloids differs from that of the broadsheets in significant ways. The thematic range of Euroscepticism is more limited and the themes themselves are considerably less defined than in the broadsheets. There are internal differences too, and for this reason we shall distinguish between the discourse of the middle-market or 'blacktop' tabloids, the *Mail* and the *Express*, and that of the 'red-top' mass-market *Sun*. The blacktops devote more of their discourse to Europe and address a wider range of issues generally. The *Sun*, on the other hand, frequently excludes almost any mention of Europe from its pages, which raises discourse issues of a different kind.

The principal differences between the broadsheet and tabloid Euroscepticism can be summarised as follows:

- Length of text: the three tabloids, and the *Sun* in particular, dedicate significantly less of their column space to European issues than the broadsheets.
- Discourse focus: the thematic range of European issues represented is significantly smaller in the tabloids than in the broadsheets.

- The discourse functions: in addition to a reduced overall discourse and a reduced range of issues presented, the informational/ representational aspect of the discourse is also diminished and more emphasis is placed upon the other two functions of identities and relations. To restate this perhaps more clearly, the discourse of the tabloids is strikingly more conversational than that of the broadsheets.

Despite, or perhaps because of, these distinguishing features of reduced textual quantity, reduced range of issues, and lower level of formality, the overt point of view is stridently expressed and the covert, underlying ideological force is intense. This intensity is striking and is derived from a narrower set of assumptions concerning the shared lifeworld of writer and reader than is the case with the broadsheets.

The reduced thematic range of tabloid discourse can be summarised as falling under the same broad range which we identified for the broadsheets above, but they are less discrete in terms of their sub-categories. They are as follows:

The economic implications
- The main focus is on the Social Chapter.

The political implications
- The principal focus is the implications of further integration for British sovereignty with particular focus upon the single currency

History and culture
- The distinguishing historical and cultural factors of Britain's European partners, particularly those relating to Germany and France;
- The effects of EU interventionism upon the British way of life.

We propose in the commentary that follows to look first at the representation of Europe in the *Express* and the *Daily Mail* together before moving in the final section to the *Sun*.

The Express *and the* Mail

The economic implications
The *Mail*, in similar vein to that of the broadsheets, focuses on the socio-economic disquiet felt by other European member states as the result of their preparation for EMU membership. Note in passing that the headline in Text 3.31 below contains a widespread ideological assumption that all is not well between France and Germany (a theme which strictly speaking could be placed under *History and culture* too).

Text 3.31   (John Langland, 22.3.97:23)

Mass unemployment and running scared of the Germans – Why France is a warning to us all

France – like other countries of continental Europe – is trussed and bound by a net of policies she has spun for herself, all inspired by the belief that European integration is a panacea ... Generally speaking they do not see that their economic woes are the direct consequences of the government's preparation for the Euro...

This lengthy article on this theme of European disquiet was, however, the only one to appear in the tabloids in the period examined and the omission of this theme elsewhere is interesting, particularly since it was used to such good effect as a telling and relevant argument of Euroscepticism in the broadsheets. The omission may be explained by the perception held by the tabloids of what they deemed to be the limited interest on the part of their readers for European issues. The assumption may be that their readers' concerns are more ethnocentrically 'British', and their interests do not extend to the unease felt by other European citizens to the consequences of preparing for EMU membership. This is, however, speculation only and would need to be checked against more recent discourse that has appeared or is appearing in the press in the run up to the launch of the single currency in 1998/9 (see for example our comments on the *Mail* in Chapter 5).

The Social Chapter and its alleged harmful effects on the British economy, does figure frequently in the discourse of both papers. In the *Express*, Peter Hitchens, in a mock address to Tony Blair links the signing of the Social Chapter with the alleged endebtedness of New Labour to the British trade union movement. The ideological assumption here is that the Social Chapter is synonymous with socialism:

Text 3.32   (Peter Hitchens, 10.4.97:18)

... Yet surely you will pay your huge debts to the union movement in other ways by making it easier to recruit and by importing continental workplace law. Isn't it time that you admitted that this is why you will sign up to the social contract? ...

This view is echoed in the *Mail* by Simon Heffer:

Text 3.33   (Simon Heffer, 9.4.97:12)

... The social chapter of the Treaty of Maastricht will load new bureaucracy on most businesses. But the damage that [it] will do to employment prospects is nothing compared to the party's [New Labour] commitment to a minimum wage...

The political implications
One of the most noteworthy features of the discourse of the *Express* for this period is the space it affords to the representation of the views of

the Referendum Party and by using the technique of direct quotation (secondary discourse) in the representation of the views of the late Sir James Goldsmith. There are four separate articles devoted to the Referendum Party in the *Express* in the period 8–15 April 1997. They project that vague yet highly emotional brand of Euroscepticism which borders upon phobia and closely resembles the Whig-imperialistic attitudes referred to by Marquand reported in Chapter 1.

Text 3.34   (8.4.97:2)

Referendum Party

Sir James Goldsmith launched his election campaign to 100 trawlermen in Newlyn, Cornwall which had been hit by cuts in EU fishing quotas ... He said 'No government has the right to give away sovereignty. Our sovereignty doesn't belong to politicians. It belongs to the people'...

The 'free ride' offered to the Referendum Party is significant in so far as it points to a lingering sympathy on the part of the *Express* towards the Europhobic views of a party to the right of the Conservatives. For further evidence of this sympathy see the *Express* discourse cited under *History and culture* below.

The *Mail* is less generous towards the Referendum Party but nevertheless shares some of the 'Whig-imperialist' nostalgia for a 'Europe-free' Britain of the *Express*. Two texts will suffice, we hope, to illustrate its profound dislike for further integration with Europe. Notice in Text 3.35 the evocation of the famous air battle between Britain and Germany in 1940 – a theme which is extrapolated to include all of Europe and which thematically overlaps with *History and culture* below.

Text 3.35   (leader, 15.4.97:1)

The Battle for Britain

...How long will it be before our mortgage rates are set in Frankfurt? A unified European VAT and income tax system is imposed on Britain...? ... Our gold reserves shipped to Germany to ensure the dubious stability of the single currency?...

The *Mail* is equally forthright on its page-one headline after a speech by Jacques Santer, allegedly critical of the British Eurosceptic camp, which was seen as an attempt to intervene in the election process:

Text 3.36   (David Hughes, 22.4.97:1)

Keep your nose out of our election...

History and culture
Under this category are located the dominant themes of the discourse of the Eurosceptic tabloids and they range from the scorning of

Commissioners and of political leaders to the evocation of a legendary Britain, independent, strong and untainted by the will of the 'Other' – in this case, continental Europe. As Marquand has pointed out, this is indeed the stuff that 'Whig-imperialist' dreams are made of. Borrowing (inter-textually) for a moment from the discourse of another medium, we wish to warn the reader that what follows contains scenes of violence and strong language which some may find disturbing. Texts 3.37–3.43, all taken from the *Express*, offer examples of the discourse of a kind of British nationalism which finally topples over into outright xenophobia.

Text 3.37 is an example of the more gentle and humorous voice of scorn aimed at an EU Commissioner. It is linked to the historical discourse (unpopular government interference in the British diet) of post-war austerity:

Text 3.37   (Matthew Mervyn Jones, 3.4.97:29)

Hop on the bandwagon and sample a sardine

...Miss Bonino, the EU Fisheries Commissioner, wants us to lay off our lovely cod and haddock. There's been nothing quite like it since Britain's post-war 'austerity' era with its whale meat ... which became national jokes...

An EU report on the issue of child labour gets an interesting and predictably negative representation as an example of EU intervention in a time-honoured British custom:

Text 3.38   (8.4.97:24)

Threat to child jobs

Two million British children should be banned from taking out-of-school jobs to earn pocket money according to a European parliament report.
It would mean a ban on Saturday jobs and paper rounds which give millions of Britons their first experience of work and financial independence...

Germany, as we have seen already, has come under attack from the Eurosceptics in the broadsheets of which the most pronounced example was the article in *The Times* cited above in this chapter (Texts 3.11–12). The tabloids carry this theme of Germanophobia to new heights, relentlessly tapping into an anti-German discourse which pre-dates the treaty of Rome by 40 years. Note in Text 3.39, in addition to the overtly negative representation of German tourists abroad, the evocative use of such items as 'Heil', 'warfare', 'master-race' and the phrase (lifted from a Churchillian speech?) 'combined might of wartime allies' which clearly recalls the historic military defeat of the most prosperous member of the European Union and looks westward away from Europe for salvation.

Text 3.39   (Paul Crosbie, 9.4.97:9)

Germany is taking over the world

Heil, big spenders! After decades of sunbed warfare with the Germans, Britain has had to throw in the towel. The Germans are the master-race at world travel and spend more money on going abroad than any other nation ... Only the combined might of wartime allies, Britain and America, could knock them off their perch ...

The content of the above discourse could be dismissed as a light-hearted joke and our highlighting of it runs the risk of being labelled humourless were it not for the raising of another voice in the leader column of the same day (Text 3.40 below) which picks up on the same topic. Its prioritised position in the leader indicates its perceived importance by the *Express*, and the rhetorical question clearly draws upon deep currents of Germanophobic discourse which prevailed at another time in our history.

Text 3.40   (leader, 9.4.97:10)

Despite the growing difficulties of their economy, the Germans spend more on going abroad ... Why is it that we are not greatly surprised to learn this? ...

Still exploiting this rich vein of Germanophobia, and on the same news item relating to German tourism in the *Express*, Peter Tory offers in Text 3.41 an additional pastiche of a German speaking English in a discourse style worthy of *Punch* in 1918. Note the feigned slip of the tongue 'Fatherland' for 'frontiers' which precedes the mock (secondary) discourse of the demonised German.

Text 3.41   (Peter Tory, 12.4.97:11)

Losing the war of words

... Germans now head the international tourist league and ... nearly one million of them abandon the Fatherland – their frontiers rather... – and enjoy their holidays abroad ...
'That' [losing the war] he said curtly, 'vas becos ve vere outnumbered' ...

Finally, here are two extracts from the *Express* devoted to the Referendum Party. The first is another example of Germanophobia and needs little introduction. It is perhaps worthwhile however to draw attention to the fact that this xenophobic outburst is not a secondary discourse (the reporting of direct speech) but apparently a comment by the journalist, where the pronoun 'we' also includes the reader. The item 'heel', and particularly the phrase after the conjunction 'and' (note the capitalised pronoun), appear to be the voice of the journalist too and one which carries a strong underlying assumption of reader endorsement of the xenophobic discourse. The reference, should anyone fail to have noticed, is to the German military 'Jackboot' worn in both World Wars.

Text 3.42   (Chris Buckland, 14.4.97:7)

Sir James and friends have a very pally rally

They all saw a plot, a conspiracy to put Britain under the heel of the Germans and we all know what sort of boots THEY wear...

The last text in this section is still on the subject of the policies of the Referendum Party and uses the same technique as is employed in Text 3.41, that is the xenophobia appears to come, not from a secondary discourse quoted from another source, but from the primary discourse. The informational/representational function of the discourse is clearly being subordinated here to the other two functions of identities and relations, involving reader and journalist in an assumed close and non-specialist relationship with each other and with the topic. Such relationships may be deemed good or bad depending on the reader's point of view of conversationalised media discourse. Since we are discussing Europhobia here as opposed to Euroscepticism Text 3.43 below also makes interesting reading.

Text 3.43   (Geoffrey Wheatcroft, 15.4.97:10)

Two Parties splash each other with mud from the same road

...Hogarth would have understood the emotions which the Refs [Referendum Party] are tapping. It is an angry, frustrated patriotism, the belief that John Bull knows best and that the British bulldog isn't going to be dictated to by the Froggies or any other foreigners...

Summary and evaluation

The Euroscepticism of the *Mail* and *Express*, and the phobias which nourish them, are integral parts of their respective discourses. This discourse plays variations on a narrower range of themes than those of the broadsheets although the ideological underpinning is considerable. This underpinning naturally shares some of the features of the Euroscepticism of *The Times* and the *Daily Telegraph* but it is also steeped (more so than in the broadsheets) with allusions to a mythical and essential 'British way of life' around which 'closure' is being sought against a tide of invasive thrusts from continental Europe.

The ideological content of the discourse can be summarised as follows:

- France and Germany are uneasy partners in Europe;
- The Social Chapter is linked to socialism and hence favoured by New Labour;
- The Referendum Party is the true champion of British sovereignty;
- The single currency entails 'surrendering' British economic independence and sovereignty to Europe and to Germany in particular;

- European legislation is interventionist and must be kept at arm's length;
- German expansionist dreams remain largely unchanged from those of the 1930s;
- Britain's destiny is still westward/maritime towards America and away from Europe;
- Britain can go it alone.

There is also a marked distinction in the discourse types where the two tabloids are concerned. Generally speaking they are more conversationalised in style with more emphasis placed upon the identities and relations functions than in the broadsheets. This change of emphasis between discourse functions mostly accounts for the headline in the *Mail* – **Keep your nose out of our election** – in Text 3.36 above – where the social identities of writer and reader are fused together and, by extension, the relational distance between them is non-existent.

The Sun

'Cry God for England, the *Sun* and St George!' (*Sun*, 22 April 1997).
We have left the *Sun* until last because, as with other aspects of its performance, it is a special case. It shares with the *Mail* and the *Express* a conversationalised style of discourse which, if anything, is more pronounced and extreme than the two middle-market tabloids. This perhaps, is not surprising since it was the *Sun* which began the process in 1969. It tends also to treat an even narrower thematic range of European issues than the other two. Relative to the *Mail* and the *Express* its representation of Europe is sparse. Nevertheless, within this sparseness of coverage, the *Sun*'s voice is wholly anti-European. This places the *Sun* in a curious position. In a much trumpeted *volte-face*, the paper announced in March 1997 that it would be supporting New Labour in the election campaign. Since 1979 the *Sun* had been a strident supporter of the Conservatives, and a particularly enthusiastic admirer of Margaret Thatcher. It is rumoured that the change of political allegiance imposed on the journalists of the *Sun* by Rupert Murdoch in March 1997 caused widespread dismay and understandable difficulties in their adaptation to a new left-of-centre line. In addition there was the question of how the Europhobic *Sun* would deal with Europe, given that New Labour's attitudes were considerably more relaxed on European issues. The resulting discourse is fascinating to say the least.

The political discourse of a newspaper cannot change overnight, not even at the bidding of such a legendary will as the one attributed to Rupert Murdoch. Nurtured in its infancy by Thatcherism and matured in later life, in the post-1990 era, by Majorism, the authentic voice of the *Sun*, in the spring of 1997, was the product of a complex set of factors. Not the least of these was a press room long versed in the demonising of such traditional old enemies of the right as the trade unions, liberal educationalists, and, importantly for this study, Europe. It is not surprising, therefore, to discover that whilst changes in its discourse began to occur in order to effect the switch of support away from the Conservatives and towards New Labour, they are superficial in nature. They focused more upon personality preferences – the perceived firmness and determination of Blair over the equivocation and alleged aimlessness of Major – than upon real political issues of substance. Thus the well springs of the *Sun*'s ideological opposition to the EU, with their sources still located on the right wing of British politics, remain unadulterated, despite a change in the direction of the surface wind.

We can still just about use the three thematic categories which we used for the other Eurosceptics above, but the boundaries between them are very blurred. This is because, with a few exceptions, the *Sun*'s discourse, of all the Eurosceptic discourse, is the most elliptical. The *Sun* rarely uses ten words of explanatory discourse on Europe when three ideologically charged items will do. Such compression produces a discourse with an ideological undercurrent which is disproportionate in force and in range to its surface properties. Thus the item 'Europe' itself is often the surface token word for a wide range of Eurosceptic notions deeply embedded in its discourse (see Text 3.44 below) which we shall now examine in turn using the same categories as before:

The economic implications

The main focus of the *Sun*'s attention, as with the *Express* and the *Mail*, is the Social Chapter. Note in Text 3.44 below the warring metaphor with reference to Europe, and the 'given' (ideological) assumptions relating to anything to do with the Social Chapter.

Text 3.44   (4.4.97:6)

Tony's trust is what we need

... The second battleground will be Europe ... Yesterday he [Blair] described fears over the social chapter as 'hooey' ... But Blair insists that he can and will veto any attempt to impose sky-high European social costs on Britain ...

Text 3.45 below, a *Sun* leader, is a good example of the compressed style, packed with ideological assumptions, which we mentioned above. Notice the implications for the workings of the European Commission, and the xenophobic reference to character and to the provenance of the Commissioner.

Text 3.45   (leader, 12.4.97:6)

By order – No! Britain didn't want the 48-hour working week

We voted against it but Europe sneaked it in by another route. Now Brussels wants to extend it to more than 1.5 million workers in Britain.

Social affairs commissioner Padraig Flynn, a busybody from the backwoods of Ireland, thinks he knows what's best for us ... Why the hell should Europe be able to impose anything on us? ... We must not be dictated to by men like Flynn ...

Finally in this section, Texts 3.46 and 3.47 illustrate a recurring link-up in the discourse of the *Sun* of the Social Chapter to left wing European politics, and by extension, to the trade union movement in Britain.

Text 3.46 *Sun* (Permission withheld)

> Interest value of this extract is in the association of John Prescott (and by extension, New Labour) with the perceived intentions of European trade unions to demand a four day week and call European-wide strikes. This 'Europe equals socialism-by-the-back-door' is an established ideological assumption in the *Sun*.
> Access via British Library on micro-film (Pascoe Watson, 26.3.97:2, ll. 1–8).

To our ears, at least, the reference to 'union barons' in the above text has a strangely hollow, outmoded ring about it. This must be because, since the late 1980s, the exclusion of the unions from the deliberations of government strips from the item 'baron' much of its old ideological force. It seems to relate it (intentionally, presumably) to a previous discourse in the early 1980s when the TUC had a much more significant voice in the public sphere than it does in the late 1990s. It is likely that the evocation of this past discourse is indeed self-consciously recalling the old ideological themes of industrial conflict which characterised the *Sun* at that time. Similarly, in Text 3.47 below, the allusion to the TUC members as 'brothers' strikes an equally antiquated note for the same reason.

Text 3.47 (leader, 26.4.97:6)

... the 1950s socialism across the Channel

The brothers there want EU-wide laws, union deals and industrial action to achieve their aim of 'social justice'...

The political implications

The political dimensions of the *Sun*'s Eurosceptic discourse are realised mostly during this period by references, in direct and reported speech, to the views of such well known Eurosceptics as Margaret Thatcher, the novelist Frederick Forsyth *and* Tony Blair. Notwithstanding the varying measures of respect and affection that Margaret Thatcher commands in the Eurosceptic discourse elsewhere in the British press, the place she has in the *Sun* is surely unique. We suggested earlier in this section that the item 'Europe' for the *Sun* is a good example of the compression of its discourse style. It is the surface 'token word' for a whole range of ideological Euroscepticism. Likewise the use of the items 'Margaret Thatcher' or (particularly) 'Maggie' appear at times to take on an ideological force all of their own, as in Text 3.48 below:

Text 3.48   (14.4.97:2)

Maggie EU poll war cry

Baroness Thatcher yesterday demanded that every election candidate should spell out to voters how they stand on Europe. She said the candidates ought to 'answer clearly' the question of whether they would hand over Parliament's power to 'the non-elected bureaucracy of Brussels'...

This call on the part of Margaret Thatcher is revealingly coloured in the leader column of the same edition as follows:

Text 3.49   (leader, 14.4.97:6)

Right, Maggie   You've got to hand it to Maggie.

...Lady Thatcher wants every election candidate to answer this: Will you hand over this country to pen-pushers in Brussels?...

Margaret Thatcher's opposition to the Eurocurrency and her preference for Britain's continued political links with the United States are also reported exclusively in the *Sun*:

Text 3.50   *Sun* (Permission withheld)

Extract taken from article by *Sun*'s political editor, Trevor Kavanagh. Interest value is the association of Margaret Thatcher with the Eurosceptic opponents of the euro and her alleged assertion that the only single currency is the dollar.
Access via British Library on micro-film (Trevor Kavanagh, 19.4.97:2, ll. 75–85).

In an uncharacteristic, extended stretch of discourse on the subject of the single currency which, its length aside, also prioritises the informative/representative function over those of identities and relations, the *Sun*'s leader links the single currency with the issue of sovereignty. The style and tone of this discourse is a rarity in the *Sun* and, interestingly, may be said to bear a fleeting comparison with the formal discourse of the *Daily Herald* cited in Chapter 1 (Text 1.1). Notice, though, how the discourse functions switch in emphasis towards the end and swing back to favour social identities and social relations, thereby restoring it to its much more usual conversational tone (the italics and bold print indicating that the importance of the particular part of the discourse are in the original).

Text 3.51   (leader, 17.4.97:6)

Big question on big issue

...It is clear that the Tory Party could never take Britain into a single currency. There are barely a handful of MPs who favour the closer political and economic integration it would require ... The national interest is about more than just whether we are better off. Our sovereignty, heritage and way of life matter too.

> *With momentous decisions to be made in the coming months, this is the election of a lifetime.*
>
> So, every candidate of every party must spell out what he or she believes on the single currency ... **Go along to a public meeting or stop your candidate in the street, and ask point blank. If they waffle, take it as yes. And tell them you'll vote for someone else...**

It is left to the novelist (and, we are told, former newspaper foreign correspondent), Frederick Forsyth to represent some of the more clichéd and emotional fears of the Eurosceptics. The following extract is placed in this category of *Politics* but it could be equally located under *History and culture* below. We drew attention, at the outset of our commentary on the *Sun*'s discoursal style to the use of the item 'Europe' as a token word for a covert set of ideological associations. In the headline of Text 3.52 below, one aspect of this ideological association (deception) is made explicit.

Text 3.52 *Sun* (Permission withheld)

> Extract is from an article by Frederick Forsyth in which it is alleged that Britain is the victim of a confidence trick bearing the name of 'Europe', wherein perceived hard won freedoms will be replaced by undemocratic secret deals struck in Brussels.
> Access via British Library on micro-film (Frederick Forsyth, 21.4.97:6, ll. 31–34).

Finally under this category, should there be any doubt as to where the editorial line is, we shall allow the authentic voice of the *Sun* in its leader column to have the last word:

Text 3.53 (leader, 16.4.97:6)

> **Revolt proves the party's over**
>
> ...We don't want our laws, and our interest rates imposed on us by unelected foreigners. That is not being anti-Europe ... it is being pro-Britain...

History and culture
As is the case with the other two tabloids, it is in this category that Euroscepticism topples over into flag-waving abuse and other disturbing manifestations of xenophobia. However, curiously and against our expectations, the *Sun*'s xenophobia, whilst ugly and inadmissible, does not focus on Germany and German politicians with anything like the same ferocity as the *Express* or even *The Times* (but see Text 3.45 above and Text 5.27 below for other variations of *Sun* Europhobia). As we have noted already, the *Sun*'s representation of Europe generally is reduced when compared to that of the rest of the Eurosceptic press, and this reduction of coverage, together with the targeting of younger consumers, perceived as possessing little sense of history and lower levels of literacy, may explain the absence of the Germanophobia

found elsewhere. Whatever the reason, the apparent restraint of the *Sun* in this one aspect, (restraint over Germany) and at this time, is worthy of note.

The Euroscepticism in this category finds its expression in two well-worn and associated themes: the perceived deception and dishonesty perpetrated by Britain's European partners. A platform is offered to Norman Tebbit and to Frederick Forsyth as well as to Tony Blair, whose voice presumably has been coloured in the same way as Margaret Thatcher's (see Text 3.49 above), in order to conform to the ideological compression of the *Sun's* discourse.

The switch of political allegiances, as we have pointed out, is problematic for a newspaper, particularly if it has been as staunch a supporter of one side as the *Sun*. One of the tactics of the paper for bridging the credibility gap created by the announcement, in the pre-election period, that it was supporting New Labour as the government-in-waiting, was to represent Tony Blair as a Eurosceptic as is illustrated by Text 3.54 below. Note in this discourse the restraint of the reference to Germany as well as its apparent unintended ambiguity and amusing contradiction.

Text 3.54 *Sun* (Permission withheld)

> Extract refers to the intentions of Tony Blair to combat aggressively fraudulant claims made upon European funding which, it is alleged, are rife among some member states. Germany is cited as being the chief offender but only apparently because it is the most honest in declaring the extent of the fraud. The 'Europe-equals-corruption' is an established ideological assumption in the *Sun*.
> Access via British Library on micro-film (Pascoe Watson, 11.4.97:9, ll. 1–3, 21–25, 32–36).

Norman Tebbit is a regular voice in the *Sun's* political discourse. We assume that this voice is sub-edited into the compressed ideologically loaded style which we claim is a defining feature of this paper's discourse. If it is not, then Mr Tebbit's mastery of '*Sun*-speak' is impressive. Notice how in Text 3.55 below, Europe is ideologically associated with the fraudulent appropriation of British money – a place where 'freeloaders' are apparently rife.

Text 3.55 *Sun* (Permission withheld)

> Interest value lies in the damaging association of foreign nationals who come to Britain, allegedly to live off the welfare state, with other citizens of the European Union who, it is claimed, also fraudulently exploit the system.
> Access via British Library on micro-film (Norman Tebbit, 18.4.97:9, ll. 16–20).

Two texts on the theme of untrustworthiness of European politicians generally are also worthy of attention. The first is the voice of Frederick Forsyth.

Text 3.56   *Sun* (Permission withheld)

> In this extract Frederick Forsyth repeats the accusation made in
> Text 3.52 that the European Union's policy making is conducted
> in secret and with duplicity.
> Access via British Library on micro-film (Frederick Forsyth,
> 22.4.97:6, ll. 1–5).

Picking up on this alleged plot, the *Sun*'s leader in the same issue offers
Forsyth some reassurance. The recurring ideological theme is of course
that *something* is indeed being plotted.

Text 3.57   (leader, 22.4.97:6)

Rumbled

> Ordinary people across Europe have rumbled what is being plotted in
> Brussels...

We end this commentary on the discourse of the *Sun* where we
began, on the eve of St George's Day 1997. In the light of all the
foregoing commentary on Euroscepticism, derived mostly from
concepts developed in critical discourse analysis, but also illuminated,
we hope, by other concepts relating to the phenomenon of cultural
identity, cultural change and closure, the final text can stand alone
without further commentary other than to point out that the author of
the discourse may cause disquiet in some quarters.

Figure 3.2   *Source:* The *Guardian,* 19 March 1997

Text 3.58   *Sun* (Permission withheld)

> This extract is from an article attributed to Tony Blair in which the headline asserts that he doesn't need lessons from John Major on dealing with the EU. Here, a future Europe which attempts to become a superstate is likened to a dragon which Blair claims he will slay in the manner of St George.
> Access via British Library on micro-film (Tony Blair, 22.4.97:13, ll. 6–8, 18–23).

Summary and evaluation

We have offered here a candid and indeed critical commentary on the discourse of the *Sun* which, for the reasons we have stated, merits special attention and distinguishes it from those of the *Mail* and the *Express*. Quantitatively, it offers less space in its columns to European issues than the other two Eurosceptic tabloids (see Chapter 5 for further discussion). When, however, the focus is Europe, the discourse is highly ideologically charged, sharing with the other tabloids comparable views but adding particular phobias of its own too. The ideological dimension of the *Sun*'s discourse can be summarised as follows:

- The Social Chapter is socialism in disguise and should be rejected;
- Europe is harmfully interfering in the affairs of Britain;
- The Irish acting on behalf of the Commission are particularly unacceptable to Britain;
- Some New Labour politicians are suspect for their sympathies towards the trade unions;
- Margaret Thatcher's policies on Europe are models for New Labour to follow if it gets to power;
- Europe is untrustworthy and is deceiving Britons about its real intentions;
- Europe is corrupt;
- Blair is Eurosceptic.

Conclusion

Our examination of the discourse of Euroscepticism in the British press has revealed a diversity of anti-European voices. These range from the presentation of reasoned and understandable concerns at the prospect of important changes to the governance of the UK, as a consequence of further integration, on the one hand, to a depressing miasma of xenophobic forebodings, on the other. For the most part, this rational/irrational division of these two extreme kinds of representations/mediations was perceived to correlate with the discourse of the broadsheets and the tabloids. But there was significant overlap too. There were in the broadsheets representations/mediations that were underpinned with a kind of extreme historicism and cultural emotionalism which added little to any rational discourse relating to

Europe. Frequently, this emotionalism rides on a discourse which avails itself of the rhetoric of the false proposition or 'Aunt Sally' as it is sometimes benignly called. In the discourse of the Eurosceptic this translates as the deliberate exaggeration of the principles, beliefs and intentions of the 'Other', first, in order to influence opinions by causing alarm, and secondly, to evoke the support and admiration of the reader by opposing them. Typical examples of such anxiety-provoking rhetoric in the case of Europe might be in relation to the single currency and unemployment (i.e. Texts 3.15 and 3.31); the 'expansionist plot theory' relating to Germany's support of the single currency (i.e. Texts 3.11 and 3.39); the US style 'superstate' version of the integration issue (i.e. Text 3.58); the 'European plot' aimed at deceiving Britain into further integration (i.e. Texts 3.35, 3.52 and 3.56). We encounter this phenomenon again in Chapter 5 where it is dealt with in greater detail.

The range of representation of events too, when compared to the potential narrative on Europe that is suggested in Chapter 2, is restricted in the broadsheets and much more so in the tabloids. The representation of European issues in the latter case, and particularly in the *Express* and *Sun* is, to put it mildly, extraordinary for its limited range as well as for the emotionalism and the ferocity of its Eurosceptic voices.

Almost without exception an overarching discourse which transcends the nation-state and places the integration question within a wider context of the post-war European 'grand vision', of peace, prosperity and democracy is missing. This is regrettable but not really surprising. There may indeed be some truth in the *Telegraph*'s assertion that, unlike the rest of Europe in 1945, the British did not feel that their institutions had failed them. In consequence, the grand vision that inspired the founders of the Common Market as well as their successors did not and does not have the same appeal for the British that it enjoys in other European countries (see Text 3.25 above). This is a worthy and serious representation of one aspect of recent British historical experience which links the past with the present within a verifiable public discourse of modern European history. It also transcends the narrowness of viewpoint which all too often characterises the voices of the Eurosceptics. Historicism of this kind has its place in the anti-European discourse but it has to be weighed against the other socio-economic and political changes which have taken place too. European institutions, and particularly those of the EU, have been transformed (some say irrevocably so) since the mid-century. What is missing in the Eurosceptic narrative is the representation of this socio-economic and political change *as a counterpoint to the lessons of history*. In short, there is an absence of a discourse which tempers historicism with the representation of how the other economies of the member states, the working of European institutions, and democracy itself within the EU, are faring. What references there are to these aspects of overarching discourse concerning Europe, are as infrequent as they are brief.

The issue of the single currency – a supranational affair if ever there was one – is for the most part represented in only two of its aspects. The first concerns the political implications for British sovereignty (but not in any detail) should Britain eventually sign up for EMU. The second represents the social ramifications and unrest in Europe currently caused by the monetary discipline imposed on member states seeking entry to EMU in the first round. These are indeed important issues, but again the 'big picture' in the form of a fuller narrative, which includes the perceivable benefits (again if only to reject them), is largely ignored. EMU is as yet untried and, for the reasons stated, opposition to it in the majority of the British press is strong but lacking in balance. As we shall see in Chapter 5, the single currency debate becomes significantly sharper and more focused from February 1998 onwards as the preparations for EMU accelerate and take on an irrevocable air.

Where defence and security are concerned, the Eurosceptics are on firmer ground. Unlike EMU, these are indeed tried issues which are close to the experience and interests of British readers. The less than resolute performance of the EU in the former Yugoslavia, and more recently the differences of opinion on how to deal with Saddam Hussein's flouting of the UN's authority, point to the evident weaknesses in the coordination of an EU foreign policy. Such irresolution has been exploited to good and perhaps justifiable effect by the Eurosceptics to subvert the grand vision of the supporters of further integration, and to point up the value of NATO and the transatlantic alliance.

We have already referred to the Eurosceptic discourse of the tabloids as being emotional and ferocious in its opposition to current and future levels of British integration with Europe. It would seem that the consumer of tabloid information is caught, voluntarily or involuntarily, in a triple bind. First, the thematic range of issues represented is risibly small, secondly these themes predominantly derive from historical/ cultural assumptions of dubious relevance, and finally they are subject to distortion through presentation in a discourse style which by excessive informalisation, obscures rather than illuminates the topic.

We shall return to most of these conclusions relating to the discourse of Euroscepticism when we discuss in Chapter 4 the discourse of the pro-European press, as well as in the concluding chapters of this book.

Finally, there is one more point to make which the reader should bear in mind constantly when reading our commentary on this particular aspect of the performance of the British press. This commentary is self-evidently *our* reading of the Eurosceptic press. It is our interpretation of the discourse and not necessarily that of the reader of this book, nor even less so, it could be argued, is it the interpretation of the news-paper-reading public, the consumers. There are strongly held views about what are perceived as exaggerated claims made by some media analysts about the influence of media discourse on the public. We shall return to this issue in Chapter 7.

Chapter 4

The pro-European press

Introduction

It is sometimes said, in relation to the great issues which have preoccupied the minds of men and women throughout history, that the devil has the best lines. This fragment of folk wisdom is particularly pertinent to the debate on European integration when voiced by the sceptic majority of the British press. Closure around a set of economic, historical and cultural features, however mythical, offers an attractive, if imaginary, identity, and all the more so for being set against a threatening, meddlesome 'Other' in the form of Europe.

Even those aspects of Euroscepticism which are perceived to be founded on less mythical stuff, such as the economic arguments against the single currency, get a better coverage than any arguments in favour. This is partly because the projected doomsday scenario of economic scepticism frequently spills over into other issues, of which the most important is the emotional question over sovereignty. In consequence, it seems that the alleged shift of economic power from London to Frankfurt, and the entailed threat to the sovereignty of the British parliament, are more imaginable than the less discernible alternatives: a more prosperous Britain with its money and commodity markets intact, and a parliament still taking vital decisions in the national interest.

The advantages of a single currency have never been fully explained to the British public by the press. There are two reasons for this information deficit, the first being that the Eurosceptic press massively dominates the sector, and the second that, even in the pro-European press itself, there are doubts about Britain's early membership of EMU. Thus under the thematic categories listed under *Economic implications* for the *Independent* and the *Guardian*, we find both papers representing the attempts of other member states to meet the Maastricht economic criteria in a light which overall reflects negatively on the single currency. We noted in Chapter 3 that this thematic treatment was also a strong feature of Euroscepticism. The difference between this negative portrayal by the pro-European press and the negative discourse of Euroscepticism would appear to be one of degree only (although we suggest that for the *Guardian*, at least, there may be another ideological reason). The Eurosceptics urge rejection (see Text 3.13 above) whereas the pro-Europeans counsel delay and caution (see Text 4.3 below).

The discourse of the pro-European press – general

The common themes occurring in the pro-European discourse of the *Independent*, the *Guardian* and the *Financial Times* (we shall deal with the *Mirror* separately) may be summarised as follows, although, as we shall see later, there is considerable variation in rhetorical and ideological force among the three titles:

The economic implications
- The European Union as a provider/facilitator at the international level;
- British business needs in Europe;
- The economic and social implications as the member states prepare for EMU.

   (N.B. There is an absence of sustained comment on the social chapter and no date is proposed for British entry to EMU.)

The political implications
- The issue of further integration with reference to Britain;
- The complexity of European politics.

History and culture
- Europe as a legitimate economic, political and social space;
- Europe as an initiator and regulator, efficient or otherwise, of the international activities of the member states.

We noted in the course of the analysis the same features of discoursal organisation here as for the Eurosceptic press – the use of secondary discourse in the form of direct quotation of sources, on both sides of the debate; the offering of space to public figures to promote their own particular point of view; and finally, the admission into the discourse of voices diametrically opposed to its dominant flow.

The discourse of the pro-European broadsheets

The Independent

The discourse of the *Independent* may be best described as predominantly pro-European with Eurosceptic undertones in certain of its aspects. Economically, it seems to take its cue from the business sector (see Text 4.1 below), but, even so, finds space to question the viability of the single currency by representing the economic and social problems of other countries in the run-up to EMU membership. What is conspicuously absent in the economic category is any consistent opposition to the Social Chapter of the kind that we found in the Euroscepticism of *The Times*, the *Telegraph*, *Mail*, *Express* and *Sun* during this period. The *Independent* does however allow the arch-Eurosceptic, John Redwood, space in its columns, where the Social Chapter is opposed for 'importing unemployment with Euro-policies' (18.3.97:18), thus admitting within its discourse a counterflow of the kind we have already noted in Chapter 3.

Politically, without getting into the charged area of sovereignty, the *Independent* somewhat equivocally asserts that Britain's future *is* Europe. Nevertheless it implies that there are limits to its political free-thinking, where Europe is concerned, which are coterminous with the Conservative opt-out clauses written into the Maastricht Treaty (see Text 4.7 below).

Finally, historically and culturally, whilst it is clearly pro-European, it could be said that this newspaper is tempted at times to represent cultural distinctions and historical precedents in a manner which suggests at least a residue of scepticism in its discourse.

The economic implications

The *Independent* has taken note of the strong opinions in British business circles relating to the economic imperative of further developing our ties with Europe (and by extension, eventually joining the single currency).

Text 4.1 (leader, 18.3.97:17)

Forget numbers – thls Is about our future

... As long as business keeps saying, however sotto voce, that Europe is our future, he [John Major] can not make use of the ready symbols of British-English nostalgic nationalism...

Sarah Helm describes Brussels as both cautious and gleeful as the Commission awaits the result of the Election. Using both secondary discourse and comments of her own, the position of this journalist, in Text 4.2 below, is clear on this day at least.

Text 4.2 (Sarah Helm, 23.3.1997:16)

Cautious, gleeful EU awaits Blair

... The launch of EMU will produce the most far-reaching economic and political integration yet seen. 'If we don't join, we will effectively be outside the union. We will be outside the decision-making block', says Roy Denman, the former EU ambassador to Washington.

If Mr Blair keeps out of a single currency he will have no chance of taking a leading role in the shaping of Europe...

But two days later, in a manner which well illustrates the frequently ambivalent attitudes of the pro-European press, the same journalist spelled out a much less than positive line.

Text 4.3   (Sarah Helm, 25.3.97:13)

Forty years on, is the European train still running on track?

...But, today, doubts about the economic aims of Europe are as deep as ever they have been. Rising unemployment and spending cuts are being blamed on efforts of the member states to meet the criteria for economic and monetary union...

On the following day, the *Independent* printed an example of the doubts mentioned above by representing Italy's problems in meeting the criteria (problems which we now know Italy overcame in time to meet the declaration deadline of March 1998).

Text 4.4   (Andrew Gumbel, 26.3.97:14)

Italy's lone play for delay on euro falls on stony ground

...But the rest of the European Union, particularly Germany, has grown more nervous in the face of Italy's efforts because it has no faith in the country's archaic economic structure and Byzantine, inefficient institutions...

The political implications

With certain significant reservations the *Independent* is in favour of pursuing further the political possiblities of closer union implicit in a single currency, although the details are not spelled out. Indeed, in many cases the negative aspects – the points of closure – are more indicative of its position than any forward-looking political vision. This ambivalence is typical of the *Independent*'s discourse but will also be found in the other pro-European papers too. But to begin with, two positive voices:

Text 4.5   (leader, 1.3.97:19)

It's time for Labour to loosen its tongue

Whatever happens to single money... Britain's future is 'European', and no political formation contending for parliamentary power can be anything else...

Andrew Marr, the then editor of the *Independent*, is also unequivocal about the political implications for Britain in Europe in the event of either a Labour or a Conservative win in the impending election:

Text 4.6   (Andrew Marr, 18.3.97:1)

An historic choice for Britain – the case against cynicism

If New Labour wins on 1 May, then our political system will alter, probably quite fast and probably for ever. From Scotland to London, from Cardiff to Strasbourg ... If Mr Major wins? It would keep us out of monetary union and ensure a glacial freeze in our relations with continental Union-builders...

But, as we have pointed out, this pro-European discourse of the *Independent* is also tempered by scepticism. Three days later, in the leader column, the paper voices a much more cautious attitude, which endorses John Major's Maastricht achievements in securing opt-outs in key areas of the treaty:

Text 4.7 (leader, 21.3.97:17)

One last bad day for parliament

...Mr Major's negotiated stance at Maastricht will be remembered as a wise, far-sighted achievement and a signal service to his country...

History and culture

It would be surprising to find the *Independent* using historical and cultural themes in the same way as the Eurosceptic papers for making unfavourable distinctions between Britain and the rest of Europe. For the most part the focus on these themes is indeed pro-European but there are nevertheless some exceptions to this general trend. To take the favourable focus first, James Roberts, although in an article which is not given great prominence, represents European education in very strong and positive terms indeed, and ones, which we suspect, would be unimaginable in a truly Eurosceptic discourse:

Text 4.8 (James Roberts, 23.3.97:15)

What Europe can teach us all

...Our near and dear rivals ... France and Germany both provide their children with a far better education than we do ... The middle classes trust their little treasures to the state ... state schools are well funded, attract good teachers...

On the same day and in a major article Neal Ascherson speaks of the British exposure to other cultures through the EU as both beneficial and irrevocable processes. Again, such a view is unheard in the discourse of scepticism:

Text 4.9 (Neal Ascherson, 23.3.97:21)

Are we the electorate they deserve?

...comparisons are made ... with French railways, German schools, Danish farming, Dutch budgeting, Italian regionalism ... but this habit ... is opening a big window on the world – and it cannot be shut again...

Notwithstanding these positive and wholly pro-European voices, notable for their transcendence of nationalism and their willingness to acknowledge good practice beyond our frontiers, there are others which, if not openly hostile, suggest reservations and, ideologically speaking, point to a need for caution and distance as Britain reconsiders its position towards Europe under a new government. Among others these include articles relating to European 'beef bans' (23.3.97:9), perceived

EU financial excesses relating to the construction of the new parliament buildings (19.3.97:18), EU 'restrictions' on citrus fruits (1.3.97:2), and imposed changes in Britain's immigration laws (9.3.97:21).

The Guardian

In many ways the *Guardian*'s pro-Europeanism is comparable to that of the *Independent* but there are subtle differences. Like the *Independent* it focuses upon the problems which other member states are encountering in the run-up to joining the EMU, although its motives for doing so may be perceived as being slightly different (see Text 4.12 below). Again, like the *Independent*, which seemed to take its pro-single-currency-with-caution line from the City, the *Guardian*'s commitment is similarly inspired, although it goes as far as to suggest that the whole EMU issue is a distraction for the EU from its primary commitment of completing the single market (see Text 4.20 below). It also partly represents the social and industrial unrest which was occurring across Europe in a positive political light, that of organised labour successfully making its voice heard with regard to the priorities given to economic considerations over social ones in the EMU run-up period.

The essentially pro-European discourse gets off to an impressive start in early March 1997 by representing a whole range of European issues which includes information on the single currency and the working of the European Commission. By mid-March however, the paper becomes centrally involved in domestic issues and in particular the pursuit of Conservative politicians on what was to become a major election issue: the so-called 'sleaze factor' perceived to be deeply ingrained in the activities of the Conservative government. At this mid-point in March, Europe is relegated to the occasional article and hardly regains its importance in the discourse as the *Guardian* sets off in pursuit of the alleged financial and other moral misdemeanours of Conservative MPs. However important these 'sleaze factors' were, it is odd, to say the least, that Europe is under-represented during the last two weeks of March. This is particularly so when in its leader of 26 March, the *Guardian* bemoans the lack of debate on Britain's future relationship with the European Union, yet on that same day it runs only one article of any import dedicated to European issues. Notwithstanding this uneven coverage, the dominant tone of the discourse is firmly pro-European, eloquent at times, and never more so than when expressed by the voices of David Marquand, Roy Hattersley and the *Guardian*'s own political correspondent, Hugo Young. We found no 'hard' Eurosceptic voices in the *Guardian* during this period on the 'invited opposing-voice principle' noted elsewhere, and which accounted for John Redwood's presence in the *Independent* as well as those of others elsewhere.

The economic implications
The *Guardian*'s position on the single currency is most clearly expressed in the leader of 12 March. Note that what follows is hardly a wholehearted endorsement:

Text 4.10   (leader, 12.3.97:14)

Kicking against the wrong goalposts
Europe has more urgent priorities than the single currency

...A single currency may be the correct thing when the time is right but it emphatically isn't a magic wand to cure Europe's ailments...

We mentioned earlier that the *Guardian* gives wide coverage to the social and industrial unrest that was affecting other member countries of the EU and which was perceived to be caused by the economic measures being taken by governments in the run-up to EMU. The representation of this industrial and social turbulence in Europe by the British press may be intended to be interpreted slightly differently depending on the origin of the discourse. From a Eurosceptic point of view the coverage of these events could constitute a warning: 'this is what happens when the EU intervenes in a country's national economy'. When the unrest in Europe is reported in a dominantly pro-European discourse, then, we can presume that it also constitutes a warning, although perhaps in a more attenuated way. This representation can be placed on an ideological continuum where, at one extreme, the political right rejects the single currency completely, and at the other the centre-left accepts the idea of a single currency but counsels extreme caution in Britain's involvement with it. This cautious version of pro-European discourse is the prevailing one by far. Nowhere in the press, in the pre-election period, did we find a single voice advocating wholehearted support for the single currency, nor of Britain entering EMU in the first round (but see the *Mirror* of 2.5.98, Text 5.54 below).

When the *Guardian* widely reports the industrial turmoil in Europe already noted in the discourse of other papers, we assume that its underlying purpose is first one of advocating caution on economic grounds along the lines suggested above (an assumption which is supported by the leader quoted in Text 4.10 above). However, we also perceive a second, ideological element not present in the discourse of any of the other pro-European papers, which links the unrest to the galvanisation of resistance by organised labour to the monetary policies of European governments.

In Text 4.11, in our view, the unrest is represented as an economic cautionary tale:

Text 4.11   (Ian Traynor, 3.3.97:1)

Germany clings to EMU

The German government yesterday sought to quash rampant speculation about an impending delay in the launch of the single currency despite unemployment figures of almost 5 million...

However, in Text 4.12, the issue – unemployment – is represented in a political context which has galvanised the resistance of organised labour across Europe. The events reported here are the threatened pit closures in Germany, a topic with distinct ideological resonance for any *Guardian* reader who recalls its coverage of the miners' strike in Britain in the early 1980s. We did not find representation of this kind in any other paper:

Text 4.12   (Ian Traynor, 12.3.97:11)

Tremors shake the heart of Europe

European workers angry at threatened redundancies took to the streets yesterday. The protests came amid wider fears that jobs will be sacrificed to meet the criteria for the single currency...

Further evidence of this ideological element is provided on the same page, this time in relation to the demonstration of the Belgian Renault workers in Brussels. As the introduction shows, this is a sympathetic discourse:

Text 4.13   (Alex Duval Smith, 12.3.97:11)

France/The Euro-demo is born
as Renault workers unite against cuts

The Belgians brought the beer, the French provided the wine and the Spanish started dancing as soon as the multi-lingual singing of the Internationale had died down...

The political implications

In a seminal article on European integration, the historian, David Marquand, was invited to examine the Eurosceptic argument in favour of Britain developing as the 'Hong Kong' of Europe, an off-shore island, benefiting from the proximity of the economic activity of the EU, but with low participatory status, and to compare it with the alternative, the argument for fuller integration. The view expressed here regarding the Major opt-outs from Maastricht, whilst it does not have the authority of a leader column, is at odds with the discourse of the *Independent* whose political stance endorsed Major's achievements (see Text 4.7 above). Note too that Marquand's discourse is also distinguished from the mainstream pro-European discourse for its positive mention of federalism, the notorious the F-word.

Text 4.14   (David Marquand, 27.3.97:21)

The real choice is here

...John Major's Britain has been a free rider on the European single market: that is the point of the opt-outs he secured at Maastricht ... If we take the European option, we move further down the road towards Europe. We accept proto-federal power sharing with our European partners and the Brussels institutions; albeit gradually, we reconstruct our European culture on European lines...

Marquand's views are important and may be said to stand at the most pro-European extremity of the *Guardian*'s discourse. His vision of a Europe whose political organisation transcends the narrower confines of *fin-de-siècle* nationalism is matched by those of the well-known former MP and journalist, Roy Hattersley. His historical summary of Britain's reluctance to become involved in the European project concurs closely with that of Marquand mentioned in Chapter 1:

Text 4.15   (Roy Hattersley, 25.3.97:17)

Euro visionaries

...It was nostalgia that kept Britain out of the partnership from the very start. Sentiment was dressed up to look like judgement and a few romantics really believed that the Commonwealth and Empire would see the Mother country into the 21st century. But it was never the economic arguments which lay at the heart of the antagonism. Then as now the problem was sovereignty...

At the beginning of March 1997, in a highly informative double page spread, the *Guardian* reports on a range of Euro-issues and sets them helpfully against a 'background' discourse which explains why the optimism of the late 1980s has given way to anxiety and loss of confidence as the end of the century approaches. It cites the primary reasons for this downturn as the perceived failure of the European Union to resolve important issues such as enlargement, reform of the CAP, competition policy, completion of the single market, and reforms of the product and labour market. The thrust of the argument is to suggest that the prioritising of EMU has been a strategic error by the politicians whose attentions should have been given to these other matters. However, the background piece inserts into the discourse one interesting comment on the possible political organisation of a Europe yet to come. Again the journalist ventures into the unmentionable territory of the F-word:

Text 4.16   (Larry Elliot, 3.3.97:15)

The Wall came tumbling down – but the walls are going back up

...But as David Currie argued ... there is no intrinsic reason why a federal Europe should not be organised on loose Swiss style lines to accommodate fears about over-centralisation of power...

History and culture

As was the case with the *Independent*, we would not expect to find in the pro-European discourse of the *Guardian* the retreat pell-mell into nationalism, historicism and dubious cultural distinctions which we encountered in the Eurosceptic narrative. For the most part our expectations were sustained. Europe is overtly represented as both a provider and facilitator for international action often in a seemingly neutral manner, which ideologically speaking implies its acceptance in the discourse. But there are the occasional exceptions too which suggest elements of scepticism, and in one case, an inexplicable phobia. As a senior journalist and political commentator, Hugo Young's voice on the nature of Europhobic discourse characterises the *Guardian's* positive pro-European cultural narrative:

Text 4.17   (Hugo Young, 11.3.97:15)

The phobia that lies behind the sneers

... but it [Europe] has become an acceptable object about which to say what would be unsayable about frogs, krauts or blacks. Arid denunciations of Maastricht give ever less cover to the message they encode: populist ravings against everything the EU does or wants to do ...

As we have already noted, international initiatives undertaken by the European Union were frequently represented by the Eurosceptic press as meddlesome, harmful and unwarranted interference in Britain's national life. For the most part, European action by the Commissioners, and by other officials, is represented by the *Guardian* in a manner which, if it does not completely endorse its legitimacy, does not dismiss it either for reasons of dark anti-British plots, or because the Commissioner is Irish or the politician German. Thus in its positive pro-European voices, we find the EU fishing resolution 'hailed as success' (15.3.97:14), Robin Cook's prediction that a new government would successfully conclude an agreement at the impending Amsterdam EU summit as being 'hailed as a breakthrough' by the Dutch (15.3.97:16), and the role of the EU as a facilitator of international trade is endorsed by such headlines as 'EU to dispel small firm suspicion' (4.3.97:17). In among these positive representations there are others which are less enthusiastic such as 'Fraud robs EU coffers of billions' (13.4.97:19) but there are none of the xenophobic references to 'Euro-swindlers' and the like which we find in other references to the same event in the Eurosceptic press. One voice stands out in this discourse which overall, as we have said, tends to normalise, legitimate and endorse the role of the EU in Britain's affairs, as indirectly, striking a discordant note. In a long article on Louis Schweitzer, the chairman of Renault in its 'At the heart of Europe' series, Alex Duval Smith relates how Schweitzer and President Chirac went to the same elitist school in Strasbourg, perhaps the most well known in France, the Ecole Nationale d'Administration (ENA). In an unaccountable but interesting foray into personal prejudice and anti-French attitudes Duval Smith describes Schweitzer as follows:

Text 4.18   (Alex Duval Smith, 8.3.97:24)

Iron in the soul of Sartre's cousin

... Its [ENA's] elitist post-graduate course turns bright social cripples, such as Schweitzer, into French bureaucrats ...

The Financial Times

Having looked at two of the leading pro-European broadsheets, it is time to examine the discourse of the third, and in many ways the most pro-European, that of the *Financial Times*.

As we have just mentioned, the discourse of the *Financial Times* on European issues is among the most interesting encountered in our analysis. It emerges as the strongest Europhile voice of all the papers examined. Its overt positiveness and directness of representation – few ethnocentric jokes at the expense of European policies and EU officials and even fewer pejorative references to 'Eurocrats', 'bureaucrats', 'pleasure palaces', 'white elephants' and the like – gives the discourse of the *FT* an ideological dimension which strongly legitimises the activities of the European Union as well as endorsing British participation within it. It does not advance historical justifications for caution on Britain's part, nor indulge in any of the negative cultural discrimination which is a feature of Euroscepticism, but whose residues can be found even in the pro-European titles, as we have noted above.

The economic implications

Predictably perhaps, this category is the most significant both from the point of view of the *Financial Times'* own preoccupations as well as from the conclusions that can be inferred from them. The representation of the economic role and importance of the EU in Britain's present and future can be separated into two principal kinds. The first we suggest is the more permanent, although, in one sense, indirect. It existed in the discourse of the *FT* long before the 1997 Election and is comprised of a plurality of voices representing the myriad deals, capital flows, EU appointments and initiatives, policy changes and financial reports which bind the economy of Britain to that of the European Single Market. Whilst these representations may be adverse at times, the majority have a quality of matter-of-factness which makes for the strong, overt, as well as ideological endorsement of Britain as a major player in Europe. Such is the frequency of this kind of representation that we propose only to assert it here, for this economic category, and leave it to our readers to check the truth of it for themselves.

The second stream of discourse is more self-consciously focused on the imminent election issues, where by this time, Europe has emerged in higher profile. We shall focus in this category on economic aspects of Europe as an election issue. In Text 4.19 below, Martin Wolf, in an extended, highly informative article, offers a view of the viability of EMU not found elsewhere. It plays down the 'European turbulence/ disgruntlement' factor, so much emphasised by the Eurosceptics and Euroagnostics alike, and this de-emphasis runs counter to the doomsday scenarios that we reported in this category for other papers. It is worth quoting Wolf at some length:

Text 4.19 (Martin Wolf, 29.4.97:22)

This EMU can surely fly

As in the referendum in September 1992, a French president has apparently entrusted the fate of European economic and monetary union to the mercies of a disgruntled populace. Many in the UK hope the French electorate will save them from having to decide whether to enter. They are fooling themselves. EMU is far more likely to go ahead as planned. There are three reasons for believing this: European political leaders have repeatedly stated how important they think the project is; they have all, including the French, already imposed all the sacrifices necessary to fulfil the Maastricht treaty's economic convergence criteria; and the pain consequent upon that austerity lies largely in the past...

In the event, as we now know, the French did return a socialist government but the vote was not regarded as anti-European, nor did Lionel Jospin, the incoming Prime Minister, alter the economic course of the French economy away from the objectives imposed by the Maastricht criteria for EMU membership in 1999. Wolf's representation of the rest of EU as poised to enter the single currency, despite the obstacles, stands in marked contrast to those of the majority of the British press sector.

In the same issue, on its European page the *FT* runs two articles on the single currency. The first deals with the unreadiness of the British banking system to deal 'over the counter' in Euros which virtually rules out Britain's entry to EMU in 1999 anyway (29.4.97:3). The second describes in detail the arrangements which Germany is making for the introduction of the euro-currency in the first round. The representation conceals neither the mistrust of the euro by the majority of the Germans nor the perceived lack of preparation on the part of the authorities for its implementation, but it offers a fascinating insight into practical preparations for an event which the rest of the British press leaves entirely unreported:

Text 4.20 (Peter Norman, 29.4.97:3)

German town halls look for lead on EMU

Germany is a land of euro-paradox. A euro-enthusiast chancellor is confronted with a citizenry that profoundly mistrusts the single currency and yet the Bonn government publicity campaign for the euro has been modest to the point of near invisibility...

The euro poses many challenges at local level. They include the physical conversion of coin-operated machines, such as parking meters, and decisions on whether to round up or down the prices charged for public transport, swimming pools, libraries and parking fines...

Finally in this category, it will be recalled that the British press during this period laid particular stress on the flagging economies of our European partners as they struggled to adapt to the imperatives of the Maastricht criteria. It is interesting to find in the European News Digest column, the good news regarding output in France:

Text 4.21   (25.4.97:3)

Sharp rise in French output

French manufacturing industry picked up sharply in February, spurred on by market improvements in the motor industry...

In conclusion, we should perhaps point out that there is some representation of other nations' anxieties about the perceived lack of preparedness, and its consequences for Italy (29.4.97:3), France (22.4.97:2) and Germany (28.4.97:3) for entering the single currency. However, these are represented once again with a matter-of-factness which carries little of the ideological baggage of the *'Beware! it could happen in Britain'* kind that we have encountered elsewhere.

The political implications

The evidence contained in the data during the week preceding the election points to the *FT*'s discourse, through the scope and detail of its representations, and its general literalness (i.e. few hidden anti-European agendas) as being most at ease with the concept of Britain operating economically and politically within a European space. Sovereignty was not an issue, but equally, neither were any of the pro-European 'grand narratives' of the kind we encountered in the *Guardian* written by such authoritative voices as David Marquand or Roy Hattersley. However, the leader of 29 April gives the key features of the *FT*'s official as well as its ideological position. In addition to the unequivocal assertion that Britain is inextricably linked with the single market, note the two friendly, if indirect references to issues which are anathema for the Eurosceptics – foreign policy and political integration.

Text 4.22   (leader, 29.4.97:23)

Europe is the issue

...The UK needs Europe, and Europe needs the UK. The fortunes of British business are inextricably linked with the preservation and extension of the single market, which rests in turn on continued UK participation in the political structures of the EU. More broadly, the UK's influence in the world is increasingly a function of its membership of the EU. Disengagement is not an option any government could responsibly contemplate...

History and culture

The most striking features of the *FT*'s discourse under this category, apart from the total absence of Euroscepticism in the forms we encountered elsewhere, are indeed its directness, literalness and distanced qualities of the kind we mentioned under *Economic implications* above. Paradoxically, it is not so much the *content* of the representations (although clearly this is important) which places them in this category, as it is the accepting, 'normalising' directness of the discourse by which the events are represented. We found no references to historical factors or to British cultural distinctiveness as reasons for the United Kingdom proceeding cautiously with our European partners.

A typical example of this 'Euro-normalising' discourse is contained in Text 4.23 below, where the EU is represented as a facilitator of international initiatives:

Text 4.23   (Charles Batchelor, 22.4.97:6)

EU hopes to put freight back on track

A project for freight 'express' and European rail freight 'freeways' could provide the answer to the panoply of problems associated with moving goods through Europe...

Another example of this normalising discourse comes in references to the EU's endorsement of subsidies to certain national shipbuilding industries. Again here we should note in Text 4.24 below, the distance and apparent literalness of the representation as well as the assumptions about mutually held knowledge between reader and journalist. We would suggest too, that this restraint in the discourse is even more noteworthy if we recall the manner in which, for almost two decades, the face of British governments has been resolutely set against subsidies, a policy which has had profound effects upon the British shipbuilding industry. Note the even-handedness in the reporting which includes the 'strategic' argument from France in reply to the protest from Britain and others.

Text 4.24   (Emma Tucker, 25.4.97:2)

EU clears aid for shipyards

European Industry ministers yesterday endorsed three big state aid packages to shipbuilders in Germany, Spain and Greece but insisted this was not a signal to other troubled enterprises to demand new subsidies ... the aid was approved only after a long debate ... that split council into two camps with the Nordic countries and Britain calling for an end to subsidies ... But southern bloc countries, led by France argued that supporting shipbuilders was not just about protecting jobs, but also about protecting a strategic industry...

Even when reporting on a massive European financial error, the tone of the discourse is nevertheless restrained and distanced; the representation is even-handed and full, and pitched to an informed reader. Note in passing the quoting of the overpayment in ecus first and sterling second in the main body of the text:

Text 4.25   (Alison Maitland, 30.4.97:28)

EU overpaid cereal producers by £12 bn

The European Union has overcompensated cereal farmers by Ecu 17 bn (£11.8 bn) in the past four years for cuts in price supports under the Common Agricultural Policy...

This article is not wholly uncritical but the criticism is implied rather than directly stated by the use of secondary discourse:

> ...Asked why nothing had been done to adjust the compensation, an EU Commission official said: 'The grain lobby is very strong with agricultural ministers'.

Readers will recall the manner in which the *Telegraph* represented the setting up by the European Commission of a unit to monitor food safety (see Text 3.30 above) as follows: 'A team of European bureaucrats is being created to police food safety throughout the EU'. Compare this hostile representation (i.e. 'bureaucrats', 'police') with the reporting of the same event in the *FT* in Text 4.26 below. Note the use of the legitimising title 'European Commission' instead of the illegitimising item 'bureaucrats' and the more neutral use of 'monitor' instead of the 'police' as typical examples of the integrating/normalising representation of the *FT*'s discourse.

Text 4.26   (Neil Buckley, 1.5.97:2)

Brussels to expand EU food safety unit

The European Commission is to set up a Food and Veterinary Service in Ireland to monitor EU-wide food safety as part of measures to guard against future 'mad cow' type health crises...

There are other examples of this normalising style whose overall effect is to integrate a European cultural dimension into the discourse of the *FT*. These include, among others, the reporting of how British computing experts, lured by big salaries and the 'European lifestyle' are in demand by European banks (25.4.97:2), the perceived benefit of the single currency to European chemical manufactures (22.4.97:7), the need for European legislation on industrial relations (29.4.97:2), co-operation on legal and home affairs issues (29.4.97:2) and banking (25.4.97:8).

This completes our commentary on this category of the *FT*'s discourse as well as, indeed, for the section generally on the pro-European broadsheets. After the summary and evaluation relating to the broadsheets, we shall turn our attention finally to the one pro-European tabloid, the *Mirror*.

Summary and evaluation

Our commentary on the three broadsheets has identified some common features of pro-European discourse as well as some distinctions which, for the most part, are more delineated by the degree of commitment to a particular issue than by real substantive differences. In one case we claim to have spotted a distinct, ideological position in relation to the *Guardian* (see Text 4.12 above) not found in the rest of the pro-European discourse. We have mostly identified the major themes and overt rhetoric around which the pro-European discourse turns.

The covert, ideological position of these papers can be summarised as follows (papers identified by initials in brackets i.e. *I*, *G*, and *FT*).

- The European Union is an efficient provider and facilitator working *acceptably* well in Britain's interests (*I*, *G*, *FT*);
- The Maastricht opt-outs offer a tactical advantage to Britain which should proceed with caution in future negotiations (*I*);
- The economic and social pressures on other member states in the run-up to qualifying for EMU signal caution as Britain negotiates on the single currency (*I*, *G*);
- The single currency is (properly) being resisted by organised labour (*G*);
- The single currency is an unnecessary diversion of the EU from other more pressing issues such as the completion of the single market (*G*);
- Britain should not enter in the first round of the single currency (*I*, *G*, *FT*);
- Britain should be prepared boldly to investigate further political integration, not ignoring certain federal options (*G*);
- Britain should be prepared to investigate further unspecified acts of political integration (*I*, *G*, *FT*);
- Europe is the most important geo-political/economic and social space in which Britain must become a permanent and major player (*I*, *G*, *FT*).

One pro-European tabloid

We shall proceed now to the final analysis in this chapter where we examine the discourse of the only tabloid pro-European paper – the *Mirror*.

The Mirror

The *Mirror* is a special case but not in the same way as the *Sun*. Unlike its rival, it was not obliged to change political colours half-way through the pre-election period. In every election since 1945 it has consistently supported the Labour Party although it is often said, with some justification that, for many reasons, not the least of which has been its life or death struggle with the *Sun*, its political stance has become significantly weakened in the 1980s and 1990s. It is a special case only because it is the sole pro-European tabloid voice in the British press sector. However, by its own admission, it did not believe that Europe was going to be an election issue in March 1997, and its discourse, whilst clearly pro-European, reflects this view. Looking at its discourse then, from the point of view of the three thematic categories, our comments are as follows:

The economic implications

The strongest pro-European argument that the *Mirror* uses at this time is in fact the same as those put forward as economic justifications by the broadsheets – that British business needs Europe. Readers will recall that one of the Eurosceptic tactics for attacking the Social Chapter and the introduction of the single currency was to evoke the fear of unemployment as one of the consequences of signing up to either. Here we find the *Mirror* using the same ploy, but this time as the perceived consequence of a reduced British economic participation in Europe:

Text 4.27   (Kevin Reilly, Clinton Manning, and Emily Wilson, 12.3.97:2)

We love £72 Bn EU Bosses warn Major

Top bosses yesterday warned that leaving the European Union could cost Britain £72 BILLION. And they said that Conservative Europhobia threatened thousands of jobs. ... And they blasted the mistaken belief that a hostile attitude to Europe is in our best interests...

This article is significantly more informative than anything appearing in the Eurosceptic tabloids over the same period. The informational/representational function of the discourse is particularly pronounced by the framing of the main piece by 12 mini-articles giving the economic stakes of 12 major British companies, ranging from British Airways through BP to ICI, in the single market. It constitutes the *Mirror*'s strongest endorsement of the benefits of Britain's continuing participation in the European single market.

Clinton Manning, one of the authors of the article quoted above in Text 4.27, contributes a further consistent and revelatory voice to the *Mirror*'s position on the economy by highlighting the fact that, despite the perceived healthy state of the British economy represented in the Eurosceptic press at this time, the British inflation rate compared badly with the rest of the EU. Again here, the referential/informational element of the representation function of the discourse is strong. What, in fact, the reader is getting here is a condensed report on European inflation published by the OECD – a commendable act of information.

Text 4.28   (Clinton Manning, 17.3.97:22)

Britain still worst in EU for inflation

Government claims to have licked inflation have been dented by the Organisation for Economic Cooperation and Development.
   Its latest figures show that Britain's inflation rate, worse than the rest of the EU through the 1970s and 80s, is no better now...

The political implications

As we mentioned earlier, the *Mirror*, at this time at least, did not believe that Europe was set to become an important election issue even though Euroscepticism was being widely brandished in the discourse of the other side (Mr Major's decision to fight on European issues was not announced until mid-April).

It will be recalled that the activities of the Referendum Party were given extensive coverage by the *Express* in early April, in a wistful mood of nostalgia, in defence of all things British, including the political system. A month earlier, in the *Mirror*, readers were treated to a no-nonsense-style report on the late Sir James Goldsmith and his alleged irrelevant obsession with Europe. Of interest here is the manner in which Europe itself, as an election issue, is deprioritised in favour of what are perceived to be more important domestic matters:

Text 4.29   (leader, 7.3.97:6)

Deluded Messiah

James Goldsmith is stinking rich and obsessed with Europe ... As an interview with him in the *Mirror* shows, he has no interest in the issues that really matter – health, education, crime, unemployment...

Direct evidence that the *Mirror* is downplaying the significance of Europe as an election issue is provided a few days later when the paper covers the defection of the Conservative MP, Sir George Gardiner, to the Referendum Party:

Text 4.30   (leader, 10.3.97:6)

Treachery by George

...Sir George's excuse is that he believes Britain's future in Europe is THE KEY election issue ... Yet, as the *Mirror*'s recent poll showed, Europe is almost irrelevant to most voters...

Thus Europe as a political issue does not receive much further representation in the discourse of the *Mirror* for the period examined. This view runs counter to the general implied importance of European issues as manifested on both sides of the European divide in the written press. Even so, the *Mirror* takes the trouble to include the European issue as being among 20 ways in which New Labour, once in power, will improve the lives of British citizens. It signals a new start for Britain in Europe whilst implying that care will need to be taken to defend Britain's interests:

Text 4.31   (leader, 19.3.97:6)

20 ways things will get better under Labour

...Tony Blair will build a new relationship with our European partners – while standing up for Britain in Brussels...

History and culture

The *Mirror* does not consciously seek to hide behind historical precedents or cultural distinctiveness in its European discourse, and indeed it would be surprising to find excessive posturing of this kind in the pro-European press, even though there are traces, as we have noted already. We suggested in Chapter 3 that *The Times* had almost benevolently represented the xenophobic outbursts of David Evans MP, Conservative MP for Welwyn and Hatfield, for dubious reasons (see Text 3.4). The *Mirror*'s report of the same event is uncompromising in its stinging attack on Evans, and its pro-European credentials are all too plain.

Text 4.32   (Peter Allen, 6.3.97:1)

Tory Nut goes mad again

Foul-mouthed Tory David Evans has let rip again with a scathing attack on Britain's European partners [France, Belgium and Germany] ... He said France and Belgium – which fought proudly alongside the Allies in the First World War – were unfit to defend Europe...

Nevertheless, as we can see, the representation of this event is pro-European, albeit perhaps for the wrong reasons, and contrasts strongly with the anti-European use it is put to by *The Times*.

Summary and evaluation
Whilst the *Mirror*'s stand on Europe, when it is represented, is firmly pro-European, it is also deprioritised as an issue. The ideological underpinning appears to be as follows:

- Britain's economic prosperity depends on its participation in Europe;
- Europe as an electoral issue (but with post-electoral implications) is low on the voters' priority lists – British interests lie elsewhere;
- New Labour means a new (beneficial) start for Britain in Europe;
- Britain needs a leader who is capable of standing up to European demands.

Conclusion

The discourse of the *Independent, Guardian, Financial Times* and the *Mirror*, as we have pointed out in the course of our commentary, is not unreservedly pro-European. There is nothing intrinsically odd in this since further integration with the European Union does pose problems for Britain of the kind that will only be resolved by robust negotiations involving solution by compromise (see Chapter 8 for further discussion).

However this pro-European discourse distinguishes itself from the dominant Euroscepticism of the British press represented by the *Telegraph, The Times, Mail, Express* and *Sun* by insisting on the economic reality of Europe as Britain's largest trading partner and, by extension, on Europe as being the natural and most obvious political and social space in which Britain should operate. Whereas the single currency question causes the Eurosceptics to fulminate against the alleged intrusiveness of the EU in the affairs of a sovereign state and to seek closure, for the Europhiles it is the occasion to halt, but not necessarily falter, in order to assess the wisdom of the introduction of the euro at this stage in the integration process. It is also the opportunity to reflect on how Britain can best harness such a potentially far-reaching initiative for its own advantage.

Without doubt, the single currency issue, as we have seen, was already becoming a major focus of attention in the pre-election period. By the beginning of May 1998, the period of the launch of the euro and of the appointment of the president of the European Central Bank, both camps have a clearer if still unresolved position to represent. We shall be looking at the discourse surrounding this particular event in the next chapter.

Chapter 5

The British presidency of the European Union, 1998

Introduction

In addition to offering perceptive insights into the quality of the devil's lines, folk wisdom also asserts that leopards have difficulties in changing their spots. It would be surprising indeed were we to discover, in the second period of the discourse of the British press that we examined – the British presidency of the Council of Ministers, January–June 1998 – that the opinions of the key Eurosceptic or Europhile press had significantly changed. Nor was it the case, with the possible exception of one tabloid.

What had changed, however, was the context in which the discourse took place. Europe is no longer just one issue among others in a greater discourse of the General Election. It emerges in the January–June 1998 period, in its own right, unbidden by the electoral ambitions of the political parties.

Moreover, the government had changed and in consequence the representation of these events is coloured by a new political reality, that of New Labour sustained by a massive majority in parliament. Of the four events covered, the preliminary procedures, between February and March 1998, relating to the eventual launch of the single currency, was the topic which most concentrated the minds of the papers of both camps. It received very extensive coverage. Apart from one tabloid and one broadsheet, and despite deep reservations, alarm, and a conveyed sense of genuine unknowingness about the future of the single currency, there is an air of inevitability on all sides. This acknowledgement of the inevitability of the euro is induced by the new and sympathetic stance on Europe adopted by the British government, on the one hand, and the implementation of procedures in May 1998, leading to the eventual launch of the single currency on the other.

This chapter differs from the two preceding ones in two significant ways. In Chapters 3 and 4, we examined each paper's representation of Europe across a wide range of issues on a title-by-title basis. First, in this chapter, whilst the commentary uses broadly the same approach as previously, it examines the press coverage from the narrower perspective of just four specific political events that occurred during the British presidency of the European Union (1 January–22 June 1998). The events we selected were the following:

- The announcement by 11 member states that they had successfully fulfilled the Maastricht criteria for entry to EMU (27 February 1998);

- Tony Blair's speech to the French National Assembly (24 March 1998);
- The adoption by the Blair government of the European Working Time Directive (9 April 1998);
- The procedures implemented on 1 May 1998, leading to the eventual launch of the euro.

The fourth event, the launch of the euro in May 1998, generated by far the most coverage of the European Union of all the discourse we examined for the whole period.

We have an opportunity of doing something different here. We are able to engage in a more in-depth commentary of the coverage of these specific matters by individual newspapers – as opposed to the broader brush approach of the earlier chapters – whilst at the same time checking to ascertain whether what we find is indeed a continuity of the previous discourse of the pre-election period (as we predicted it would be) or whether it constitutes a change in direction. Secondly, Chapters 3 and 4 were written by a media analyst informed by politics. This chapter is undertaken principally by a political scientist informed by the techniques of media/discourse analysis. We shall therefore be concentrating more upon the political/economic themes of the discourse than upon the others mentioned in the earlier chapters.

By way of a preamble, we should say that Britain's influence on the events which occupied its attention during the period of its presidency was significantly affected by its opt-out position on EMU. As we might expect, its occupancy of the presidency, and its position as one of the four largest states, was often eclipsed by the initiatives of the other EMU participants. Britain will inevitably suffer in terms of the influence it has on this crucial stage of European development as the result of its voluntary self-exclusion.

The fulfilment of the budget deficit criterion by 11 member states, February 1998

We begin our commentary with an examination of the way in which the press covered the announcement that 11 member states had met the budget deficit criteria for EMU entry. In some ways this coverage is the most significant of all. On 27 February, the member governments published figures showing in the words of the *Financial Times*, 'unexpected strong economic convergence'. The importance of this event is considerable because it appears to have been accepted by much of the press as evidence, whether they liked it or not, that EMU would go ahead in 1999 with the large majority of the member states on board. Given the charged significance of this announcement for the most ideologically committed papers in both camps, it seems reasonable to assume that their coverage will reflect their core attitudes on the desirability or otherwise of EMU, and of the further integration that will accompany it. This assumption, if correct, gives the evaluation of this particular day's events a higher level of significance than it might otherwise possess. In short, this commentary has a particularly useful 'benchmark' significance. We begin with the broadsheets and go on to the tabloids, placing the papers within each category in an order which roughly reflects their place on the Eurosceptic–Europhile continuum as broadsheets and tabloids.

The broadsheets

The Daily Telegraph

The *Telegraph* carried three substantial items on the EMU convergence criteria announcement and one shorter one. The more substantial ones are examined below. Of the three reports, the first is the most objective. It contains a concise coverage of the extent to which a representative selection of member states had or had not satisfied relevant convergence criteria and focuses in particular on Britain's position as an opt-out state. It explains briefly some of the key ways in which EMU will have an impact across Europe. It mentions also Liberal Democrat fears that Britain's self-exclusion from the first wave of EMU will result in Britain being excluded from important decisions made by the first wave entrants. The article also covers Lord Hattersley's call for a pro-EMU campaign by the government, together with demands for a referendum on the single currency. Having presented all this in an even-handed manner, the piece concludes with four paragraphs which effectively accuse several leading EU states of 'creative accounting' and of having 'fudged' their figures. Three of the four paragraphs are devoted to the views of 'leading German Eurosceptics'; a sample extract is as follows:

Text 5.1 (George Jones, Toby Helm and Alan Gimson, 28.2.98:2)

> Tony Blair and Gordon Brown ... have said they will play the role of 'honest broker' and do their best to ensure a successful launch of the euro even though Britain will not be in the first wave. All the indications are that they will turn a blind eye to what has been described as the great euro 'fudge', creative accounting measures that have enabled several leading EU states to claim they have met the strict economic criteria for membership of the single currency.
>
> Leading German Eurosceptics reacted with disbelief yesterday to the claim that the budget deficit last year was only 2.7 per cent, within the 3 per cent limit...

The effect of the final four paragraphs on economic considerations makes very clear the writers' view that there has been some creative accounting, also identified by the more pejorative item 'fudge' in order for some countries to comply with the criteria. It gives the article the overall slant that fully corresponds to the *Telegraph*'s March–May discourse of the previous year.

The second article starts off with an apparently up-beat assessment of the major states' alleged success in meeting the Maastricht criteria. Germany and Italy, for example, are said to have 'both breezed in comfortably'. However, in paragraph four, an element of doubt is introduced, which from that point on builds up to a crescendo of rhetorical criticism in which Italy is accused of being a 'fiddler of the rules', Germany is accused of having engaged in a 'ruse' with regard to its deficit figures and the development of the economies of Portugal and Spain are described as being 'equally miraculous but no less questionable' than those of Germany and Italy. This scepticism and its ideological sub-text imputing dishonest practice to some EU members, come to a head in the final paragraph:

Text 5.2 (Toby Helm, 28.2.98:13)

> The Maastricht figures game – and that is what it has become – is proof that economic and monetary union is a political rather than just an economic project. With political will the figures are simply made to fit.

Once again the *Telegraph*'s Eurosceptic rhetoric and its accompanying ideology are completely in line with its position in March–May 1997.

Should the reader of the *Telegraph* be left in any doubt as to its views of the announcement by the 11 member states that they had met the Maasticht criteria, then the leader of the day should dispel them. Here it sets out its position with true Eurosceptic fervour. It starts off by stating that 'massaging the figures' is unable to hide the fact that most of the EU states have failed to meet the Maastricht conditions. It asserts that the EU's decision to give Italy and Belgium a 'free pass' on the debt ceiling of 60 per cent of GDP criterion has been justified on 'hilarious grounds' and that EMU will proceed without any sustainable convergence of the EU states' economies and warns of bitter resentment as people discover that the European Central Bank is not subject to democratic accountability. For the *Telegraph* the euro is a more of a political than economic expedient aimed at achieving Helmut Kohl's declared belief that the single currency means:

Text 5.3 (leader, 28.2.98)

> ...the federal unification of Europe ... By abandoning the most crucial convergence criteria, the EU has shown that it is willing to sacrifice Europe's economy for the sake of its grandiose political dreams...

No change here whatsoever from the Eurosceptic discourse of the pre-election period of which the ideological sub-text can be summarised under three items: 'great Euro-fudge' (*Euro-deception*), single-currency (*political plot*), political dreams (*federal plans*).

The Times
The Times of Saturday 28 February contained three articles on EMU, of which one is commented upon below.

Text 5.4   (Charles Bremner, 28.2.98:18)

> ... In Brussels EU officials were taking satisfaction from the vindication of their forecasts of recent years, which had been widely criticised as overoptimistic notably in Britain...

The tone of the discourse is, initially, even-handed and includes quotes from Helmut Kohl and Jacques Chirac in which they congratulate their countries on having met the Maastricht criteria. Bremner asserts that the convergence data virtually guarantee that a 'broad' euro will be launched which will include all EU states except Britain, Greece, Sweden and Denmark, and goes on to make the same point about 'creative accounting' as we found in the *Telegraph*. The article covers both economic and political considerations and although we can perceive in it the ideological scepticism that characterises *The Times'* previous discourse, this scepticism is relatively restrained.

In this article, and in the other two, one of which repeats the 'fudging' accusation (28.2.98:28), we find that there is a general continuity of the sceptic discourse which characterised the earlier pre-election period.

The Independent

The *Independent* of 28 February contained four articles on the EU announcement which were centred around a large and possibly controversial photograph of Chancellor Kohl. Controversial because Kohl is photographed against a backdrop of a large Roman Catholic Pilgrim banner depicting a variety of medieval and New Testament scenes. The construction of the photograph appears to have been intended to evoke resonances of the Holy Roman Empire, especially as the halo around Christ's head appears also to be roundly placed upon that of the German Chancellor.

The overall tone of the article, of which Text 5.5 below is an extract, is one of moderate scepticism about the economics of the EMU exercise. While acknowledging that months of 'belt-tightening' have been part of the explanation for the 11 EU member states having met the key public deficit entry criterion, it also mentions that 'creative accounting' and possibly even 'statistical fudging' have played a role.

Text 5.5   (Katherine Butler, 28.2.98:14)

> ... The three big players, France, Germany and debt-strapped Italy, said they and eight other hopefuls had scraped through the key entry criterion set by the Maastricht Treaty ... France had the narrowest escape, weighing in at 3.0 per cent of GDP limit...

The article goes on to assert that ultimately the decision on which states join the euro is a 'political one' and that most EU governments now seem prepared to accept the notion of a widely based euro rather than one built around the core of the EU's strongest economies. It mentions doubts about the likelihood of the economic discipline demonstrated in the convergence figures being sustainable and discusses the possible implications of this for sterling. It mentions too the fact that pressure from big business for Britain to join the single currency is likely to grow as the launch date draws closer and outlines what are perceived as some of the political/economic obstacles in the way: these include a revamped ERM on one hand, and social unrest on the other.

The tone of the discourse of the second article – see Text 5.6 below – is remarkably more up-beat than that of the first. It too sees the political factors as being crucial in deciding the fate of the euro. While acknowledging that there has been some 'sleight of hand' in squeezing some of the economies of the member states through the narrow gates of the public deficit criteria, particularly with regard to Italy, there are fewer reservations, and indeed the journalist goes so far as to mention the word 'honest' in relation to the calculation of the figures. In a comparable manner to the *Guardian*, this article explains the success of the convergence operation with reference to global economic factors pointing to low inflation around the industrialised world, and states that the two largest EU economies are in the process of picking up speed. It concludes that the advent of the euro will further reduce the scope for independent economic management for opted-out states such as Britain.

Text 5.6   (Rupert Cornwall, 28.2.98:14)

> ... What is remarkable is that, given the political capital at stake, the book-keeping has been relatively honest ... no one doubts that the Euro will start on schedule in January 1999, or that it will have 11 members. The fighting henceforth will be over the details ...

Note here too that the discourse addresses both economic and political issues as they apply to Europe as a whole rather than to Britain in particular. Such a global perspective gives it a distinctly pro-European tone.

The final article taken from the *Independent* for this day focuses upon the accomplishment of Theo Waigel, the German finance minister, in bringing the German economy safely home to EMU membership. What begins as a moderately praising piece outlining Germany's success ends in an account of the perceived ploys of Waigel to squeeze Germany through. The discourse is rich in metaphorical allusions and (Eurosceptic) ideological assumptions. This particular article stands in interesting sceptical counterpoint to the one by Cornwall commented upon above.

Text 5.7   (Imre Karacs, 28.2.98:14)

> ... the gnomes of the Bundesbank who at one point refused to allow Mr Waigel to walk away with their hoard. The attempted gold robbery was the most desperate of ploys he devised to fatten up the books ... At the last minute, the government slashed expenditure, trimming public investments

by 10 per cent. That desperate action, representing 0.4 of GDP, might be construed as the kind of 'one-off measure' specifically forbidden in the Maastricht Treaty...

We noted in the pre-election discourse of the *Independent* a kind of mixed discourse, less sceptical than those of the *Telegraph* and *The Times* but more equivocal than that of the *Guardian*. In its representation of this event we find the *Independent*'s discourse is consistent (i.e. pro-European, on balance) with its previous position.

The Guardian

The *Guardian*, as we have noted from our previous commentary on its discourse during the pre-election period is pro-European, but as we have also noted, being in favour of further integration does not necessarily imply wholehearted acceptance of the single currency. Indeed, we saw that the *Guardian*'s position was qualified in two ways, one of which suggested that the EU had got its priorities wrong in pursuing what were perceived as elitist ambitions of a political nature rather than those of a more citizen-friendly, social kind. The second counselled economic caution with regard to the euro anyway. In the article of which an extract, Text 5.8, is printed below, the *Guardian* journalists Martin Walker and Mark Milner begin by noting that 11 member states have announced that they have met the Maastricht criteria for EMU entry. They mention the perceived role of 'creative accounting' which helped key states meet the criteria, citing Italy's Euro-Tax, France's one-off pensions payment from France Telecom and Germany's raising of taxes and removal of billions of marks of hospital debt from the public sector. They also note that EU officials were quick to 'brush aside' the debt problem stating that the convergence policy was already fostering a budgetary discipline. The pejorative item 'fudge', beloved of the true Eurosceptics, is conspicuous here for its absence although it occasionally occurs in the *Guardian*'s overall European discourse. The article covers political as well as economic considerations as the following extract shows:

Text 5.8   (Martin Walker and Mark Milner, 28.2.98:1)

> ...the figures released in Brussels yesterday will boost the project's political momentum and are expected to allow the EU's heads of government to clear all eleven to sign up for the single currency when membership is decided at the beginning of May...

The dominant perspective of this discourse would appear to be in line with the perspective that we identified in the *Guardian*'s March–May 1997 coverage. However this lukewarm, qualified response to the EMU announcement of 27 February becomes even more tepid when it recurs in the leader column. Consistent with its pre-election position, the *Guardian* too takes note of the perceived 'creative accounting' and notes that the cost of fulfilling the Maastricht criteria has been 'the terrifying rise in unemployment', and it asserts unequivocally that

Britain is right to sit out the first round. It is important to note, however, that the implications of its discourse are that we shall eventually join (thus separating it from the truly Eurosceptic press) as the following extract shows. Note first the apparent acceptance of the political goals:

Text 5.9   (leader, 28.2.98:18)

> ... Two things need to be done to prevent economic malfunctions from undermining the political goals. First labour markets must be made more flexible so workers can move to where the jobs are and to enable companies to be more confident about employing new recruits. Second there is a desperate need for new investment to create new employment...

Thus as we noted in its pre-election coverage of the European question, the *Guardian* maintains a certain coolness towards the single currency, but a close reading of its discourse reveals the acceptance that ultimately Britain will join, or as it says itself, 'The euro will come to us even if we don't go to it'.

The final article of *Guardian* coverage of this event appears in the Finance and Economics section and is also written by Mark Milner and Martin Walker. The discourse is detached and the least critical of the event of the three pieces we examined. This may be explained by the article's position in the paper – in the section assumed to be read mostly by persons whose interests in the EU are primarily economic – where, in a discourse comparable to that of the *Financial Times*, the underlying ideological element is both distanced and legitimising. Note in Text 5.10 below how in explaining the success of the 11 members in meeting the Maastricht criteria, the emphasis is placed not on politically motivated reasons (the Eurosceptic 'fudge') but upon economic factors:

Text 5.10   (Mark Milner and Martin Walker, 28.2.98:22)

> ... Yesterday's announcement that the majority of European Union member states had hit the deficit target for monetary union laid down in the Maastricht treaty owed much to a combination of lower interest rates and moderately faster growth...

The *Guardian*'s coverage of the event falls squarely within the political boundaries set down in its earlier pre-election discourse. It simultaneously takes the EU to task for placing too much emphasis upon the political objectives of the single currency and for neglecting social issues such as unemployment, whilst accepting the 'noble aim of a unified Europe' and by extension the inevitability of EMU.

The Financial Times

We have already shown in Chapter 4 how the discourse of the *Financial Times* is by far the most pro-European of all the British press. In Texts 5.11–13 below, the representations of the announcement of the successful convergence of 11 members of the EU are unique in their positiveness and the strictly economic gloss that they place upon the event. Not a single reference here to 'creative accounting', 'fudges', or 'tricks'; the discourse focuses narrowly instead upon the positive economic factors (as opposed to the alleged 'creative' one-off economic measures which get prominence in all the other papers). Twice in its opening article – see Text 5.11 – the *FT* uses direct quotes (secondary discourse) in support of the single currency – there is no countervailing secondary discourse:

Text 5.11   (28.2.98:1)

> ...Helmut Kohl of Germany said, 'I am certain that the euro will come punctually as planned on January 1999. It will be a stable currency just as we have grown accustomed to with the Mark for almost 50 years'...

The second article is dedicated to a full economic account of the events surrounding the successful convergence. Again the so-called 'creative' measures relating to Italy and France are treated lightly and those adopted by Germany ignored, whereas in other papers they are represented as being the true explanation of the success of the convergence exercise. Instead the latter is unequivocally accounted for in legitimising economic terms, that is 'budgetary rigour' and a 'pick-up in economic activity', as the extract in Text 5.12 below illustrates:

Text 5.12   (Peter Norman, Robert Graham, James Blitz, Greg McIvor, Wolfgang Munchau, 28.2.98:2)

> ...The success was due to a combination of budgetary rigour over several years and an unexpected pick-up in economic activity, especially in the final quarter of last year...

It could indeed be argued that this report, based on contributions from correspondents in Bonn, Rome, Stockholm and London, sticks rather closely to the official version of events as presented by the various member states' governments. The absence of the kinds of criticism we have encountered in all the other broadsheets so far distinguishes this discourse from the rest. The discourse focus is ostensibly economic; there is no overtly political rhetoric but there is a case which could be argued for a political (pro-European) dimension at the ideological level. By this we mean that the representation of the event is at face value (apparently based on official 'releases') with only the very limited questioning of Italy's position and the total absence of any consideration of the questions surrounding Germany's efforts to fulfil the convergence requirements raised in all the other papers we examined. This absence of any real questioning of what elsewhere was qualified as 'creative accounting' or 'fudge' may appear curious in such a paper as the *Financial Times*, specialising as it does in financial affairs. The *FT*'s position, however, becomes clearer in its coverage of the launch itself in May 1998 where events surrounding the eventual launch of the single currency are represented as the means for the achievement of a necessary long-term economic objective (see Text 5.45 below and commentary).

In the final article we examined, some of the doubts concerning the single currency, though by no means all, are given an airing. The sustainabilty of the rigour which membership of EMU will demand is questioned. The self-imposed economic and social privations of Germany are mentioned too – see Text 5.13 – along with Italy and Belgium's huge debts, with the prediction that there are problems ahead. Also the point so emphasised by the *Guardian* relating to the neglect of structural reforms in areas like labour markets, emerges for the first time in the discourse.

Text 5.13   (The Lex Column, 28.2.98:48)

> ...Sustainability remains an issue. Germany, for example crunched its deficit through a huge squeeze on public expenditure. This will surely bounce back. Moreover zeal for financial convergence has been unmatched by structural reforms like labour markets...

Whilst this report does confront the existence of these issues, it makes comparatively light of them, which again suggests a covert ideological bias in favour of EMU. As such, along with those of the other articles for this day, its discourse is a continuation of similar arguments expressed in the pre-election period of 1997.

The tabloids

In the last section we concluded our examination of the broadsheet coverage of the EMU announcement of 27 February with the most pro-European of all the British press discourse – that of the *Financial Times*. What follows is the examination of the other extreme – the discourse of the *Daily Mail*, the *Express* and the *Sun* all in full Eurosceptic voice. The proximity of the two extremities of British European discourse in this chapter facilitates the comparison between them. For reasons that the reader will soon discover, the commentary on the *Mirror*'s representation of this event will be brief.

The **Daily Mail**

The *Mail* of 28 February contained two articles that were directly focused on the single currency. We shall look at both below. As we observed in an earlier chapter the Eurosceptic tabloids take no prisoners in matters relating to Britain's current and future participation in the EU. In the first of the *Mail*'s articles the headline states that the 11 applicant countries have scraped home 'by bending the rules', a metaphor which appropriately sets the tone for the rest of the article:

Text 5.14   (David Hughes, 28.2.98:26)

> The final countdown to the single currency began yesterday as economic statistics were massaged and manipulated across the EU in a desperate attempt by member states to qualify . . . countries such as Italy, Belgium, and even Germany will meet the conditions only through the loosest possible interpretation of the Maastricht rules of entry . . .

The journalist asserts that, despite considerable concern over the way in which Italy's figures have been 'fudged', EU officials will give the Prodi government the benefit of the doubt. It concludes that it proves 'once again' (a term which frequently refers to an ideological assumption between reader and writer) that the single currency is a political rather than an economic project.

The second article is more extreme in its representation of the announcement. It undermines the event generally by association with the activities of 'dubious firms in the auditing trade', and Italy's achievements in particular by comparing them with the activities of Robert Maxwell.

Text 5.15   (Andrew Alexander, 28.2.98:67)

> Data published by European governments . . . will excite admiration among some of the more dubious firms in the auditing trade . . . It is a dismal, even ridiculous background against which to launch a new currency. But of course the motivation has all along been political, not economic.

The tone of Alexander's discourse is negative and presents the whole exercise first as dubious practice, secondly, as wholly problematic – there is liberal usage of problematising terms such as 'liabilities', 'worries', 'fears', 'margin of failure', 'political crisis' and others – and thirdly, as a political not an economic exercise anyway. This view echoes the one expressed by David Hughes in Text 5.14 above. Both articles stand in marked contrast to those of the *Financial Times* which we looked at in the previous section, but are a direct continuity of the *Mail*'s pre-election discourse.

The Express

The coverage of the *Express* of the announcement relating to the potential membership of EMU is less substantial but in some ways more strident than that of the *Mail*. The main article is divided into two distinct parts, each of which can be read in isolation; the first focuses heavily upon the perceived illegalities of the qualification for EMU membership, and the second (less likely to be read) gives some basic 'facts' about the EMU project. The headline in its main article uses the term 'cheats' (used in quotation marks to designate a source outside the *Express*) to describe some of the successful applicant states. The source of the term 'cheat', interestingly, is not revealed beyond the vague qualification of 'Eurosceptics'.

123

Text 5.16 (Jon Craig, 28.2.98:22)

> The clock started ticking in the countdown to the euro yesterday amid claims of cheating and cooking the books ... The process was branded a farce by Euro-sceptic critics who claimed EU chiefs in Brussels have bent the rules and some countries cheated...

This is a curious article where there are, as we have said, a series of strong assertions predominantly related to the alleged illegalities surrounding the exercise, but containing little substance to back them up in the manner we have encountered elsewhere in the Eurosceptic press. As such it is the clearest example we have come across, in the representation of this event, of the myth of the 'untrustworthy foreigner' which in its palest and most ghostly form appeared in the discourse of both camps as a creative accountant and subsequently re-appeared in the form of a fudger, fiddler, masseur and cheat. We discern no difference in the discourse of the *Express* at this point from that of the earlier period we have already examined.

On this note of controversy concerning the propagation of Euro-myths let us now turn to the discourse of that other bastion of British culture, fair-play and Euro-ghost busting, the *Sun*.

The Sun

The *Sun*, as we have noted already, neither pulls its punches nor wastes words, particularly if the latter are directed at the European Union. Its discourse is brief but nevertheless pulls in its wake a heavy ideological undertow of Euroscepticism and phobia. But the discourse of the *Sun* is not only noteworthy for the concentration of its anti-European message; it is characterised also by the omission of information of the kind which this paper could, if it so wished, present to its readers in a form that they found accessible and useful. In its leader of 28 February the EMU announcement receives the following cursory treatment. Cursory enough to warrant our quoting it at length (see also coverage of European Working Time Directive below).

Text 5.17 (leader, 28.2.98:8)

> ... From Italy to Spain, Portugal to Germany, France to Belgium the message is the same ... Our economies are all performing identically and impeccably.
>
> If you believe that, you'll believe in fairies.
>
> The Italians have supposedly halved their national debt.
>
> Would you buy a car from an Italian finance minister?
>
> The French have supposedly sorted out their problems caused by huge state subsidies to inefficient industries.
>
> That's why the unemployed have been laying siege to benefit offices and posh restaurants.
>
> The Germans have supposedly solved the economic turmoil of reuniting West and East.
>
> That's why they've had riots in the streets and bankers and economists fighting the euro.
>
> Forget the politics. Just think about the cloud cuckooland economics of the single currency...

If the *Sun*'s summary dismissal of the convergence announcement gives cause for concern it is not so much for its negativity as for the ideological implication in its discourse that the whole of Europe has lied about the convergence process.

The Mirror
The treatment of it by the *Mirror* (deemed to be pro-European) of the same day may well evoke even greater alarm since it carried nothing at all (see note 2). We shall return to the issue of omission in Chapter 7.

The coverage of Tony Blair's speech to the French National Assembly of 24 March 1998

On 24 March 1998 Prime Minister Tony Blair delivered a thirty-five minute speech to the French National Assembly, most of which was devoted to setting out a 'third way' for the politics of European states, the desirability of (in the words of the *Daily Telegraph*) 'ploughing a middle ground between the free market conservatism and old-style left-wing corporatism'. What interested the *Telegraph* and much of the Eurosceptic press, however, was not so much this as the comments made towards the end of his speech concerning current and future directions on European integration. The *Telegraph* went so far as to make the EU angle its main story on page one, and the two Murdoch titles, *The Times* and the *Sun*, made it their main stories on their second pages. It would seem therefore that this coverage of the Blair speech would be a useful second point of comparison of the various discourses in the press during the British presidency and those of the earlier March–May 1997 period. We also print the complete official translation of the speech in Appendix II so that readers may compare the press representation with the text (in English translation) of what Blair actually said.

The broadsheets

The Daily Telegraph
The report in the *Telegraph* of the Paris speech is the main item on the front page and the article devotes most of its coverage to EU-related aspects of the speech. Whilst acknowledging that the speech was 'generally pro-European', the article emphasises those parts which suggested that there should be clear limits to how far further integration should go and also points to passages of the speech likely to alarm the Eurosceptics. The report goes on to note that Mr Blair warned against policies that could lead European electorates to rebel against the Union and that he urged understanding of the people, of their concerns about their national identity, and the remoteness of Brussels from their needs. It also reports that Mr Blair foresaw the need for major institutional changes to the EU and expressed a desire to see a

new project for Europe. Despite the acknowledged pro-European tone of this speech, the *Telegraph* manages to maximise what it perceives as the sceptical elements: Text 5.18 below is the opening of the article. It has a distinctly Eurosceptic representation – note for example how the opening sentence implies a separateness between Blair and 'EU leaders' (he is in fact one of them himself), where the use of the item 'other' or 'fellow' before 'EU', or the substitution of the item 'colleagues' for 'leaders', would have rendered the sense altogether more inclusive of Britain. Note also the implication that these 'leaders' are indeed seeking to extend their power particularly into the British way of life:

Text 5.18   (Robert Shrimsley, 25.3.98:1)

> Tony Blair warned EU leaders yesterday not to try to extend their power into British taxes, social policy or matters affecting national culture and identity ... While he favoured more European integration in some areas, Mr Blair tempered his enthusiasm by stressing that he saw clear limits to the extent of EU involvement in national life...

The Times

The Times of 25 March contained three items on Tony Blair's speech to the French National Assembly, each of which is examined below. The first, in a more direct way than the opening lines of the *Telegraph* article, uses once again the metaphorical symbolism of separateness in the headline referring to 'a line in the sand' being drawn by Blair. The article then opens with a sentence that has a familiar Eurosceptic ring to it:

Text 5.19   (Philip Webster and Ben Macintyre, 25.3.98:2)

> Tony Blair placed a firm limit on European integration yesterday, making plain that there could be no European Union encroachment on policies covering education and health, the welfare state, personal taxation and culture...

An ideological feature which characterises the 'European' discourse of the British press (not only the Eurosceptic side) is the representation of the European Union as a separate and unwelcomed interventionist superstate. Chapter 3 is full of such representations (the tabloid voices are particularly emphatic on this point) and we encountered yet another example in Text 5.18 above. In *The Times'* article – Text 5.19 above – this ideological line recurs. In reality it should perhaps be borne in mind that Britain, far from being a passive recipient of the policies of a separate supranational organisation, is after all an integral participant of the EU and its policy making, with the power of veto in many crucial areas. The second article is an elegant, insightful and culturally informed leader column. Here the leader writer mischievously parallels Blair's perceived values of democracy, diversity and flexibility with the revolutionary rallying cry of *liberté, égalité et fraternité* and speculates upon the possible interpretations that may be placed on Blair's three watchwords. It is a clever, informed and perceptive piece written from the perspective of the Eurosceptic and which probably is not far off the mark in its view of Blair's European stance. Text 5.20 illustrates well the balanced scepticism of the discourse:

Text 5.20 (leader, 25.3.98:19)

> Although he paid tribute to his hosts and prayed in aid of his own youthful enthusiasm for the European ideal, Mr Blair came not to praise the model of integration which had driven the continent, but to bury it . . . The vision he outlined was not integrationist on the past model of Monnet or Schuman, although both received their ritual nods, but neither was it intergovernmental in the manner outlined by Margaret Thatcher in her Bruges speech of 1988...

The final voice on the Paris speech is that of Peter Riddell. Readers may recall that it was Riddell's voice which stood out as the sole representation of a pro-European perspective in *The Times* overall scepticism of the pre-election period (see Text 3.5 above). This later article reports on and predominantly discusses the meaning of the so-called *Blairisme*, set out in the Paris address, as it has unfolded in the national context, and it makes only limited references to the EU. It does, however, pick up on Blair's call for a new political vision for Europe but notes that he did not spell out what he meant by a new political framework that would be dramatically closer to the European electorate than the present one (but see Michael White's interpretation in the *Guardian* below). This is perhaps some of the most interesting discourse contained in all the articles focusing on Blair's speech in Paris that appeared in *The Times* on this day. As we have noted, it mostly focuses on the practical application of the 'third way' to Britain during the first year of the New Labour government. Text 5.21 illustrates its tenor and argument with which, it has to be said, some members of the New Labour Party might not disagree:

Text 5.21 (Peter Riddell, 25.3.98:10)

> . . . If you look at the Government's record since May as opposed to its rhetoric, the third way boils down to government activism on the cheap, financed by limited redistribution aimed to benefit the working poor...

What we have in these three articles is a range of discourse which goes from the orthodox, exclusive Eurosceptic position, which implies that Britain is being threatened from without, to the more inclusive and relaxed position of the leader and of Peter Riddell suggesting that the British point of view relating to Europe will have a place in its future development. Compared with some of the more extreme voices of *The Times* encountered in the pre-election period, this discourse, whilst not moving in a different direction, is relatively restrained.

The Independent

The *Independent*, along with the *Telegraph*, holds little affection for the Murdoch press. This disaffection is easily explained by the aggressive price cutting campaign launched by News International which for over a year has sold *The Times* at half its usual price on a Monday, thereby biting into the readership of the two other papers. This situation may explain the reference and useful insight concerning the *Sun* made in the *Independent*'s main report of Blair's Paris speech. Generally speaking, the article stresses the ambiguity of the event and the way in which it appealed alternately to both the left and the right of the French parliament. John Lichfield's article does not extract either pro or sceptic arguments from Blair's speech, but it does point to a trick of the Eurosceptic discourse, deliberate or unconscious, which is to argue fervently against a non-existent threat to British sovereignty, or other aspects of cultural concern to the British people. The originator of the discourse which prompts Lichfield's comment will no doubt, not go unnoticed by the reader:

Text 5.22   (John Lichfield, 25.3.98:12)

> But in a passage which might have fallen out of a *Sun* editorial, he [Blair] rejected a 'Europe of conformity' and any European move to harmonise education, health, personal taxes and identity. Fortunately no such proposals exist...

This is a truly perceptive insight into part of the discourse of Euroscepticism and we shall return to it a little later in this chapter.

The Guardian

We noted in Peter Riddell's article the assertion that Tony Blair did not spell out what he meant by the need for a new political framework for the EU. It will therefore be of interest to learn from the *Guardian* that this was not the case. Michael White, the political editor, represents the speech not in the predominant 'separateness' or exclusive sense of the Eurosceptics of building 'curbs' or drawing 'lines in sand', but instead as an appeal by Blair to the French to embrace his 'third way' for the reforming of the EU. White's voice, unlike those of the Eurosceptics, is inclusive in the important sense that it places Blair's views within a discourse which is not so much about 'closure' around British interests (although there is clear evidence of this tendency elsewhere in the speech), as it is about Britain wishing to opt in to reforming the political structures of the EU. Although the item 'warning' is used, there are no other references to the exclusive Eurosceptic language of British separateness encountered elsewhere in the reporting of this event. Instead the generally inclusive tone of the discourse is achieved by the use of items such as 'appeal', 'plea' and 'pledge' – all terms associated with conciliation and cooperative acts. The most interesting pro-European interpretation to emerge from this article is the one placed on Blair's call for the reform of the EU as signalling a specific reference to the Parliament and the Council of Ministers:

Text 5.23   (Michael White, 25.3.98:10)

> 'We have had the courage to create the European Union. We must now have the courage to reform it.' – a clear reference to stronger powers for the Strasbourg parliament and more responsiveness by the Council of Ministers...

If the reference to increasing the powers of the European Parliament and making the Council of Ministers more responsive is indeed so clear, then logically we must assume that its omission in the discourse of the other papers we have examined above was deliberate. In fact we rather doubt that the reference is as clear as White would have us believe. It could be argued, however, that the apparent omission in the Eurosceptic press of such a specific and positive call for political reform, which implies taking Britain further into Europe, is at least plausible. If this is the case then the omission in the Eurosceptic press takes on a definite ideological significance rather than one of carelessness. More of this later.

The second *Guardian* representation of the Paris speech comes in the leader column and focuses almost entirely on the fact that Mr Blair addressed the National Assembly in French and it uses this event to launch into a lament about the poor competence of the British in foreign languages. In an aside which is a long way from the specifics of the Paris speech, the *Guardian* manages to insert into its discourse its oft repeated view that the single currency is not a solution to Europe's many current problems and that the question of employment has greater priority (see Text 4.10 above).

Text 5.24   (leader, 25.3.98:19)

> Economists argue that European monetary union – with a European central bank deciding one rate of interest – won't work unless there is labour mobility on a European scale. But what use mobility if you can't speak the language of your employer let alone your customer?...

The Financial Times

Having noted the fulsomeness with which the *FT*'s discourse supported, at an economic level, the EMU announcement (and thereby legitimised the EU in the single currency project) in the first section of this chapter (see Texts 5.11–13 above), it is with some interest that we read its main report of Blair's Paris speech in the edition of 25 March 1998. The headline, which reads 'Blair warns Brussels on interfering in state affairs', could be as well located in one of the middle-market Eurosceptic tabloids as in the generally pro-European *FT*. Note here the Eurosceptic discourse of exclusion (the warner and the warned) as well as the imputing to the EU of the desire to interfere in national state affairs. In reality, as John Lichfield pointed out in the *Independent*, no such intentions can exist at any level in the EU (without the consent of the member states). Such a headline, we suggest, puts a surprising and revealing Eurosceptic gloss on Blair's speech, but in fact does not set the tone of the whole article, which is not hostile. This gloss in the headline appears to stem from the part of the speech quoted in Text 5.25 below:

Text 5.25 (Robert Graham and George Parker, 25.3.98:1)

> ...On the question of how we run our education, and health systems, welfare state, personal taxation, matters affecting our culture and identity, I say: be proud of our diversity and let subsidiarity rule...

We would imagine that as far as the majority of pro-European civil servant politicians in the Council, Parliament and Commission are concerned, Mr Blair would appear to be hammering on a wide open door. There is a certain irony that this point should be made in the generally more sceptical *Independent* and missed by the *FT*. So, what are we to infer from this apparent outbreak of scepticism in the discourse of the *Financial Times*? It could be argued that it supports the EMU on the grounds of economic pragmatism alone but to take this view would be to impute a political naivety to this newspaper not supported by the facts: its previous discourse has consistently urged further economic and political integration with the EU (see Text 4.22 above). It should be borne in mind however that our comments relating to Euroscepticism here are directed mostly at the headline and that the article itself is positive enough in its pro-Europeanness. Nevertheless the headline representation of the particular part of Blair's speech (quoted in Text 5.25) by the *FT* is puzzling and strikes a dissonant note when compared with its previous discourse.

The tabloids

We mentioned above, in the coverage of this event by the broadsheets, a rhetorical trick in the discourse of Euroscepticism. This device sets up a false assumption between writer and reader in order defiantly to assert opposition to it, and even at times to claim triumph over it. It is an old trick well known to politicians and journalists alike and what we had in mind when we observed earlier that, frequently in the grand narratives of history, the devil seems to have the best lines. At its most pronounced extreme it forms part of the black art of propaganda; in more attenuated guise it is the very stuff that political discourse is made of. We perceive the discourse of the press, regardless of the manner in which it is received, to be highly political and ideologically charged. As such, the fact that the discourse of Euroscepticism is frequently given to setting up these false assumptions should neither surprise nor shock us particularly. But they need to be spotted, as Lichfield has done in Text 5.22, and conclusions drawn about the quality of the discourse in which they occur. Since the protagonists of these dark myths are indeed illusory (can any British citizen truly name any European – British or otherwise – who is calling for intervention in our educational system or seeking to change our cultural identity?) within limits, they can be accused of almost anything and precisely because they don't exist they do not answer back.

This would seem an appropriate moment to examine the manner in which the tabloids represented the Paris speech, starting with the *Daily Mail*.

The Daily Mail

In the *Mail*'s main piece, dedicated to the reporting of Blair's Paris speech, we once again encounter the interventionist Euromyth in full flight. The headline reads 'Blair "hands off" warning to EU', implying presumably that someone in Brussels has got their hands *on* British assets who should not. In the article itself the tone is dominantly Eurosceptic, as one might expect from the evidence of the *Mail*'s pre-election views. More Euromyths are released into the discourse too. The areas of education, health, welfare, taxation, culture and national identity, mentioned in the part of his address which is quoted in Text 5.25 above, are represented as responsibilities that 'he would never surrender'. As we have pointed out already, to our knowledge, no one has asked him to.

Text 5.26   (Paul Eastham, 25.3.98:2)

> Tony Blair warned Europe last night to keep its hands off Britain's taxes and identity ... he declared that rushing headlong into a United States of Europe run by bureaucrats risked creating such resentment that people would rebel against them ... there were areas of national sovereignty that he would never surrender.
> They included education, health, welfare, personal taxes, culture and national identity...

The Express

Blair's speech was given short shrift by the *Express*. Its main report concentrates more on the context – the fact that he was speaking in French – and his asides about the World Cup than it does on the content of the speech itself. We find the Euromyth relating to the extreme version of federalism (a United States of Europe) recurring here, but since Blair did in fact raise this one himself we can hardly blame the *Express* for repeating it in what is otherwise a discourse lacking in focus.

The Sun

Again Euromyths swarm through the *Sun*'s representation of this event and, for good measure, these are nourished by some liberal helpings of xenophobia. With all the Eurosceptic implications we have already mentioned above, the headline of the main report reads 'No surrender to Europe, PM warns French'. In the main text the 'hands off' term we encountered in the *Mail* is repeated and with it the same ideological assumption that someone 'out there' has got their hands (or eyes) on Britain's assets. Curiously, the *Sun* also asserts that Blair 'lashed out at the left-wing economic policies of French Premier Lionel Jospin', an assertion that the British Prime Minister might himself find at odds with the gloss he may have intended to be placed on his speech. But the full force of the *Sun*'s Europhobia is reserved for its leader column. We print it here in its entirety, allowing it literally to speak for itself although we would direct the reader's attention to the factual inaccuracy (Greece will not be joining EMU in 1999) and the inadmissible xenophobic nature of the final line which compares with a similar tone found in Texts 3.45 and 5.17 above:

Text 5.27   (leader, 25.3.98:8 italics are in the original text)

> There are other ways of doing things. That is the message Tony Blair delivers – in French – to Europe. He is right.
>
> If Europe doesn't change its working practices, reform its labour markets, stop feather-bedding workers and end subsidies to inefficient state industries, then it will never be able to emulate the success Britain is enjoying.
>
> *The only fear we have is that Europe may refuse to listen to Blair's good advice. He believes he can revolutionise the EU and hopes that then it would be safe for us to join the single currency.*
>
> But by signing up for the Euro we would be dragged down to everyone else's level.
>
> With corrupt Italy and poverty-stricken Greece in it, the Euro is a lame duck...

The Mirror

The *Mirror*'s reporting of the Paris speech is pro-European although it uses the same language in parts as some of the Eurosceptic press, and in particular repeats the charge (allegedly made by Blair) that Europe was 'meddling in our taxes, schools and hospitals'. The pro-European ring of the *Mirror*'s discourse is unmistakable in its leader where the headline, 'Let's follow Tony's lead into Europe' sets the tone of the whole piece. Blair is represented as a strong supporter of the EU although the *Mirror* notes that he has reservations in some areas and is against 'a superstate run by bureaucrats'. Unlike the *Sun*, which has consistently opposed the single currency, the *Mirror* does not take issue with what it perceives as Blair's position of not 'if' but 'when' Britain joins EMU. The leader is remarkable less for its firm pro-European leanings, which are undoubtedly in evidence, than for the absence of the 'exclusive' ideology and phobic distrust of the EU which is palpable in the *Sun* and other papers in the Eurosceptic camp.[1] As a 'red-top' tabloid, the *Mirror*'s discourse is often likened to that of the *Sun*, and in some areas (sport, scandal, leisure) and to some extent, the comparison is deserved. This is because the *Mirror* as the *Sun*'s biggest competitor, has had little choice but to follow the down-market lurch of the latter in recent years. However, in its political discourse we perceive a real attempt at times to inform in a manner which suggests that it does assume some intelligence on the part of its readers, as well as a desire to understand events in the wider world beyond these shores. But the discourse on Europe is intermittent and occasionally, as we have noted already in the first section of this chapter, crucial events appear to be given scant attention or even ignored. Such omissions, in our view, are as puzzling as they are inadmissible and we shall return to this issue in Chapter 7.

Text 5.28 below is more remarkable for the absence of jingoistic ideology than for its content, although in our view, the discourse strikes a balanced note which characterises the *Mirror*'s voice:

Text 5.28   (leader, 25.3.98:6)

> There can no longer be any doubt about the strength of Tony Blair's feelings on Europe. Yesterday the Prime Minister proclaimed his support for the European Union ... He is not blindly in favour. He does not believe in a superstate run by bureaucrats. And he understands that every country needs to keep its separate national identity. But Mr Blair was quite clear about his attitude to the EU: 'Britain's future lies in being full partners in Europe', he said ...

Readers are reminded that the full text of Blair's speech to the French National Assembly is located in Appendix II.

The implementation of the Working Time Directive, 9 April 1998

One of the more serious criticisms of the European Union is that, by following policies conceived by political elites and relating to the grand design for a deeper and a more integral form of European polity, it fails to capture the hearts and minds of the ordinary people. There is, as we shall see in the next chapter, some justification for such criticism. How then does the British press respond to what clearly looks like good news for the citizens of the UK?

The European Working Time Directive will benefit millions of British workers from October 1998 in important areas ranging from compulsory rest breaks, and a statutory 48-hour working week, to health checks and the right (currently denied to two million, mostly part-time, female workers) to three weeks of paid holiday a year. The significance of the directive for the policies of New Labour is mostly related to the concept of the 'flexibility of the labour market', itself inherited largely from the previous Conservative government. It should be noted that, though resigned to accepting the directive, the former Major government had negotiated certain 'derogations' or relaxations of certain of its clauses deemed to damage the interests of employers. These pre-existing derogations were also accepted by the Blair government. We examine below how the directive was received and represented in the press, starting with the broadsheets. For a large number of ordinary people this news from the EU is good. This places the Eurosceptic press in a dilemma which, as we shall see, provokes some predictable results. First the broadsheets:

The broadsheets

The Daily Telegraph

The *Daily Telegraph* of 9 April covered the event in a substantial manner. The discourse is informative – listing the main provisions of the directive and indicating their relevance for the British workforce – but it plays down the role of the EU (no mention of it in the headline nor in the two opening paragraphs) whilst at the same time emphasising the steps taken by the two governments (Conservative and New Labour) to reduce the impact of initiative upon flexible working in the UK.

Text 5.29   (George Jones, 9.4.98:2)

> The Government unveiled plans last night to implement a maximum 48-hour working week but admitted that nine out of ten workers affected by the new rules will still be able to work extra hours ... the Government has taken full advantage of so called derogations to ease the impact of the directive which were secured by the previous Tory administration ...

The Times

In many respects the coverage of this event by *The Times* is comparable to that of the *Telegraph*. Its discourse is informative and indicates the directive's principal relevance for the British workforce, but here again, any mention of the origins of this legislation as being from the EU is delayed for a full three substantial paragraphs (i.e. 130 words into the text) with again no mention of the EU in the headline. Despite the listing of the directive's provisions, much emphasis is placed upon the mitigating effects of the derogation clauses upon the British workplace, for example Text 5.30:

Text 5.30   (Jill Sherman, 9.4.98:2)

> ... The Tory Government was initially adamantly opposed to the EC directive on the 48-hour working week but drew up plans towards the end of its administration to include the maximum number of derogation ...

The Independent

The *Independent*'s voice in the reporting of this event is both similar to and different from those of its two Eurosceptic predecessors. Its discourse is informative and relevantly covers the provisions of the directive and like the *Telegraph* and *The Times*, it delays any mention of the EU for two paragraphs. Equally, like them, it opens by representing the government's opting 'to take advantage' of the derogations negotiated by the Major government. But this government policy is then represented not so much as a triumphal curb on the directive than as a compromise which has been accepted alike by the CBI and the trades unions, although much less wholeheartedly in the latter case. Text 5.31 below picks up part of the discourse dedicated to the major representation of union concerns which, whilst mentioned in the *Telegraph* and *The Times*, are given less prominence. The *Independent*'s voice stops just short of criticising the Blair government for adopting the Tory derogations although it could be argued that the criticism is present in the secondary discourse, as the extract below illustrates:

Text 5.31   (Barrie Clement, 9.4.98:10)

> John Monks, general secretary of the TUC, welcomed the enhanced rights delivered by the directive, but said that allowing individual opt-outs would not give people sufficient protection and that 'undue pressure' could be applied to staff. 'This underlines the need for an effective union recognition law so that employees can call on their unions for help against exploitative bosses'...

The Guardian

Predictably, and perhaps significantly, the *Guardian*'s representation of the European Working Time Directive differs from its predecessors in two important ways. First, at the outset, in its headline, it attributes the improvement in working conditions for the British people directly to the EU. In this it stands alone among all the papers we examined. Secondly, unlike any of the others, its discourse is critical of the derogation clauses adopted by the British government. The *Guardian*, as we have noted previously, is particularly concerned about the perceived failings of the EU to reach out and touch the lives of the ordinary citizens in tangible ways. On this occasion, where it perceives a European initiative to be wholly beneficial to millions of working people in Britain, its pro-European discourse is given full rein:

Text 5.32   (Seumas Milne, 9.4.98:9)

> Four million workers will gain extra paid holiday rights this year and millions more will benefit from the first national legal controls on long working hours ... To the delight of the CBI and concern of the TUC, the government has taken advantage of all the exemption and derogation allowed under the directive which will weaken the impact of the directive on Britain's marathon working hours, by far the longest in Europe...

The Financial Times

The coverage of the adoption of the directive in the *FT* is predictably pro-European although the focus of the discourse is upon less polemical aspects of the event than that of the *Guardian*. The attribution of the reform to the EU, whilst absent from the headline, appears early in the text and there is no emphasis upon the perceived (Eurosceptic) mitigating effects of the derogations upon the impact of the directive on the British workplace. The discourse is informative, sets out the main provisions in detail and also lists the exempted groups. The positive reception by the CBI and the reservations of the trades unions are appropriately represented. Text 5.33 gives some idea of the overall pro-European tone:

Text 5.33   (Robert Taylor, 9.4.98:2)

> Workers will for the first time have a legal right to paid annual leave, regular rest breaks, and protection from being forced to work excessive hours by their employers ... The proposals will transpose into UK law the European Union working time directive ...

The tabloids

We referred above to the rhetorical device beloved of the Eurosceptics of erecting imaginary threats to the British way of life in order to oppose them, often by grandiose discoursal gestures and mock heroism of the 'over my dead body' variety. Another Eurosceptic tactic is to play down the importance of its role in the particular event, as we have suggested above, by casual or delayed attribution. Yet another is to ignore Europe altogether.

So far in this commentary this ignoring of good news from Europe has been noted in the *Mirror* on 28 February relating to the announcement of the member states of their fulfilment of the Maastricht criteria for EMU membership. We can only explain this omission by a previously noted observation by the *Mirror* during the run-up to the election that the British were not so much interested in the European issues as they were concerned with domestic ones. All true no doubt, but it cannot justify the complete omission on 28 February of the 27 February convergence announcement.

When we turn to examine the tabloid version of events surrounding the adoption of the directive in British law, we are struck first of all by the paucity overall of the representation, and secondly by its complete omission in one instance. As if to emphasise the ignoring of the 'glad tidings' from Europe, the *Daily Mail* ran a 'bad tidings' spoiler piece in its leader on 9 April relating to the decision of the British Appeal Court to uphold the rights of Spanish fishermen over those of their British counterparts. The European Working Directive gets no space at all in the *Mail* on this day.[2] It gets little better treatment in the *Sun* and the *Mirror*; both consign it to the news-in-brief columns of their inside pages. Given the truly extraordinary significance of this event, particularly for working people, the very same people, indeed, who read the tabloids, its omission or scant treatment of the kind we have noted below is inadmissable.

The **Daily Mail**
No representation on 9 April but the leader is devoted to the fishing ruling going against British fishermen, featured instead on page 10.

The **Express**
The *Express*'s coverage of the event occurred a day earlier than the rest of the dailies. It adopts a similar tactic to the one used by the other

Eurosceptic representations – the playing down of the importance of the EU's role in obliging the British government to adopt the reforms relating to working conditions at a cost of £1.9 billion. The directive is referred to as 'controversial' and the subject of 'a long wrangle between the British Government and Brussels'. Although the piece is clearly Eurosceptic, some important information relating to the provision of the directive and the outcome for relevant groups of workers is given. Text 5.34 offers an example of the Eurosceptic tone of the discourse:

Text 5.34   (Roland Watson, 8.4.98:12)

> ... Margaret Beckett, President of the Board of Trade, will announce details [for the incorporation of the directive] as she sets out plans for the introduction of the controversial working time directive. It could cost industry up to £1.9 billion, but ministers believe improved workplace conditions will benefit not only workers but employers in the long run...

The Sun

The *Sun* devotes 82 words to the event in the third item of a news-in-brief box on an inside page. The tone of the piece is not particularly Eurosceptic, no mention is made of the derogations nor of the trade unions' reservations. It is the low status location of the piece in the paper and its brevity which downgrade the importance of the discourse. More significant, certainly is that, in the place where one might expect to find the *Sun*'s views on the event, in the leader column, there is instead a strident attack on the single currency, allegedly as the result of a truly important event in the form of a *Sun* poll.

The Mirror

The *Mirror*'s coverage of the EU directive is startlingly similar to the *Sun*'s in two respects: its brevity (85 words) and its placement in the in-brief column of the inside page. However, unlike the other tabloids, there is no 'spoiling' anti-European piece in the leader. Even so, the coverage of such an important event for so many *Mirror* readers, who are clearly affected by the directive, is – to put it mildly – lamentable.

The preliminaries to the eventual launch of the euro, 1 May 1998

Having announced the names of the countries who had successfully met the specified Maastricht Treaty criteria for joining EMU in February, the European Union duly launched the euro two months later at the beginning of May 1998. At the same time at a special summit in Brussels, Wim Duisenberg, the first President of the European Central Bank (ECB) was appointed, as the result of intensive and robust negotiations between France and Germany, in a deal over which Britain's Prime Minister, Tony Blair, presided. Foreign exchange markets, contrary to the predictions of the Eurosceptics, reacted calmly to the prospect of the new currency; there was no flight into sterling, and indeed, the pound began to fall against the deutschmark to the relief of the British Chancellor and to exporting industrialists alike. The appointment of Wim Duisenberg was controversial in the sense that France had forcefully put forward its own candidate at the last minute, throwing the summit into a spasm of heated negotiations which ended in a compromise. Amid an atmosphere of perceived controversy, it was announced that Duisenberg would not be completing the full eight-year term of office and would be succeeded by the French candidate, Jean-Claude Trichet.

The smell of 'fudge', so beloved of the Eurosceptics, was in the air and moreover Mr Blair was directly associated with the brokering of the deal. The British press sensed a field day and gave the event very extensive coverage. The Eurosceptic press found themselves in a dilemma. They know that the euro, with so much hanging upon its success, will be driven forward by the two strongest economies in the EU. Notwithstanding the rivalries between France and Germany, therefore, there is an overwhelming political and economic imperative for the single currency to succeed. Thus the issue of whether or not Britain joins is now subordinated to the euro's official arrival in the markets and the effects, largely out of British control, that this will have upon the British economy, political system and social life. To be both against the single currency and yet powerless to stop it poses a difficult problem for the Eurosceptics. Some pursued the old arguments (but sharpened by its launch) against the euro, and in some instances, sometimes in the same discourse, we perceive the first signs of a very reluctant acceptance of the inevitable: Britain's eventual signing up to EMU.

Some of the more characteristic examples of this extensive pro- and anti-single currency discourse figure in our commentary which follows.

The broadsheets

The Daily Telegraph

The discourse of the *Telegraph* was extensive and wholly consistent in its opposition to the euro which it sees as the forerunner of 'creeping "federalisation" of budgetary and tax policy' (2.5.98:25), and the paper seized upon the compromise ECB appointment as further justification for extreme caution in Britain's attitude to the single currency. On the day following the launch, Anne Segall raises the popular British Euromyth of the untrustworthiness of the other member states:

Text 5.35   (Anne Segall, 2.5.98:33; see also Text 3.18)

> ...They [the 11 members of EMU] have struggled and cheated their way to the shortlist and would not take kindly to being bumped off at this late stage...

In a leader entitled 'The currency of failure', two days later, the *Telegraph* puts the dead hand on the euro in the form of a poem. The leader then goes on to make the point, not surprising in itself, but relevant to the ECB because the bank is supposed to be independent of the political pressures, that the compromise appointment of Duisenberg is highly politicised:

Text 5.36   (leader, 4.5.98:19)

> 'I am yet unborn: O fill me with the strength against those who would blow me like thistledown hither and thither. Otherwise kill me'. With apologies to Louis MacNeice, if the euro were allowed a prayer at birth, this would be it ... This particular wrangle was no different from hundreds of other meetings of the Council of Ministers, in which promises and principles are regularly sacrificed to the need to cut a deal. It is further proof however, that everything touched by Brussels becomes political ...

Finally, in terms of examples of the *Telegraph's* Eurosceptic perspective, there was the reporting of the views of the ex-Chancellor Nigel Lawson. In the secondary discourse of this text, we find some of the more technical and more telling objections to the single currency: the lack of labour mobility in Europe and the absence of fiscal transfers of the kind which exist under a federal system such as that of the United States:

Text 5.37   (Christopher Fildes, 2.5.98:32)

> ... 'What it takes to make a monetary union work successfully over a large and diverse area can be shown by the example of the United States. There's a high degree of labour mobility – people move to wherever the jobs are – that's facilitated by a common language. And there's a highly flexible labour market – wages can move down as well as up. All this is buttressed by very substantial fiscal transfers' ...

The Times

This paper's stand against the single currency will be recalled from Chapter 3 (see Texts 3.1–3.4). In May 1998 nothing had changed except that the launch of the euro had concentrated the mind of *The Times*, so that the more technical arguments of the kind we encountered in the *Telegraph* are presented. Text 5.38 below, for example, presents aspects of the anti-single currency argument which we explored in Chapter 2, relating to the use of interest rates currently by national governments to smooth out the unevenness of their particular economic cycles. The leader then reprises part of its pre-election discourse to remind the reader of the alleged price that the citizens of Europe have paid for EMU in terms of unemployment:

Text 5.38   (leader, 2.5.98:21)

> ... At the most basic level, treasuries and central banks will no longer be able to change either interest rates or exchange rates as shock absorbers to

> smooth out the bumps in the economic cycle ... dole queues, which in Italy,
> France and Germany are the highest in living memory. People are tired of
> sacrifice in the name of the single currency...

William Rees-Mogg, as we have noted already, is given to outspoken opinions and colourful language (see Text 3.10), and his anti-single currency discourse is given full vent on the news of the Duisenberg appointment. Taking an historical view that evokes the shadows of Bismarck and Napoleon, Rees-Mogg thunders against the compromise ECB appointment, asserting that 'All Europe will pay for this folly' (imputed originally to Jacques Chirac) which he claims will do more than anything to see Helmut Kohl removed from office by the German electorate in the autumn of 1998 and replaced by Gerhard Schroder of the CDU. Rees-Mogg also takes up a familiar Eurosceptic line that Britain, too, has been let down by the weakness of successive governments:

Text 5.39   *The Times* (Permission withheld)

> Contains emotional references to what is perceived as British
> appeasement in Europe and an exhortation to EU countries to
> (metaphorically) give France one in the eye for causing the problem
> – the issue of the appointment of the president of the ECB – in the
> first place.
> Access via CD-ROM and micro-fiche (William Rees-Mogg, 4.5.98:20,
> col. 1, ll. 23–30, col. 4, ll. 7–8).

We noted in Chapter 3 that during the pre-election period the voice of Peter Riddell offered opinions which ran almost entirely counter to the prevailing Euroscepticism of *The Times* (see Text 3.5). On the same page as the Rees-Mogg article we encounter again the voice of Riddell still extolling the wisdom of Britain's early joining of the single currency:

Text 5.40   (Peter Riddell, 4.5.98:20)

> ...World weary Euro-enthusiasts say we have been here before. Offered
> the opportunity and indeed pressed to join earlier moves towards
> European integration, Britain has stood apart. This has been a consistent
> theme from the Schuman plan of 1950, through the negotiations of 1955–
> 57 leading to the Treaty of Rome, and to the formation of the European
> Monetary System in 1978–79...

This influential discourse from a regular *Times* journalist which opposes its official line is characteristic of this paper. We did not come across such countervailing discourse from staff journalists in the other papers that we examined.

The Independent

The *Independent*'s position on the single currency issue during the pre-election period was cautious and ambivalent. Without setting its face against the project – its pro-European stance ruled this out – it was careful to point out the many perceived pitfalls that existed along the road to monetary unity (see also Texts 4.1–4.5 and 5.5 and 5.6 above). In its leader of 4 May 1998 this discourse of 'pro-European scepticism' (a new qualification in our terminolgy of discourse evaluation) is confirmed. The appointment of Duisenberg is represented as a 'fix' and a 'fudge' and as the political compromising of the ECB before it even assumes its functions. But the *Independent* is nevertheless accepting the inevitability of Britain joining EMU at some point, as the extract in Text 5.41 illustrates:

Text 5.41   (leader, 4.5.98:14)

> ... Mr Blair's position is not easy, but it is right: to postpone entry until there is genuine convergence, while trying to ensure the constitution of the euro emphasises openness and transparency...

The *Independent*'s cautiousness and critical attitude with regard to the May launch of the euro is reaffirmed in a major article of the same day of the leader quoted above. Here the political strains on Helmut Kohl during the eleven hours of intensive negotiations are emphasised – 'his government almost collapsed' – along with the perceived profound disquiet among other member states at the sight of France and Germany allegedly at loggerheads over the ECM appointment. It also reveals that there was criticism too of the way in which Tony Blair handled the matter in his role of Chairman. Text 5.42 suggests the tone of the discourse in which terms such as 'cobble', 'shabby' and 'fudged compromise' can hardly be described as euro-friendly:

Text 5.42   (Katherine Butler, 4.5.98:8)

> ... It took 11 tortuous hours to cobble together the shabby backroom deal on who would run the central bank. But the fudged compromise now faces constitutional legal and political challenges which could still mar the euro's launch...

The Guardian

The *Guardian* of the pre-election period was, as we have noted, distinctly cool in its attitude towards the single currency, not so much from anti-European sentiments as from a conviction that the priority given to the single currency over other objectives by Germany and France was ill-judged (see Text 4.10). The launch of the single currency provokes the recall of little of the previous discourse of this paper. It is critical of the manner in which the president of the ECB was appointed and on this issue its discourse, whilst not as negative as the *Independent*'s, is nevertheless hardly euro-friendly. It suggests that there will be political and legal challenges to the Brussels agreement for the alleged way in which it breaks the terms of the Maastricht Treaty.

In what amounts to an extensive and informative coverage of the event by several journalists, the key discourse of the *Guardian* can be found in its leader of 2 May 1998 where the potential wealth-creating force of the euro is examined in detail and is compared with the single currency of the United States. Of interest here is the repetition of the points made by Nigel Lawson in the Eurosceptic context of the *Daily Telegraph* (see Text 5.37 above) – that any comparison of the European single currency with the dollar reveals three major differences in the latter's case: a common language, flexible labour markets, and the power of fiscal transfer to redress regional economic disparities. In spite of the non-similarity of the two currencies, the *Guardian's* overall position is also one of pro-European scepticism. Text 5.43 gives an example of this cautious acceptance of the single currency:

Text 5.43 (leader, 2.5.98:24)

EMU arrives on time: We must make it work

Europe has a lot going for it. The 11 candidates for EMU have a combined GDP of almost 80 per cent of the US and a balance of payments surplus where America has a deficit. Maybe the biggest thing going for Europe is the unexpected ... Europe doesn't look to be on the brink of technological renaissance. But it certainly is in a state of change. Who knows? Maybe, like America, it will surprise its critics ...

The Financial Times

As might be expected, the *FT*'s coverage of the launch is full, detailed and favourable with a characteristic, detached economic perspective which distinguishes it from the reports in all the other titles. On 2 May the front page headline asserts 'EU leaders near deal on top bank job' and is followed by an explanatory article which puts the French case into a political context. At this point, although the intentions of Jacques Chirac relating to the French candidate are known, the negotiations have not begun. On 4 May, the day after the German–French bargain was struck, the tone of the *FT* changes but not significantly. Whilst describing the event as 'bruising' and quoting some strong criticisms of the compromise from Germany itself, there is little of the negativity here of the kind we encountered, for example, in the *Independent* (see Text 5.42 above). Moreover, as if to off-set the quarrel between the two main players against more favourable events, the report goes on to focus positively on the appointment of five other members to the ECB, as shown in Text 5.44:

Text 5.44 (Lionel Barber, Wolfgang Munchau and Robert Chote, 4.5.98:1)

Europe's single currency faces a critical test of credibility this week after a bruising weekend compromise over the appointment of Wim Duisenberg as president of the European Central Bank ... EU leaders appointed five other executive board members whose qualifications and expertise won immediate backing among analysts and central bankers ...

In its leader of the same day we find the key to the *FT*'s position where the events are referred to as 'undignified' and 'disappointing' and the fault laid at the door of the French. But for the *FT* these are the unfortunate means only which, whilst they confirmed the 'inability of the European Union to resolve the appointments of top people without a public squabble', nevertheless produced a satisfactory long-term outcome. This is a good example of the distanced, overarching political/economic perspective we mentioned above which is character- istic of the discourse of this paper:

Text 5.45 (leader 4.5.98:17)

> ... If the markets take the whole affair amiss, it will be understandable, but nevertheless unjustified. For the outcome is that the ECB will be governed by an impressive line-up of central bankers and economists, none of whom has a track record of pusillanimity in the face of political pressure ...

The tabloids

The Daily Mail

In answer to an enquiry by the authors in which we requested confirmation of the *Mail's* position regarding the single currency, we were told that the paper urged 'extreme caution' about entry because it was not merely a fiscal question but involved issues of sovereignty, the supremacy of parliament and federalism. This is a perfectly reasonable and accurate assessment of the implications of EMU membership for all the member states, but we believe that the *Mail's* discourse goes beyond the 'extreme caution' position that it has officially declared to us, to one where it paradoxically both strongly rejects the single currency yet acknowledges the inevitability of its influence upon Britain.

In its leader of 4 May the *Mail* takes the opportunity to represent the ECB appointment in the worst possible light:

Text 5.46 (leader, 4.5.98:8)

> Two dogs fighting over a bone could hardly have launched the single currency with less decorum ... Of course, at the eleventh hour the impasse was predictably overcome by shameless resort to the fudge-bucket ... first the pass marks for entry into monetary union were rigged. Now with a Dutch front half and a French hind quarters, the presidency of Europe's central bank has been made to resemble a pantomime horse ...

In its leader of 2 May the *Mail* had already set out in detail its reservations concerning the single currency; it repeats the 'untrust- worthy Europe' and the 'superstate' myths before giving voice to more legitimate concerns about varying economic cycles, social unrest and the future limitations on national governments to act individually in times of recession. Then comes the admission that despite the *Mail's* reservations, the euro still might succeed. It glosses over the position in which Britain will find itself in this event: presumably even if the economics of the euro prove to be sound, then an economic decision will still need to be made, and there are still the unresolved questions of sovereignty and the supremacy of parliament and federalism to be confronted. The problem appears to be for the *Mail* not, as it claims, that the euro goes wrong, but that it goes right.

Text 5.47 (leader, 2.5.98:12)

> ... Though the *Mail* has profound reservations, it cannot be denied that the launch of the euro is a remarkable achievement of imagination and the political will. Indeed that is precisely the trouble. For the primary purpose of this vastly ambitious project is political and not economic. It is to lay the foundations of a European superstate, one that will be inevitably dominated by Germany ... Yes it is possible that the euro may succeed in spite of all these problems [mentioned in our preceding commentary] But the unedifying squabble between Germany and France over who should run the European Central Bank hardly inspires confidence. At least Britain has had the good sense so far to stay out of the single currency. But make no mistake. If the euro goes wrong, Britain will suffer too, even though we remain outside. The great experiment has begun ...

The Express

Compared with some of its previous statements, the discourse of the *Express* which represents the launch of the euro is relatively restrained. Roland Watson, the political editor, in a major article, seems to go out of his way to avoid the sensationalism we encountered in the *Mail*, in Text 5.46 above. No mention here of 'fudge-buckets' or 'fighting dogs'. No attacks either on the manner in which Blair handled the affair. Instead this matter is dealt with in a positive manner by representing Downing Street as going on the 'offensive' and 'insisting that Tony Blair's brokered deal of splitting the first term of the European Central Bank's head was not a fudge'. Text 5.48, which is an extract from Watson's piece, gives some idea of what we perceive to be a more restrained voice in the discourse. It should be noted that the date is 4 May and that the intensive negotiations which resulted in the ECB appointment are available to all the papers for comment. It is too early to speculate about the reason for this perceived restraint although perhaps it is worth noting that a new editor of the *Express*, Rosie Boycott, formerly of the *Independent*, was appointed on 27 April 1998 just before the Brussels summit. Note in Text 5.48 below the understated references to the disagreements between France and Germany and Mr Blair's role in the brokering deal. Is this a continuation of the strongly Europhobic discourse that we encountered in the *Express* of the pre-election period or has it taken a new direction?[3]

Text 5.48 (Roland Watson, 4.5.98:6)[4]

> The newly-launched single currency was making its debut on the money markets today, with a nervous Europe waiting anxiously to see if EMU would fly ... With Germany and France disagreeing about who should run the new European Central Bank, the body which will run the euro, it was down to Mr Blair – in the EU President's chair – to oversee a deal ...

However, any speculation that might tempt us to believe that there is a change in the previous discourse of this newspaper should be tempered by the voice of Peter Hitchens. Here the discourse is more reminiscent of its former pre-election self:

Text 5.49   (Peter Hitchens, 4.5.98:11)

> Do I hear a child weeping? The vanity and folly of our leaders is rushing Europe towards misery and violence and it is today's infants and teenagers who will pay for it in the black future we are preparing for them ... when it [the single currency] leads to unemployment, wage cuts, savage tax increases and the re-birth of fascism ...

The Sun

Rupert Murdoch has made no secret of his vigorous opposition to the single currency, and if proprietors do indeed influence the editorial policies of their newspapers then there can be little doubt about the origin of the *Sun*'s voice on this issue. Its face, as we have noted, is implacably set against the euro. In consequence, the May launch provokes the paper to ascend new heights of Europhobia and abuse of EU officials. Note in passing the concentrated ideological references to the EU overpaying its officials and its alleged undemocratic nature:

Text 5.50   (leader, 2.5.98:6)

> ### A lesson for dim Santer
> ### Arrogant Euro-Twit Jacques Santer has proved
> ### his ignorance of democracy yet again
>
> ... According to Santer, unaccountable to the voters who pay his £160,000 wages, the decision has already been taken to scrap sterling ... the euro is a disaster waiting to happen, a fraudulent stitch-up of secret rows, sordid deals and broken rules. We're well out of it. And soon the government will have to admit it.

The well-publicised, heated negotiations of the Brussels summit plays once again into the hands of the *Sun*'s leader writer of 4 May 1998. The leader, entitled 'Euro bunglers', is one of seven articles spread over two pages – such rare and extensive treatment of a political/economic event is an indication of the measure of the paper's opposition to the object of its discourse. One of the main pieces by the political editor, Trevor Kavanagh is headed 'Born in a Brawl' and focuses relentlessly upon the alleged 'row' between Germany and France. The sub-text, in case anyone may have missed it, is printed towards the end in the *Sun*'s own italics:

Text 5.51   (Trevor Kavanagh, 4.5.98:3)

> A blazing row between French President Jacques Chirac and German Chancellor Helmut Kohl nearly wrecked the launch of the euro, it emerged yesterday ... *But the row exposed deep divisions over the way it will operate.*

In a second article by the political editor, the French are treated to the full blaze of the *Sun*'s overblown metaphors:

Text 5.52   (Trevor Kavanagh, 4.5.98:8)

> ... Tony Blair rejects any suggestion of a 'fix' in Brussels over the birth of
> the single currency. He is right. The word 'fix' is completely inadequate to
> describe this week's display of blatant eye-gouging and arm twisting in a
> political power play...

The Mirror

The *Mirror*'s discourse on Europe, as we have noted, whilst intermittent, is positive. When the announcement was made in February
naming the 11 member states which had met the Maastricht criteria,
the *Mirror* was unaccountably silent. The launch of the euro itself
two months later provoked a positive and informative, if brief,
discourse.

Whilst the urgency and heated nature of the event is mentioned, note
the contrast between the measured tones of the discourse quoted in
Text 5.53 below, particularly the restraint and distance of the writer
in relation to the French and German views on the functioning of the
European Central Bank, and those of the *Mail* in Text 5.46 and of the *Sun*
in Text 5.50 above:

Text 5.53   (Robert Gibson, 3.5.98:6)

> #### Peacemaker Blair clinches euro deal
>
> Tony Blair saved Euro chiefs from humiliation last night as he brokered a
> last-minute deal to launch their new currency ... The Germans want him
> [the head of the ECB] to follow the example of their Bundesbank and take
> financial decisions on interests rates and inflation independently of the
> politicians. But the French want the bank chief to be 'sensitive' to what
> politicians want – and that means politicians would have control in the
> end...

The leader of the day before is also the very model of pro-European
sentiments. Far from urging caution, the *Mirror* complains that Britain
is not moving fast enough:

Text 5.54   (leader 2.5.98:6)

> A historic step forward is being taken this weekend by most European
> countries. They will set the seal on plans to introduce the single currency.
> Although our prime minister will preside at the meeting, this country is
> being left on the sidelines ... In a few years the euro is expected to rival the
> mighty dollar as the greatest international currency. Britain cannot be still
> on the sidelines then...

This leader is characterised by the lack of any reservation on the part of
the writer about the need for Britain to sign up to the single currency.
As such it is the most pro-European of all the pro-European discourse
we have encountered on this topic.

Conclusion

This effectively marks the end of our commentary on the European discourse of the British press which we began in Chapter 3. In general the examination of the coverage of the four events contained in this chapter confirms our findings of the previous commentaries with regard to the ideological position of the individual papers, with the possible exception of the *Express*. This paper, owned by the New Labour supporter, Lord Hollick, and with a new editor appointed in April 1998, appears to have changed direction, if not completely its colours, and to be heading towards a more restrained representation of European issues. The rest ran true to form. However, the imminence and the eventual implementation of the single currency, in particular, provoked some serious and worthy arguments against it (e.g. Text 5.37), and these were not wholly restricted to the acknowledged Eurosceptic camp (see commentary on Text 5.43). The implications for Britain of the single currency are a matter of concern, too, for the pro-European titles.

In closing, we would identify in particular the following frequently used devices for the misrepresentation of the European Union which dominated the Eurosceptic discourse but which sometimes found their way also into the discourse of the Europhiles. These devices can be summarised as follows:

- The denial of, and/or opposition to, the false proposition, for example the alleged threat to cultural identity proposed in Text 5.26 (which subsequently translates into ideology and Euromyth);
- The downplaying of the EU's initiatives by casual, delayed or non-existent attribution as in Text 5.29 in relation to the Working Time Directive, or by low-status locations in the paper such as news-in-brief columns;
- The frequent non-representation of significant European events as in the case of the *Mirror* on 28 February relating to EMU and the *Mail* in relation to the Working Time Directive on 9 April.

The use of these devices and the resulting ideological implications relating to Europe that flow from them are significant. The press is not bound by any statutory requirement to be impartial, as is the case with the BBC and ITV, and in consequence there are no restrictions on the use of such manipulative rhetoric. We shall return to this topic in Chapter 7.

Notes

1. The *Mirror*'s discourse has not always been deemed to be so free of Europhobia. In 1996 the Press Complaints Commission received dozens of complaints relating to its alleged anti-German coverage of the European Cup. Although the PCC found in the *Mirror*'s favour the editor felt compelled to print an apology.

2. The additional running of a spoiler in the form of an 'anti-European' leader by the *Mail* 9 on April 1998 distinguishes the omission in the reporting of the European Working Time Directive in this paper from the earlier omission of the reporting of the convergence announcement on 27 February by the *Mirror*. The *Mirror* did not print any anti-European piece on that day which may point more to oversight in the non-representation of the European Working Time Directive than to Euroscepticism.

3. Our view that the *Express* had taken a new direction involving a more pro-European stance was confirmed to us subsequently in unequivocal terms by the deputy editor, Chris Blackhurst, who told us that both he and the new editor Rosie Boycott were 'passionately pro-European' and that in time they would like the paper to reflect those views.

4. In the event too, the doubts raised by Watson and others about the predicted flight of currencies into sterling from continental Europe did not materialise. In fact the opposite happened: the foreign currency markets remained calm and the pound weakened against the dollar.

Chapter 6

The Great Public Relations Disaster?

Introduction

The European Union has been successful in many respects which are crucial to the lives of ordinary citizens in Britain and elsewhere. It has played a key and leading role in fostering a level of political and economic cooperation among old adversaries that has proved capable of long surviving the end of the superpower-imposed disciplines of the Cold War. In this very important sense it has made a real and substantial contribution to the peace and stability of Europe. The full importance and the continuing relevance of this role has been explained already in Chapter 2. Furthermore, in a manner which has gone almost unnoticed in mainland Britain, the European Union has extended this 'mission' down to the most local of levels, indeed right into the heart of the most troubled area of the United Kingdom, via funding which it provided for the sustaining of women's groups in Northern Ireland in an attempt to encourage the reconciliation that is vital for any lasting peace settlement.

Whilst, ironically, its own institutions have been criticised for an alleged 'democratic deficit', the EU has nevertheless proved itself to be a beacon of democracy in a continent where democratic traditions have a very short history within many of its component states. It already provides a backbone against which the political systems of Greece, Spain and Portugal are able to rest. The fact that they would face expulsion should they cease to be democracies is a strong deterrent to any group within these states which might in future contemplate a coup or other measures designed to push them back towards authoritarian regimes. And while the perceived prosperity, stability and prestige of membership is a useful magnet that is drawing Eastern European states towards the EU, the desire to join that this is fostering is itself a powerful factor helping to wed these societies to the idea of democracy as their long-term way of doing things. Democratic credentials are, after all, one of the basic admission tickets to the EU. Moreover, for some of the existing members of the EU, advocates of the Union have argued that membership has provided a level of prosperity which they otherwise might not enjoy. This is particularly true of the poorer states and regions which have benefited significantly from the main structural funds and/or the CAP, and it is a benefit in which the aspirant states from Eastern Europe hope to share.

So why, after this impressive beneficial impact that the European Union has had upon the old continent, is it possible for a leading 'think tank' report to describe the EU as the 'ultimate public relations disaster' (Leonard, 1998:5)? In response to this question this chapter will do several things. First, it will present the main charges which the Demos Report lays against the European Union in a public relations and communications context, followed by our comments relating to these criticisms. This commentary will be divided into three sections, one relating to the Commission, one relating to the European Parliament and one to the Council of Ministers. In the case of the first of these, the function and activities of the Commission's London outpost, in particular its press office, will be examined with regard to its role in presenting the EU to the British press and public. Secondly, we shall attempt to evaluate the European Parliament's ability to make its activities accessible to the press and public. Thirdly, given that the member states are largely in the driving seat with regard to the nature and the breadth of the EU's political agenda, even if the making of specific proposals is still left largely to the Commission, we shall attempt to evaluate the extent to which they, through the Council of Ministers, are succeeding in addressing the business of producing and promoting policies which target the needs of the ordinary citizens of the Union.

In this respect, we shall make an assessment of the role of the British presidency of the Union during the first half of 1998 which will include, among other things, an evaluation of its Internet site and its handling of the European Working Time Directive. We shall conclude the chapter by considering the extent to which greater success in the domain of public relations on the part of the EU would improve its image in the eyes of the British public if the dominant discourse of the Eurosceptic press were to remain as hostile as we have found it in our previous analysis.

The Demos critique

The Demos report begins by stating that the British presidency is faced with having to deal with the two biggest challenges which have ever confronted the Union – monetary union and enlargement in the east – at a time when the EU's legitimacy has hit rock bottom. It cites a damning array of statistics (see Figure 6.1): only 46 per cent of EU citizens now support their state's membership of the Union, only 41 per cent believe that EU membership benefits their country, less than 50 per cent support the single currency, and only 50 per cent identify with Europe as a whole or with the EU's institutions. Contrary to a generalised belief in this country that Euroscepticism is mainly confined to Britain, it points out that this disaffection has spread right across the EU. It states that:

> ... The EU is unpopular because the troubles stored up over 40 years of technocratic integration by a political elite are now catching up with it. It has failed to use the elements which give national governments legitimacy: increasing awareness of their activities; being relevant to citizens' concerns; delivering practical benefits; offering leadership; and having an identity which citizens can feel part of ... (Leonard, 1998:5)

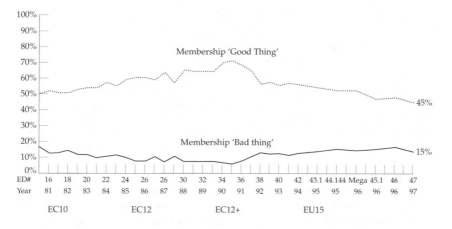

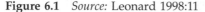

Figure 6.1   *Source:* Leonard 1998:11

With regard to the first part, the report argues that there is a high level of ignorance concerning the EU among its citizens and it identifies a number of causes of this situation. First, it sees it as partly the result of the fact that most of the EU's policies are not perceived to stem from the Union but to be mediated by local and national government. Indeed, it points out that some governments even take credit for the measures themselves (Leonard, 1998:5–14).

Secondly, it argues that the EU has been 'spectacularly bad' at claiming the credit due to it for its successes. While being bountiful with grants and subsidies it generally forgets to shout about them, despite the fact that the polls reveal that one of the most powerful legitimising forces that has helped the EU in the past has been the simple device of billboards publishing its role on EU-funded roads and other projects.

Thirdly, and most importantly, it argues that the EU has often not helped itself by investing in the wrong projects, claiming that the evidence of opinion polls clearly reveals that the Union devotes most of its time to matters of least concern to its citizens, namely EMU and the Common Agricultural Policy. Both of these are perceived as priorities by only 9 per cent of the population. According to the Demos Report, poll findings show that what people want the EU to resolve are the 'problems without frontiers' – 68 per cent support a common defence and military policy (a priority which the British presidency in particular has gone out of its way to ignore), and 72 per cent see tackling international crime and terrorism and the protection of the environment as important and urgent priorities (Leonard, 1998: pp. 5, 13). The report notes that the electorate's response to the EU's effective downplaying of these priorities has been a falling voter turnout at elections on a grand scale for the European Parliament. According to Demos, the people find the EU not only irrelevant but remote, noting that 97 per cent of EU citizens have never had any direct contact with it. This it considers to be

151

partly related to the earlier mentioned point about the EU's actions being largely mediated by national and local governments (it should also, of course, have included regional governments).

The image of the EU, it is alleged, has also been seriously damaged by the publicity given to fraud and waste scandals and by the failure of important EU initiatives in the former Yugoslavia. Here, where the fundamental issue of bringing peace to Europe is concerned, only half the British people think that Europe has a good record whilst 22 per cent believe it has a bad one (Leonard, 1998:14). In addition, it is argued that the member states have found it easy to blame the EU's institutions for multiple sins because of the lack of will on their part for their rebuttal.

The report identifies another perceived serious weakness in the position of the EU in so far as it appears to show no leadership or sense of mission. In consequence, it alleges that the EU's clarion call of 'peace, prosperity and democracy' has lost its purchase within the EU (even though they are the main reasons why states from Central and Eastern Europe wish to join). It makes the valuable point that a generation that has never known war directly seems to take peace for granted: when asked what the EU meant to them less than one in four of those between the ages of 15 and 24 cited peace. It is noted that the failures in the former Yugoslavia have also weakened the EU's claim as a peacemaker. Furthermore, it is claimed that the association with prosperity has also been weakened by unemployment and recession.

The EU's third role, that of the protector and promoter of democracy, has been seriously damaged by the complexity and opaqueness of its own decision-making system. This situation has been worsened by the fact that democracy seems less attractive to a generation unimpressed by mainstream politics and which has had no experience of totalitarianism (Leonard, 1998:15).

The process of European integration is also perceived to have little sense of direction; Demos observes that policy issues such as EMU tend to become bogged down in 'micro-wrangling'. This prevents them from being linked to the major clarion call relating to the grand European narrative of 'peace, prosperity and democracy' mentioned earlier. It places part of the blame for this situation on what political analysts frequently refer to as neo-functionalism, the idea of integration proceeding by stealth, wherein each measure taken hopefully leads to another of increasing significance, until a closely knit economic and political unity is achieved. Among other things, this quiet, determinedly incremental progress by mundane means, has, according to Demos, deprived the EU of a sense of strategy and made it impossible to rally the people around a commonly desired endpoint. The report argues also that instead of trying to build positive support for the integration process, the leaders of the EU have too often exploited popular fatalism and inertia to enable them to push integration forwards. The problem with this approach, it concludes, is that it stores up popular resentment to continuing integration and that it therefore cannot be sustainable in the long term.

Finally, and by way of summarising the findings of the Demos Report, we include below its own five key recommendations for ways in which governments can facilitate EU legitimacy. These are:

- increasing awareness and understanding of its activities;
- being relevant to its citizens' concerns;
- delivering practical benefits to its citizens;
- offering leadership and a sense of mission;
- having an identity which its citizens feel they are part of.

So much then for the Demos critique. We propose now to look at the three main decision-making institutions and to assess the extent to which each is guilty of the charges laid against them by the report.

The role of the European Commission in promoting the EU within the United Kingdom

The European Commission first established an office in London in the late 1960s. This was effectively a kind of 'embassy' to the British government prior to the latter's membership of the then EC. Once Britain had become a member of the Community, this 'embassy' became a fully fledged press and information office with the explicit task of promoting the EU within the United Kingdom. This promotional role was changed yet again during the second half of the 1980s when the office became known by its somewhat prosaic title of the European Commission's Representation in the UK. It was simultaneously effectively downgraded, with the promotional role taken away from it, and this role transferred to the British government itself. In an interview with senior officials at the London, Storey's Gate headquarters, we were told that the two current main functions of the office are to download much of the task of information distribution to a variety of regional intermediary information distributors and public libraries, and to feed back information on what is happening in Britain to the European Commission in Brussels. The head of the EU's London office still retains a diplomatic representational role of sorts in so far as he is expected to make speeches concerning Commission policy and to mix with the media, politicians and other opinion formers in the UK.

The role of the Commission's press office, also at Storey's Gate, is now a relatively small one. The press still expects to receive basic information and this is provided, via briefings, press releases, and access to EU publications via the Internet. However, the office's role is non-promotional since this aspect of EU representation now rests with national governments. However, an important task of the press office is that of monitoring and countering factual or other inaccuracies in the representation of the EU in the British media. This is undertaken on a regular basis via personal calls to editors, letters to the papers themselves, and corrective circulars and occasional publications such as *Press Watch*, all of which are designed to lay to rest the Euromyths as they are released by the Eurosceptic press.

Frequently we were told that the press office experiences difficulty in getting the tabloids, in particular, to publish its rebuttal letters or to correct the inaccuracies. A somewhat better relationship was reported with the broadsheets. A particular problem for the press office was the phenomenon described as 'editorialising' within articles and reports: a style of writing which avoids straight factual error but which seeks to mislead by more subtle devices.[1] This means that, from the point of view of making a formal complaint to the Press Complaints Commission, there are few official grounds for doing so. However, we were informed that the press office does take periodic preventative initiatives with the British press and that, for example, prior to the last election the office warned the British papers that if the Commission was attacked 'the office would hit back'. In the view of the press office, the kinds of measures outlined above have together produced an improvement in the reporting of EU affairs.

Whilst we accept much of this assessment of its activities on the part of the Commission's London press office, we nevertheless find its overall functions, and the wider role of the Representation of the European Commission in the United Kingdom unclear and unquantifiable in terms of their effectiveness. For example, the Commission's London office, as we have mentioned above, asserts that it has a 'non-promotional remit'. Yet we learned that such offices, which are distributed across the EU, do retain some promotional roles. One example is the 30 million ecus that have been set aside for the promotion across Europe of the euro. However, in the case of the UK, the British government's opt-out of the single currency had led the Commission to delegate to the government, and not its own London office, the promotional responsibility. Our understanding is that, while such promotional roles do exist, they are rather few in number.

As far as the effectiveness of the press office is concerned it is clear that its role is more one of an information source and reactive monitor, than of a pro-active and persistent initiator of potential 'good news' for the British people. Its own briefings, we are told, are poorly attended by the press who prefer to take their stories from UKREP, the British government's permanent civil service office in Brussels. Its corrective circular *Press Watch* appears to get no acknowledgement in the press itself, and indeed when we pointed out to the Chairman of the Press Complaints Commission that the PCC appeared on the circulation list of *Press Watch*, we were informed that he had never seen it before. The reason for this is that because *Press Watch* is not submitted to the PCC with the status of a formal complaint, it is not brought to his attention. He stated also that no formal complaints have been received from the European Commission's London office during his time at the PCC.[2]

Regardless, then, of its other functions, of which the most important appears to be the relaying of information picked up in Britain's formal and informal corridors of power back to the Commission in Brussels, the impact of the Commission's London office upon the British media appears to be distinctly limited. There is a plausible but naive argument which asserts that if Britain, or indeed any other state, is a member of the EU, then it should also be the logical delegate to assume the promotion of the Union. But there is also of late a voice of experience which suggests that to do so, particularly in the light of the Thatcher and Major governments' antipathy for Europe, was comparable to leaving Herod in charge of the orphanage. While the Blair government is indeed a very different prospect from the EU's perspective, there are still noticeable lacunae in the manner in which it refers to Europe. The narrow and restrictive remit of the Commission's London office is insufficient to fill these gaps.

Having offered this view, we are aware that critics within the EU might accuse us of not having taken the realities of its own policy-making rules and structures into account. On the contrary, we do acknowledge fully that the Commission at all levels – from London and all EU capitals to Brussels itself – has to ensure that it does not overstep the mark with promotional policies for fear of provoking an adverse reaction in the Council of Ministers. However, the Commission is officially charged with the task of promoting European integration, of 'thinking European' in order to balance the frequently dominant national preoccupations of the Council. It has not only the right, therefore, to be less timid than it is currently being in the UK, but the duty to point out emphatically to the British government that, if nothing more is done to promote the EU in a manner which captures the imagination of the people, then the Union is in danger of being abandoned from below. New Labour may declare frequently its desire to take Europe to the people but, at best, the extent to which it had done this by June 1998 was very limited – no matter how great the Prime Minister's claim at the end of the British presidency. Even an elite-driven project of the kind so far experienced within the EU needs a minimum level of support to sustain it within liberal democracies. The Commission at all levels needs to point out to governments the existence of warning signs – of which the Demos Report is one – that all is not well among the citizenry and its feelings towards the Union.

The role of the European Parliament in promoting the EU within the UK

Whereas the Commission and its London Representation office might be said to have serious problems as a promoter and protector of the EU's image within the UK, the problems of the European Parliament with regard to its relationship with national electorates might be seen as infinitely worse. Even before we examine its public information and public relations strategies, we should note in passing the obscure and complex cooperation and codecision procedures by which it tries to exercise real influence within the EU's policy making processes. These are in themselves a major obstacle to, it being either understood or related to by ordinary voters (this sentiment is echoed by the Demos Report, Leonard, 1998:15). An understanding of the arcane workings of the Parliament is possessed only by well-informed members of specialist groups who see it as a potentially useful part of the policy-making process. They understand its arcaneness usually because they are paid to do so.

Although they are incomplete, research evaluations suggest that Members of the European Parliament in many cases are simply not very good at maintaining meaningful contacts with the voters upon whom they rely (McLeod, forthcoming). It has also been said, over the years, that the lack of the career opportunities available within comparable national parliaments has greatly reduced the number of politicians with any significant public profile who are prepared to stand for the European Parliament. In addition, while it has a president, the profile of this office is much lower than either the Commission or the Council presidencies. In consequence, the Parliament lacks a high-profile figure upon whom the media can focus in a manner comparable to the incumbents of the other two institutions. Finally, while the Parliament has had significant increases in its powers during the last twelve years, it still remains much less powerful than the Council, and much less encompassing than the Commission in terms of its effective influence over EU affairs.

All of these factors, and indeed others not mentioned here for reasons of time and space, militate against the European Parliament being an obvious source of interest to the mass of the public and to the media on all but a very few, occasional issues.[3] However, the Parliament stands accused of having added to these problems in its attitude towards information policy. Well-informed sources with a personal knowledge of the workings of the EU Parliament's Information Office in London tell us that in their view there are real problems of under-resourcing, and the blocking of innovation within the system. Such innovative ideas, for example, as how to get information and understanding about the Parliament's activities to the public, by by-passing the press, have been proposed but finally blocked from within the Parliament's internal decision-making machinery. The result has been an operation that has remained low-key and relatively ineffective when compared to the scale of the task confronting it. There are rumours too that the Commission and the Parliament's information operations might be merged in future, although this has been denied by the Commission's London office. It was pointed out to us, however, that the relatively small-scale operation of both the Commission and the Parliament in London was attributable to the Parliament, given that it was one of the two main participants in the EU's budgetary process.

In terms of visibility, the results are not impressive as far as the European Parliament is concerned. The Parliament does occasionally succeed in getting noticed by the British press. Its attitude to the compromise over the appointment of the head of the European Central

Bank did, for example, achieve useful coverage in the British papers in early May 1998. It also made its presence felt in the media during the debate that surrounded the choice of Jacques Santer as the new President of the Commission. However, for most of the time its profile in the British press is very low, with the greater focus being upon the Council of Ministers and the Commission. Moreover, this low profile is not compensated for in any of the other media sectors such as radio or television.

The British public, therefore, sees very little in the media of the activities of the one body that is supposed to give them a direct voice in the EU. If we add to this the fact we have already mentioned, that the Parliament's London information office is under-resourced, it becomes clear that the public gets to learn very little about how the European Parliament might be of use and relevance to it. Ironically, what is perhaps the most crucial body in helping to achieve legitimacy for the EU within the UK is almost invisible to the voters whom it represents. That the Parliament's information budget and strategy should be so under-developed in the face of this critical situation is lamentable. While the British press may be legitimately accused of gross under-representation of this important and most evidently democratic institution (i.e. the people actually vote in its members), the Parliament might equally stand accused of mismanagement of its own representation. When the charges of the Demos Report referred to above are laid at the door of the Parliament, it may be perceived to be guilty on every count. Both the Parliament itself and its UK office are failing to raise public awareness in all five areas. People are unlikely to identify with the political, economic and social proximity of Europe through a body of which they are little aware and for which in turn there is a poor turnout at elections.

The role of the British government and the Council of Ministers in promoting the EU within the UK

In the UK, given the reduction in the role of the Commission's London office which occurred during the second half of the 1980s, the extent to which the British government promotes and represents the activities of both the Council of Ministers, of which it is a leading member, and the EU as a whole, is crucial. It does this by a variety of means which include press conferences given by UKREP, its permanent official representation in Brussels, or by the Foreign and Commonwealth Office in London. In addition there are statements, speeches, interviews given by ministers and prime ministers, the issuing of information and promotional booklets [4] and the posting of large quantities of information on the Foreign and Commonwealth Office's (FCO) website. Let us begin then with an examination of general promotional policy by the British government.

Broad British policy on the promotion of the EU under the Conservatives

The Thatcher and Major governments seemed often to be characterised by their determination not to promote key aspects of the EU and indeed to try to constrain and even remove them altogether. The tirades of both against the alleged evils of first the Social Charter and then the Social Chapter, and the determination of the Major government to secure an opt-out for Britain on the EMU, were episodes in which the disapproval of these governments for crucial aspects of the EU was made crystal clear to the public via the media. Mrs Thatcher's verbal wars with Britain's European partners over the British budgetary contribution during her first administration and Mr Major's much less successful beef wars during his term of office, together with Mrs Thatcher's frequent references to the EC as the 'European Economic Community', seem much more characteristic of the attitudes of these leaders towards Europe than any attempt at its more positive promotion. Yet it should be remembered that it was the Thatcher government that vigorously promoted the 1992 programme, albeit for the perceived underlying economic ideology which dovetailed neatly with aspects of government policy. Equally, it was John Major who placed his reputation on the line by defending Britain's membership of the European Monetary System in a series of widely reported speeches right up to the point where the markets forced Britain to leave the EMS. Despite their governments' opposition to much concerning the EU and its works, the Conservatives did actively promote those few aspects of the Union which they believed to be advantageous to the party and the public interest.

The objectives of the EU promotional policy under New Labour and the press issue

The New Labour government which took office in May 1997 is very different in key respects from its predecessors. It rapidly signed up to the Social Chapter and started moves to implement such measures as the Working Time Directive within the UK. In December 1997, the BBC's *Newsnight* programme revealed that the government was setting out to use its forthcoming presidency of the EU to achieve real successes and so demonstrate to the British public the advantages of British membership. By so doing, it was claimed, the government hoped that it could begin changing attitudes and gently push public opinion towards a more positive perception of the European Union. These obviously well-sourced rumours also appeared in the *Guardian* shortly afterwards. The underlying approach to this new policy became apparent when it was revealed by Andrew Rawnsley that some government advisers appear to have been saying early on that Britain should be making rapid moves to join the single currency. However, according to Rawnsley, other advisers warned Tony Blair that New Labour would lose a referendum if it moved too early on this issue.[5] It would first need a sympathetic majority within Britain for the EU and its objectives.

According to Roy Hattersley, the government was also being told that it could not hope to achieve its cherished second term of office without the support of the tabloids. Blair's acceptance of these last two facts in which the tabloids, in both cases, were believed to play a crucial 'make-or-break' role explains in part his wooing of the *Sun's* proprietor Rupert Murdoch who is strongly opposed to EMU in any form. The Blair government therefore, saw as an immediate task the targeting of the Murdoch press and of Murdoch himself in order to persuade them of the advantages of the EU and of EMU in particular.

However, it became rapidly apparent that Murdoch and his UK press subordinates were not susceptible to any early wooing. Our own interviewing at the EU Commission's Representation office in London in April 1998 revealed that the *Sun's* editor had recently stated that New Labour would not succeed in changing his paper's policy on EMU (a fact borne out by the *Sun's* negative coverage of the single currency launch in May 1998 examined in Chapter 5, and by its totally hostile and renewed declaration under its new editor David Yelland on 24 June 1998). By April 1998, the government's chief presentational guru, Peter Mandelson, appeared to have only modest hopes of changing Murdoch's opinions. Mandelson's view was that if Murdoch saw the single currency implemented and Britain losing out economically through not participating in EMU, he might then change his mind. The outcome of this was that, despite some key members of the government being strongly in favour of Britain's early joining of EMU, it was unable to promote such a view through fear of the Murdoch press, and its perception of the *Sun's* ability in particular to swing the electorate against it in the referendum or next election. The government under Blair therefore found itself in the embarassing position of holding the presidency of the Council of Ministers at the time when the most crucial decisions on EMU were being taken without being able to promote EMU to its own voters or to the press. Given the Maastricht 'opt-out' requirement that the government alone should take the responsibility for the promotion of the euro within the UK, no other body could have filled that gap even if it wanted to.[6]

What New Labour did do was to try to make progress on policies that, in line with its previously mentioned strategy, would demonstrate to the electorate the benefits of EU membership directly affecting their daily lives. A notable success took the form of the proposal to implement the European Working Time Directive which, with one or two exceptions which we identified in Chapter 5, received widespread publicity in the press and other broadcasting media. The New Labour government also made much of its attempts to bring ordinary people real benefits in it presidency half-term report, released, among other places, on the Internet (Foreign and Commonwealth Office, 1998). However the list of the 45 achievements which are mentioned in the report, for the most part, is unlikely to light the flame of Euro-love within the heart of the the British voter.

Implications for the promotion of the EU raised by Britain's 'special relationship' with the USA

The government had a failure right at the beginning of its presidency with regard to the promotion, or rather non-promotion, of the common foreign policy when the Iraq crisis arose over weapons inspection. Given the close relationship between foreign policy and defence/ security policy, this was particularly significant, if the Demos Report is to be believed. As noted earlier, Demos claims that 68 per cent of EU citizens believe that defence and security policy is better handled at a European level. The government's failure to promote any EU common policy was so blatant as to be unmissable. Blair, as the sitting president of the EU during early 1998, gave the impression of simply discounting any possible significant role for the EU in helping resolve the crisis. Instead he moved immediately towards the role which British governments have so often adopted in the post-1945 period, that of being a loyal ally and lieutenant of the United States. For Britain, it seemed, Washington was the only significant player in town, and its policy on Iraq was made in conjunction with the USA rather than with the EU.

This episode highlighted neatly a core problem in Britain's relations with the EU and one which continues to hamper both its attempts to promote fully the latter or to be a complete partner within it. In short, several key elements of the close military alliance that existed between Britain and the United States during the Second World War still remain in place, even though some of these have been temporarily abandoned or devalued in the past, and despite the fact that militarily Britain is worth much less to the United States than it was half a century ago. The relationship is complex and only partially visible. For example, the two states are closely integrated in some core aspects of their intelligence operations;[7] their nuclear forces are now so closely interwoven that in many respects the British deterrent is perhaps better thought of as a small part of the American one – it is certainly difficult to argue that the Trident system is in any credible way independently usable or targetable. The British will frequently, although not always, provide forces or the use of bases when requested to ensure that the USA does not have to stand alone among UN Security Council members when it threatens to use force.[8] Publicly the present government has made no secret of its belief that Europe's defence arrangements lie exclusively within the remit of the American-led NATO alliance and not in an EU context.

Defence is not the only dimension to the 'special relationship'. There are also clearly linguistic and cultural linkages of a strong nature which continue to be important together with periodic close ideological and personal relationships. The three most obvious examples of the latter in living memory are the Kennedy–Macmillan relationship in the early 1960s, the Reagan–Thatcher relationship during the two Reagan presidencies of the 1980s, and the current Clinton–Blair friendship. Clinton and Blair are extremely close in key respects ideologically and personally in a way that neither enjoys with other EU heads of State.[9]

In short, in their relations with Europe, British governments have been pulled in two only partially compatible directions. On the one hand, they have been prepared to integrate militarily with the United States in a number of key ways, and in consequence have been prepared to harmonise crucial aspects of their foreign policy when this seemed appropriate. On the other, they have shown a strong attraction to some of the central features of the EU's economic integration policy and have been prepared to consider a joint but intergovernmentally agreed EU foreign policy where this does not cause serious disagreements with the USA. Because both of these directions in which Britain is pulled have deep political implications in so far as the 'spillover' into areas of high politics requires some degree of political coordination and even integration between the UK and the parties involved in each, Britain periodically has found itself faced with choices between incompatible options at the highest political level. This has most often happened when the EU has wanted to move forward in a way that conflicts with Britain's policy of close linkages with the USA.

On defence and security matters, with the exception of the Heath government, the British have usually come down on the American side of the fence. The problem with this is clearly that by so doing, they suggest that the EU is insignificant in a foreign policy and security context. It is hardly unreasonable to suppose that this undermines one of the key grounds on which it might be possible to build support and legitimacy for the EU in the eyes of the British public. By offering to the media such clear examples of the evident non-importance of the EU in this vital area, the government does the work of the Eurosceptics for them. The Demos statistic of 68 per cent of EU citizens wishing to see defence and military policy handled at a European level is not necessarily reflective of the balance of opinion in the UK. However, it is not unreasonable to suggest that if the EU is portrayed by a British government as virtually worthless in such a key area, then this will cause British citizens to regard it as an insignificant body internationally, little able to protect their interests. This is not to deny the difficulty of the task which UK governments face in trying to juggle simultaneously with their EU and US policy objectives. But given that the present government deems each to be important in different ways, it needs at least to find means of reconciling the two in cases like the Gulf crisis of early 1998 to a degree that is sufficient to prevent damage to the public image of the EU.

In summary of this section, the Blair government's EU presidency of the Council of Ministers in 1998 was one that as much undermined (or at best, left unchanged), the image of the EU, as dominantly represented by the media, as it succeeded in promoting it. While it is clear that important members of the government supported the single currency privately, their fear of the Eurosceptic press, and particularly of Rupert Murdoch's News International, prevented them from promoting early British membership. It is likely that, had certain key members of the cabinet been prepared to come out in favour of EMU in a way that explained persuasively its perceived advantages for ordinary people, then this in itself would have promoted in its wake a more positive image of the EU than is currently held by the public. The 'wait-and-see' policy, it could be argued, simply reinforced the apparent gap (the implied separateness we noted in the Eurosceptic discourse in the press) between the interests of the UK and the rest of the EU in the minds of the people.

Equally, whilst, by its adoption of the European Working Time Directive, the government to some degree met its objective of showing how the EU can directly benefit ordinary citizens, it also undermined the image of the Union by portraying it as irrelevant to the protection of British interests externally during the Gulf crisis of early 1998.

Like all other previous British governments it appears that New Labour under Tony Blair has been selective in representing key aspects of EU policy to parliament and to the media, and this is a simple continuation of past secretive habits within the Council of Ministers. To put it bluntly, the government, true to the tradition of the past, reveals information about the EU which is deemed to be mostly in its own interests to promote.

So, overall, it is clear that during the British presidency of the Council, the British government fulfilled part of the task of promoting the EU to the British press and public. But equally, it left a large part incomplete. By so doing it seems to be in sympathy with some of the Demos recommendations and to be completely at odds with others. The Blair government, along with the Commission and the European Parliament, must share some of the responsibility with the British press for the continuing adverse representation of the EU which occurred in the run-up to the launch of the single currency in May 1998.

The wider Council

It is now necessary to turn to the role of the Council as a whole (remembering always that its voice is that of the member states) in order to explore the extent to which it has shown in its operation concerns for the ordinary people of the Union. The Demos criticism in this respect is quite damning. It points out, as already mentioned, that despite the fact that only 9 per cent of EU citizens see EMU and the CAP as priority policies, the EU prioritises EMU and spends massive amounts on the CAP. While the Blair presidency made some attempt to draw Europe's attention to other cross-border issues such as unemployment (see Appendix II), it was nevertheless EMU that continued to grab the headlines right across Europe and so this issue, perceived as of little relevance to people's lives, consumed most of the EU's time and attention.

There is the related question in this context of how ordinary people feel about making their voices heard at the level of the Council. It is true certainly that the Council made strides towards greater openness during the 1997–8 period. However, the member states' failure to get to grips with the democratic deficit issue within the EU's institutional structure has still left the people with little visible means of influencing the Council's deliberations. This in turn inevitably has encouraged the perception that European integration is an elite-driven process which excludes the participation of the citizenry. The result has been, as Demos points out, a falling turnout 'on a grand scale' at EU parliamentary elections.

The overall picture is very clear and for the pro-European lobby very depressing. Until the Council does something radical about the democratic deficit through institutional changes, giving ordinary voters a clearly visible means by which they feel they have a voice that counts, and until it starts to introduce policies which have a much clearer and more positive impact on people's lives, it will be difficult to promote the EU in Britain and other member states in a manner that builds long-term popular support. There are other things that Demos argues the Council needs to do as well, but the above requirements seem to us to be the most fundamental.

In short, part of the reason why it is easy for the Eurosceptic press to thrive on negative reporting of the EU is because the Council has failed to build the level and quality of popular respect and support that would otherwise limit the scope for such action.

Talking to the people in their own homes – the Internet

As a coda to this chapter we propose finally to mention a new source of information which, because of its simple and direct mode of access, as well as the technological ease by which it crosses frontiers, is becoming an important communications network in its own right.

Our intention here is to look briefly at the nature and effectiveness of one of the key means of communication which the UK government has used during its presidency to try to bring Europe closer to the people – the Internet.

The full potential of this relatively new electronic communication system is still the subject of considerable debate. It is not in widespread use among the population but access to it in the UK is among the highest in Europe. It is certainly available to professional writers, journalists and students, who in turn distribute the information it carries via other more conventional means. The British government used the Internet during its presidency in 1998 to draw attention to its activities, and the Foreign and Commonwealth Office also maintains a permanent web-site.

The overall quality of the information contained on the 'presidential' web-site, in our view at least, was not particularly good. The front page was uninformative with a slow-loading logo, there was no site map, and the list format did not encourage users to move around the site through the links. In addition, it was cluttered by a certain amount of trivia and a message that to many might appear as a self-promotion exercise by the Prime Minister.

By contrast, the main FCO site, which also contained EU information and links to the presidency site, was of a very different kind. It had a precise and informative introduction, instant access to the latest events, and a good on-line reference section containing the transcriptions of foreign policy speeches on Europe and background briefings on such topics as 'Europol and the EU's fight against serious and organised crime'. Furthermore it had very useful links to all UK government material on the web. The site presentation was clear, orderly and stylish and uncluttered by photographs, graphics, or moving logos. The site in short was highly informative and accessible. As a tool for journalists or indeed anyone else seeking access to information on the British government's perspective on EU matters, the main site is of considerable interest. Its future potential as a source of information on Europe, particularly in Britain where there is significant growth in the number of subscribers to the Internet, is very considerable indeed.

Conclusion

Our conclusion is necessarily brief and blunt. A significant part of the blame for the degree to which the EU receives negative coverage within the British press must be laid not just at the door of the Eurosceptic proprietors, but also at the doors of each of the Union's major institutions and their representation in the UK. Until they start to spend some time and effort on addressing the question of why this is the case and how they might make some real progress in changing matters, the situation is unlikely to improve. While it is unlikely that the diehard Eurosceptic press will ever be persuaded to like 'Brussels', it would certainly find it more difficult to be quite so damning if the EU was succeeding in presenting itself more successfully in key areas such as the broadcast media. The risk of an uncomfortable credibility gap opening up between the representations of the EU within the Eurosceptic press and those of the broadcasters might be such that the more astute proprietors and editors were obliged to bridge it with more even-handed representation on their own part. Equally, more successful self-presentation by the EU through more voter- (rather than elite-) friendly effective policies would provide it with a chance of building a solid base of support via the Europhile press that other-wise will remain under-developed and under-exploited. If the EU continues to ignore such possibilities then it does so at its long-term peril.

Notes

1. This could be indeed a general description of the rhetorical devices we have identified in our own analysis described in previous chapters.
2. It was also pointed out to us that the Commission may deliberately avoid making complaints against the press to the PCC since the result may be counterproductive in itself.
3. Recent debates in the Parliament on genetic and tobacco issues did attract press attention.
4. There was an impressive informational drive in this respect, for example, under the Thatcher government which was dedicated to the promotion of the single market even if it loathed other aspects of the EC.
5. Andrew Rawnsley, *Now we are one: Blair's year*, Channel 4 documentary (19 April 1998).
6. It should be remembered, however, that such a state of promotional limbo may not have been such a setback for New Labour as it may have appeared at the time. According to the Demos Report, only 9 per cent of the EU's citizens see EMU as a priority.
7. The intelligence relationship is more complicated than it is possible to show in a short study such as this. See, for example, Aldrich (1998).
8. In return, during the Falkland/Malvinas conflict the Americans showed how close the relationship can be when there is sufficient rapport between US and British leaders. On that occasion, the British were provided with crucial satellite intelligence and ammunition supplies and were even promised an instant US replacement should they lose an aircraft carrier during the conflict.
9. The import of all this was ironically highlighted when, on learning in May 1998 that the EU single currency was likely to go ahead, a prominent Republican Congressman called for Britain to leave the EU and sign up to the North American Free Trade Agreement instead.

Chapter 7

Producers, consumers and users of information

Introduction

In the preceding chapters we outlined what we perceived to be the characteristic features of a discourse which, for convenience, we have called 'Europe'. These features ranged from the emotional and frequently irrational expression of an identity, often described negatively in terms of an unacceptable European 'Other', to more positive, distanced and legitimising voices which engage with Europe as an essential space for British economic, social and political activity (see Figure 7.1).

This outline picture is the result of some considerable time spent reading literally hundreds of newpaper articles, categorising their principal themes and identifying what we perceive as the ideological assumptions which underpin their discourse. From the point of view of research this approach has yielded a fascinating perspective from which to get an overall view of the range and nature of this particular discourse for the periods mentioned.

But what can we say about the factors which have produced the discourse types that we have encountered along the way and what are the effects that these types may have had upon the readers of the newspapers from which they originated? The latter question is a matter of recently renewed debate among media specialists, and in consequence some considerable care should be taken to understand the issues at stake when claims are made (as they are here) about the effects that media discourse has upon its audience/readers. From the point of view of our own work, we should indicate, at the outset, some fairly obvious considerations which need to be noted before approaching the complicated issue of how a particular discourse may or may not be interpreted by audiences, or more concretely, by readers of the British press.

First, the range and features of the European discourse that we have outlined in the preceding chapters and summarised in Figure 7.1 are rarely, if ever, available to the public as a whole. People usually read one, or at most, two papers on a regular basis, hence their exposure to, and occasional participation in the discourse of the press is fragmentary – they do not have (nor desire to have) an overview of the kind we are offering here, although they will naturally encounter a fuller version from other (broadcast) sources.

Secondly, and associated with the point just made above, the discourse of the written press is but one of several sources of information through which the public gains access to the representation of

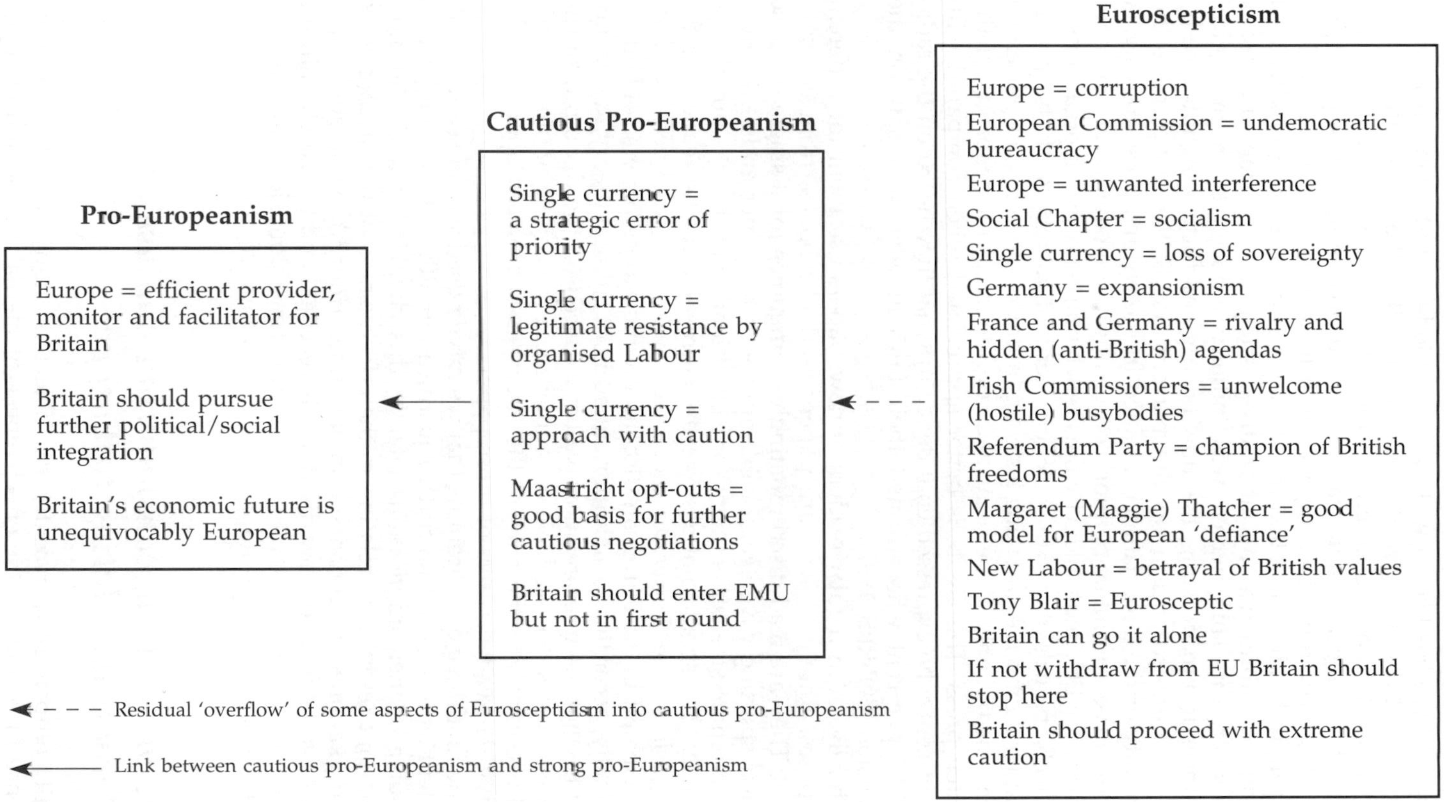

Euroscepticism

Europe = corruption

European Commission = undemocratic bureaucracy

Europe = unwanted interference

Social Chapter = socialism

Single currency = loss of sovereignty

Germany = expansionism

France and Germany = rivalry and hidden (anti-British) agendas

Irish Commissioners = unwelcome (hostile) busybodies

Referendum Party = champion of British freedoms

Margaret (Maggie) Thatcher = good model for European 'defiance'

New Labour = betrayal of British values

Tony Blair = Eurosceptic

Britain can go it alone

If not withdraw from EU Britain should stop here

Britain should proceed with extreme caution

Cautious Pro-Europeanism

Single currency = a strategic error of priority

Single currency = legitimate resistance by organised Labour

Single currency = approach with caution

Maastricht opt-outs = good basis for further cautious negotiations

Britain should enter EMU but not in first round

Pro-Europeanism

Europe = efficient provider, monitor and facilitator for Britain

Britain should pursue further political/social integration

Britain's economic future is unequivocally European

- - - Residual 'overflow' of some aspects of Euroscepticism into cautious pro-Europeanism

——— Link between cautious pro-Europeanism and strong pro-Europeanism

Figure 7.1 Three kinds of European discourse

events. There has been a widely acknowledged and pronounced shift away from the written word, in the latter half of the twentieth century, in the direction of spoken and pictorial modes of representation. It is difficult to gauge the importance and the precise nature of the input from the written press in the overall 'information picture' available to the public, but it is clear that the written word has been overtaken as a source of information by alternatives such as television and radio. Moreover, this shift, which was initially induced by technological advances in broadcasting, has now been given further significance by the apparent scepticism on the part of the British concerning the reliability of the information contained in the written press anyway. A recent survey of public opinion concerning the media in five member states of the EU, undertaken by the French market research organisation SOFRES, reveals that whilst 86 per cent of members of the public consider themselves as taking a strong interest in the news as presented in the media, only 48 per cent had confidence in the reporting of the written press. This figure is better appreciated when compared with 79 per cent who expressed confidence in what they heard on the radio and 85 per cent who affirmed their faith in what they saw on the television (SOFRES, 1997).

Thirdly, even regular readers of newspapers use them for different purposes. Rarely, if ever, are papers read like books, from cover to cover. They are read discriminatingly, sometimes for a single purpose – their sporting coverage, for example – or for wider ends – politics, general interest, entertainment (or a combination of these) – but always partially. We should not assume therefore that all the readers of the *Telegraph* or the *Mirror*, to name but two, have received, used or participated in the European discourse which these papers contain.

Finally, according to an important body of cultural theory, we cannot be sure that the interpretation we have placed on the discourse of the various voices that we have encountered in the course of our analysis will necessarily be the same as the interpretation placed upon it by the individual readers/users of those papers.

The first three qualifications that we have raised would seem so self-evident as to warrant no further justification although we shall return to some of their implications later in this chapter. Perhaps the most important reservation relating to the effectiveness of the discourse we have examined is contained in the final (fourth) point above and concerns the issue of how discourse is received and interpreted. In the following section, we shall examine this issue alongside those related to the production, consumption, and use of information.

The production, consumption and use of information relating to Europe

Until comparatively recently the object of study in communication science in relation to the effectiveness of media representations upon the public was focused firmly upon the senders or, as they are now referred to, the producers of information, rather than upon the receivers or consumers. The intended force of the communication was inferred, not just from the discourse or text, but also from the known status – political, economic, and other – of the sender or producer. Such emphasis as this generated, in the immediate post-war period, a powerful and persuasive critical literature wherein mostly passive mass audiences were depicted as being simultaneously exhorted by cultural elites and exploited by the forces of capitalism. The foundation of this dominant ideological perspective was laid in the UK by the work of Raymond Williams and Richard Hoggart. As Garnham rightly puts it:

> ...The founding thrust of cultural studies ... was ... the revalidation of British working class or popular culture as against elite, dominant culture, as part of an oppositional, broadly socialist political movement. Thus cultural studies took for granted a particular structure of domination and subordination and saw its task as the ideological one of legitimation and mobilisation ... It knew both who the enemy was and who its friends were. (Garnham, 1997:57)

In continental Europe, a similar more identifiably Marxist perspective was proposed by Gramsci (1971), Althusser (1971), and most recently by Habermas (1989).

However, over the last two decades or so, theoretical developments in Britain and in the United States particularly, have distanced themselves in significant ways from these earlier ideological formulations of mass audiences dominated by elites by prioritising instead the importance of the receivers or consumers of information and placing a new emphasis upon the perceived (variable) interpretation of discourse. The result has been that research in cultural studies, which has focused on media discourse, has been prefaced on two important assumptions which distinguish it from that of the earlier period. The first is that audiences are active and discriminating in their interpretation of media discourse, that is to say they are far less gullible and manipulated than was suggested by earlier theorists; and the second is that media discourse itself is intrinsically polysemic and open to a wide range of possible audience interpretations. These recent insights into the manner in which audiences receive and make sense of media discourse are important, but there is increasing evidence to suggest that the claims made for them in cultural studies may have been exaggerated and the importance of the producers underplayed or neglected altogether (see Kellner, 1997; Morley, 1997; Garnham, 1997). Our view, which is also encapsulated in the critical discourse analysis approach used in our commentary in the preceding chapters, also sees consumers of information as being less liberated and autonomous than has been claimed in some quarters, and, equally, perceives discourse as being less open to interpretation than some observers, over the last two decades, would have us believe.

169

In order to support this view, it will be necessary to examine the main socio-cultural events which have impacted upon European society during the second half of the twentieth century with special reference to the last two decades. By so doing we are proposing a causal link between these socio-cultural factors and the manner in which producers (and specifically newspaper proprietors) have altered the modalities of information delivery in order to serve a new generation of consumers. We shall also comment briefly upon the ways in which the latter have received and used these modes of delivery.

The producers and their adaptation to socio-cultural change

For the particular purpose of media study, it is useful to identify two periods of development since 1945. The first runs from 1945 until approximately 1975, and the second from 1975 to the present. The earlier period, according to Hobsbawm, was characterised by political, economic and cultural changes so profound that they amount to what he calls the 'post-war social and cultural revolution' (Hobsbawm, 1994). These factors of change include, among others, the now well-documented shifts from rural to urban living, improved educational standards, the emergence of a youth culture in the 1960s, sexual liberation, immigration, and the arrival of women permanently on the labour market. Technological advances in communications naturally straddle both periods. In the first, the most significant of these were the coming of television in the early 1950s and the arrival of the mass-produced transistor radio which became emblematic of the burgeoning youth culture of the mid-1960s.

By 1975 the social and cultural revolution was both slowing down and accelerating simultaneously. Immigration was ebbing in response to rising unemployment triggered by the oil crises of 1973, but second and third generation ethnic minorities were establishing themselves as permanent communities across Europe. The former solidarities engendered by strong social class membership were under siege from several quarters, not the least of which was the decline of traditional employment patterns where the old, 'rust-belt' industries were being replaced by those of the technological 'sunrise'. The collective rallying points of the nation–state of the earlier period – the Church, trade unions, the workplace, the mainstream political parties, even the marriage bed itself – were less frequented (or frequented and soon abandoned), than earlier in the twentieth century. The relative poverty of the collectivity and the mass culture which served it in the first two or so decades of the post-1945 period gives way thirty years later to relative prosperity as well as to socio-cultural fragmentation. As Hobsbawm aptly puts it: 'Prosperity and privatisation broke up what poverty and collectivity had welded together' (Hobsbawm, 1994:307).

The extent to which the media create and manipulate audiences, or are created and manipulated by them, is open to question, but this process of reciprocity and mutual invention was about to change significantly by the late 1970s. The media, particularly the British media, were not slow in responding to the fresh phase of socio-cultural development. The new-found prosperity which some (but not all) the people enjoyed, today finds its expression in alternative forms of communication, coincidentally provided by, among others, the technologies of fibre-optics (cable and satellite), on-line communication, CD-Rom, and digital transmission. Newspapers themselves have become facets of multi-media operations serving different and often individualised tastes of smaller groups of consumers. These new groups of consumers are perceived to be as distinct in their tastes and lifestyles, and as active in their participation with new media forms, as the audiences of the former mass-media were viewed as undifferentiated and passive.

Today's *Mirror* readers may well frequent several sites of information during the course of a single day, which could include specialist magazines, two or more radio stations, three television channels, including cable or satellite, and the Internet. Moreover, they will use each medium at different times and for different purposes – the newspaper in the commuter train and during breaks from work, the radio in the car or while working, the television in the evening for relaxation and news, and the on-line facilities for booking a holiday in Turkey. There is indeed a significantly larger range of information outlets from which to choose and, in this sense certainly, consumers are freer and more active than audiences of the former period. As we noted above, the newspaper is but one source of information among several competing sources, and not the most important at that.

However, as we have also noted in previous chapters, it does contain a discourse which, in varying degrees of objectivity, comprehensiveness and, indeed, passion – there are no statutory regulations about impartiality – focuses upon European issues. Moreover, unlike other media forms which may be more impartial, but which are also transitory in nature, newspapers are available in hard, semi-durable copy. If the SOFRES report is to be believed, the 48 per cent of readers of the press who believe the information it contains still amounts to well over 13 million people who read on a daily basis (i.e. the gross sales figures), plus an unknown but sizeable number who read a paper at second or third hand.

The producers of information: the commercial drive

How, more precisely, has the production of information changed over the last two decades? Generally speaking, changes have occurred in four important ways which can be summarised as follows:

- A very significant increase in the quantity of media outlets and the modalities of communication as the result first, of technological advances, and secondly of the availability of more socially fragmented audiences.

- A tendency towards niche marketing, targeting consumer groups categorised under 'lifestyle' rather than social class or political affiliations.
- The intervention of private capital, the influence of global market forces and the prevalence of commercial values in the communications system generally.
- An overall tendency in all the discourse of the media towards the conversationalisation of information.

The written press sector in Britain over the last two decades has been the site of considerable turbulence characterised by technological adaptation, industrial unrest and bitter commercial in-fighting. There have been profound changes in consequence. The newspaper industry has struggled to maintain sales to a distinctly fickle and less attentive group of consumers within an overall context of declining circulations.

Despite the repackaging of the 'product' into ever-increasing niche sections, special travel offers, money prizes, the outbreak of price wars and the prevalence of more personalised discourse styles, the public is still tempted literally to look elsewhere. It can be justifiably claimed, therefore, that there have been few, if any, periods in the history of the written press, when producers of information have been more actively engaged in capturing the elusive consumer-reader.

One consequence of the increased pressure upon newspapers to market a commercial product has been the attempts of the editors to make their papers more accessible, first, in terms of their layout with designated pages/sections for particular types of discourse, and, second, in terms of the conversationalisation of the various discourse styles themselves. An associated consequence which is particularly evident in the mass-market tabloids, the *Sun*, the *Mirror* and the *Star* (but which is present in all the other tabloids too), has been the reduction of the topic range of communicable events in the public interest and their replacement by ones of a distinctly personal interest kind. Readers are presented with a limited range of topics which cover less than a dozen categories and include for example, scandal stories relating to the rich and famous, sport, crime, certain high profile public interest topics such as the Health Service, unavoidable political events – elections, summits, peace talks – international disasters, leisure pursuits and cash competitions.

Paradoxically, this development, existing in its most pronounced form in the mass-market tabloids, and to a lesser extent in those directed at the middle market, occurs at a time when standards of education and taste have never been higher, or, at least, so it is said. One explanation for this apparent paradox must be that the effects of commercial competition both internally, between newspapers themselves, as well as externally, between the press sector generally and other information sources, have had a negative influence on press performance. Another explanation would challenge the over-generalised perception of rising educational standards among all social groupings in Britain and, in particular, with relation to standards of literacy. Despite the overall trend of significantly improved educational standards in the post-war period, mentioned already in a previous section, Britain still trails behind other European countries with regards to standards of literacy. In a comparative study carried out by the International Adult Literacy Survey (IALS), it has been shown that Britain has a significantly higher proportion of young adults occupying the lowest levels of achievement when compared with countries such as the Netherlands, Sweden and Germany (Carey *et al.*, 1997:67). The existence of significant numbers of adults at the lowest level of literacy in Britain suggests some kind of link between this group of consumers and the targeting strategies of the mass-market tabloids. We may usefully recall the examples we gave in Chapter 1 of the distinctly different discourse types occurring in the *Daily Herald* of 50 years ago and that of the *Sun* in 1997. We inferred from the discourse of the former (regardless of how this discourse was inter-preted) the assumption that persons traditionally associated with low levels of literacy (the working class) nevertheless *wished* to be informed and educated simultaneously. This kind of social responsibility undertaken by predominantly middle-class, male journalists was a characteristic of the immediate post-war period and in some senses represents the culmination of what may be termed the prevailing 'modernist' aspirations of the time. In consequence of more recent socio-cultural changes and the prioritisation of market forces over others of a more social kind, we must infer a different set of values from the evidence of the *Sun*'s discourse (and indeed those of the other tabloids too). Whilst there may be no direct causal link between the discourse of the mass-market tabloids and low levels of literacy, it is surely the case that their primary targets are located in those groups of young adults identified by the literacy survey mentioned above. As we have already noted, the emphasis in the discourse of these papers is placed upon entertainment, pleasure and self-gratification as opposed to information or education.

What we have, in short, is the purveying to a particular group of consumers of a *product* marketed and delivered with scant attention paid to wider social needs (i.e. information or education), but where, instead, a dominant emphasis is placed upon the perceived personal desires of the consumer. There is, in consequence, as we have already suggested, a downward pressure exerted upon informational content in favour of other personal and allegedly more marketable aspects of the discourse by processes we have described already. It would seem that there is little chance in these circumstances of Europe ever receiving a fair hearing, not in the tabloid press at least.

Nevertheless, despite commercial pressures to entertain and to conversationalise the discourse of the press, we have argued, and we hope, demonstrated by our commentary on its representation of Europe, that this discourse is driven by an intense political agenda set in varying measure by government, proprietors, colluding editors and a quiescent public alike. Given our comments below, relating to the limited possible readings of press discourse available to the public, we would conclude that the importance of the role of the producers of information in the opinion-making process, which has been neglected over the last two decades, is due for re-examination (see Appendix I).

The producers and the question of omission

We noted generally in our commentaries on the Eurosceptic and Europhile discourse how the press sector's representation of European issues was not comprehensive when compared with the potential for public debate as outlined in Chapter 2. This applies as much to the broadsheets as it does to the tabloids, although much more so to the latter. In coming to this conclusion we are perhaps setting our standards too high. There is after all, presumably, a limit to the interest value of Europe for British citizens beyond which they will not go. This must be the case, but in our view, those limits are rarely, if ever tested by the press.

Notwithstanding the regular coverage that Europe is given in the broadsheets, it can at best be described as adequate in the case of some papers, and in the tabloids it is quite inadequate. We perceive the general tendency to exclude European issues from the public in the Eurosceptic press to be partly derived from commercial assumptions about what the public wants, but also to stem from a pronounced inclination, deliberate or otherwise, to ignore or deprioritise the existence and function of the European Union. Whatever the case may be for a 'qualitative' ethnographic approach to the analysis of how readers understand and use information presented in the media, there can be no interpretation of information if it is omitted from the discourse, other than of it being unimportant and irrelevant to the public interest. The phenomenon of omission is evident generally across a whole range of communicable events relating to the EU – social, economic, political – which touch people's lives, either directly or indirectly, but which go largely unreported. The explanation for this, or at least the one most likely to be offered by the producers themselves, is likely to be the commercial one – that the reader-consumer has little interest in, and even less tolerance of, the more sophisticated aspects of the issues surrounding European integration. We would not accept such explanations – they are unconvincing and disingenuous.

There is some truth in the criticism of the EU by the authors of the Demos Report, discussed in Chapter 6, that it has too frequently pursued the wrong (elitist) political objectives which have served to distance it from, rather than bring it closer to, the consciousness of the people of Europe. And yet many of its policies operate in net beneficial ways, at a local level, for the everyday lives of millions of European citizens. More often than not they are played down or ignored in the British press.

We noted in Chapter 5 how the representation of the European Working Time Directive in the dominant Eurosceptic discourse of the press de-emphasised or ignored the role of the European Union in this reform which benefited millions of British workers. The distribution of the European Structural Funding also provides potentially an ideal opportunity for the EU to promote itself or be promoted as a benefactor to the British people in all kinds of ways. Such practical representations would bring Europe closer to the collective consciousness of the people in a potentially very effective manner. The money from Structural Funding is directly aimed at regional and urban regeneration, the creation of employment and the encouragement of equal opportunities. In the period 1989–99 the UK received approximately £14 billion to support socio-economic development from Structural Funding (EC, 1996:1). Moreover, 40 per cent of Britons live in areas benefiting from funding from this source. Clearly this structural initiative amounts precisely to the pragmatic, tangible, hands-on version of the European Union demanded in the Demos Report. But where is it represented in the media? Certainly in the press for the pre-election period there was little or nothing to be found representing these concrete benefits bestowed upon the ordinary people from this quarter. It could be argued that one reason at least for this distinctly understated import-ance of EU intervention in regional development is the fact that Britain is only recovering from the Regional Fund a part of the money it has already paid into the EU by way of its national contribution. Also, as was pointed out in Chapter 2, the British government in the past was not slow to claim the credit for some EU initiatives for itself rather than for Europe. All perfectly true. But what is striking about the European discourse in the immediate pre-election period, is that first, not only are the benefits that may accrue to the British regions from EU structural funding not mentioned, but neither are the counter arguments regard-ing whether or not Britain is getting value for its overall contribution generally. This criticism posed in this somewhat unadorned manner can be dressed up in finer clothes.

Over the last 20 years the British economy has undergone some sharp and in some cases, painful transformations. Manufacturing now accounts for less than 25 per cent of total employment whilst the service sector now employs over 70 per cent of British people. This movement from manufacturing towards the servicing sector has provoked a rapid and painful decline in former industrialised regions such as the North East, eastern Scotland and South Wales as well as a slowing down of activity in certain rural regions including, among others, those of Northern Ireland and the Highlands and Islands. All of these regions receive socio-economic aid from the EU aimed at sustaining existing levels of jobs and creating new forms of employ-ment. The total figure for aid from the forecast relating to Structural Funding for the period 1994–99 amounts to 12.9 billion ecus compared with 12.1 billion ecus contributed from government funds. Such important EU initiatives which, as can be seen, exceed the national contribution, should be much better represented in the British press but they are mostly ignored.

We conclude, therefore that, in addition to the limited range of European topics represented in the British press, and to the dominant

Eurosceptic readings proposed by the majority of titles, there is also the exclusion for commercial, political or other reasons, of information relating to practical policies which touch the lives of large numbers of British people in beneficial ways.

The consumers as readers of the discourse

For the readers of several of the broadsheets, deemed for the most part to be located among the more educated social groups, the discourse on Europe, whether anti- or pro-European, may be said to be both adequate and relatively varied thematically. These readers are also among the more socio-economically privileged in British society and will generally have both more time as well as the financial means to access information. Collectively they account for about 5.43 million[1] out of the total of 28.5 million daily and Sunday paper readers (Peak and Fisher, 1997:42), that is to say, less than 20 per cent of the total readership of the press in Britain.

For the readers of the remaining 80 per cent, the mass-market tabloids, and to some extent of the middle-market tabloids too, there are at least two disempowering consequences which flow from the kind of production policies outlined in the sections above. The first we have touched upon above already and concerns the narrow range of choice of topic coverage which characterises the mass-market tabloids, and to some extent the middle-market tabloids too. In our view, this restricted range is dictated much more by commercial values – its perceived saleability – than by those of 'communicative responsibility' – the public's right to be informed over a wider range of communicable events. For this reason, and for others which we shall deal with shortly, the consumer/reader's choice is severely restricted.

The second force of disempowerment concerns the available 'readings' of the discourse. It has been persuasively argued that in other mass-cultural media such as television and film, commercial interests, particularly those of Hollywood, are such that programming and films are produced strictly to formulaic structures, mostly involving conflict resolution and set within clearly marked ideological boundaries – latterly, for example these have included the advocacy of black, gay and feminist causes in American society. Such structuring, it is argued, both encourages and facilitates a dominant reading of the TV programme or movie (Kellner, 1997:112).

Whilst we do not invite a direct comparison between the meanings that cinema audiences and readers place upon the respective discourses of the film and the newspaper – that is a study in itself – we would nevertheless point to some similarities operating in the interpretation of texts and of tabloid texts in particular. Among the latter titles, commercial considerations dictate a limited range of topics which are underpinned by clear and recurring ideological boundaries indicating and delineating only a limited range of possible interpretations. Can media discourse such as 'Keep your nose out of our election' or others which contain references to 'Euro-swindlers', 'Froggies' and 'Krauts' be so variably interpreted that all xenophobic sentiments are extirpated? We would suggest that they cannot. There is here only a dominant, xenophobic reading available, and moreover we suggest that consumers are encouraged to read such texts for their dominant interpretation potential. In partial support of our view, Fowler describes what he calls 'discursive competence': '... they [*Sun* readers] know the discourse and its meanings in advance, predictively bringing relevant mental models or schemata which are to be confirmed in the act of reading...' (Fowler, 1991:44).

The extent to which these dominant potential interpretations do indeed dominate is open to question and is the subject of much contemporary research involving the close questioning of reader/consumers in order to determine their particular interpretations of the news as represented in the media (see Gavin, forthcoming). Again, our view is that in certain domains of press performance, and in particular in the discourse of the tabloid press, the potential for the variable interpretation of certain discourse-types is limited. If we add to this limited interpretation factor the other important one of omission, discussed in the previous section, then the likelihood of the reader engaging with an informative discourse on Europe through a tabloid paper is remote.

Note

1. That is, *The Times, Telegraph, Guardian, Financial Times, Independent, Sunday Times, Sunday Telegraph, Observer, Independent on Sunday* (ABC, 1996).

Chapter 8

Insulting the Public?

A cultural predisposition towards Euroscepticism?

One cultural illusion at least denied to the peoples of the continental member states of the Union is that they are not essential players within the geo-political space of Europe. Part of the Eurosceptic media discourse in Britain does appear to take this view. This attitude is partly explicable in terms of the interplay of three factors. First, there is the undeniable fact of Britain's physical separateness from continental Europe. Britain is not crossed and recrossed by the great arterial routes that link Barcelona to Strasbourg or Paris to Berlin, with their periodic or routine movements of peoples – workers, students, tourists – that throng the European continent in ways that give Europe a significance it does not enjoy in Cardiff, Barrow or Dundee. Secondly, there is the undeniable fact that Britain and its institutions have not felt the lash of hostile occupation by a foreign power as the consequence of military defeat in modern times. The latter is an experience all too common on mainland Europe [1] and provides one of the fundamental motives for Europeans to seek peace and security through integration in the post-1945 period. Finally, partly as the result of the above but also because the English language dominates in so many global activities, the British are poor speakers of foreign languages which means that, unlike significant groups of other Europeans, they engage less with the cultures of other countries at the most fundamental of levels, that of their national tongues. Mr Blair's speech to the French National Assembly was in this respect less remarkable for its content than for the fact that it was delivered in French, making it the first speech sustained in a foreign language by a British Prime Minister for decades. These widely acknowledged factors are fundamental to the shaping, in part, of the Euroscepticism which we perceive in varying measure to be innate in British culture and by extension in the contemporary media discourse which we have been examining in this study.

But beyond these fundamental factors which shape British attitudes towards continental Europe, there are naturally many others. We drew attention in Chapter 1 to Marquand's views on what he perceives to be the residues of 'Whig-imperialism' in British culture which he claims have a disproportionate influence upon political-cultural attitudes, and which may be seen as running against the current of events in Europe at the end of the twentieth century. As the reader will have noted, there is ample evidence in the data we examined of the kinds of attitudes which Marquand describes, even if the degree to which they actually influence public opinion may be contested. Identifying a particular ideological stance in a newspaper is one thing, assessing its significance is another.

These thoughts should be kept in mind by the reader and will be returned to later in this chapter. What we intend to do now is offer a dual set of conclusions deriving from our study. Our book has brought together the perspectives of a media specialist and a political scientist. Below, we present the major conclusions on our findings that can be drawn using the lenses of our respective disciplines.

A political science perspective: the press, the EU and British sovereignty

We have seen in previous chapters how a strong security-centred argument can be advanced to support existing and continuing integration within the EU, and how in particular ideological perspectives, various economic and social arguments might be added to this fundamental rationale for further British integration (see Chapter 2). We have noted also in Chapter 6 what, in our opinion, is a poor record in effectively promoting the core values of the EU during recent years on the part of its own institutions. This latter observation means that the dominant responsibility has fallen to the press for evaluating and mediating the security dimension of EU membership, the crucial significance of which we have stressed in the course of this study. As we have noted, the underlying security issues of the European debate are in fact poorly represented and this inadequacy, we suggest, is due to a serious misunderstanding of the implications of further integration for British sovereignty on the part of a large section of the written press. There is a belief in some quarters that the EU is more of a threat to British security than a benefit due to the sovereignty which it 'takes away' from Britain. Other more positive security implications tend to be forgotten in the preoccupation with this perception. However, much of the concern of the Eurosceptic press misses the point that, with the right policies, rather more sovereignty for Britain could be gained by continuing integration than would be lost. In short, the Eurosceptics are engaged in the wrong debate. Rather than calling for a reduction or a halt in Britain's involvement with continuing European integration, they should be focusing on ways in which British sovereignty could be increased through such involvement. In order to do this there must be a distinction made in the discourse of the press between *real* and *theoretical* sovereignty. In making such a distinction, and indeed in several key parts of the discussion that follows, we are ourselves following precedents which have already been well established within the literature of international relations and European studies, even if we do not use the identical terms to those employed by many writers in these fields. What we offer here then are some provocative and potent ways of thinking about and understanding the sovereignty

179

issue which to our knowledge are rarely, if ever, represented in the British press.

To put the matter as simply as possible, real sovereignty is the degree of control which a nation can exercise over its own destiny, while theoretical sovereignty can be best described as symbolic control, signifying little if any substance. An example of the latter takes the form of Britain's nuclear arsenal. For much of the post-war period the fiction was maintained that it was an 'independent' deterrent, despite the fact that, as was pointed out in Chapter 6, from the late 1950s onwards it moved increasingly under shared American control. It is inconceivable now, for example, that Britain's nuclear weapons could be fired in anger without American permission. This is because the UK's small nuclear armoury is dependent upon, and informally integrated with, its vastly larger American counterpart. The deterrent, in other words, is very clearly little more than a symbol of Britain's theoretical sovereignty as defined within the Polaris agreements during the early 1960s.

The pound sterling has also for some time been a symbol of Britain's theoretical sovereignty as opposed to the real. While short-term adjustments can be made via UK exchange rates, for a number of years its medium to long-term average value has been greatly affected by decisions taken within the German economy, the Japanese economy, the United States economy, and within the rest of the global economy as a whole. Equally, Britain's ability to make a variety of decisions on matters as varied as taxation and social welfare is constrained by how they will be perceived by global market forces and the likely impact that such perceptions might have upon the inward investment that has been so crucial to the health of the British economy in recent years. So, real sovereignty has for some time been heavily qualified in these areas also.

The extent to which there has been a deterioration in Britain's real sovereignty as the result of reasons independent of the EU is something that the Eurosceptic press has never been good at explaining to the British electorate. It is perhaps necessary that this deterioration should be reiterated here. In 1999 Britain does not retain the military capability to act in any significant way without American approval or the assistance of its European allies. As we have already pointed out, even the Falklands War of 1982 was dependent upon American ammunition supplies, intelligence help, and a US guarantee to provide a replacement aircraft carrier should the British lose one, as well as upon the political support of its European partners. The UK is a much reduced part of the global economy in proportional terms and much of its significance within global economic bodies now derives from its status as a leading member of the EU and not as a function of its own separate economic power. Politically its continued retention of a seat on the UN Security Council is becoming increasingly contentious in the light of alternative claims for Britain and France to be replaced by Germany, Japan or the EU.

Diplomatically the embarrassment of Britain's reduced influence is frequently exposed. Most recently such embarrassment occurred during the Queen's 1997 tour of India during which there were frequent snubs and the Indian Prime Minister was widely alleged to have referred to Britain as a 'third rate' power. Similarly during the 1997 US–Iraqi crisis, Tariq Aziz referred to Britain as an American stooge to some effect. When during the autumn of 1997 it was announced that Russia would henceforth be holding regular summits with leading EU members, Britain was excluded in favour of Germany and France. Britain's much vaunted special relationship with the USA, which the Blair government has done much to try to reawaken, is now dependent mainly upon ideological/personality factors (although military considerations still play a reduced underpinning role) and as such is periodic and highly fragile. While the Reagan–Thatcher and Blair–Clinton relationships may look impressive, the Major–Clinton relationship was an example of just how unimportant Britain can become to the USA when there is no personality/ideological match. As in the case of India, Britain may well be perceived as a third rate power internationally. On its own this gives it only a correspondingly third rate control over its destiny. Within Europe, as the continued dominance of France and Germany, and Russia's failure to include it within its list of EU summit partners demonstrate, the UK is now a second rank power. Britain's real sovereignty within the global arena is but a shadow of its former self and much of that sovereignty that the press implies still exists is little more than theoretical. As Britain's independent power and influence continue to decline relatively, it becomes increasingly necessary for it to harness itself to other, more powerful bodies and to persuade them to pursue interests favourable to itself. It is in this respect that the EU possesses so much potential as a means of restoring some of Britain's lost real sovereignty. It offers Britain the chance of regaining some of its former control over its own destiny, if the British can be persuasive enough bargainers within the power channels of Brussels and can use the EU effectively in their own interests.

Where the EU can be used by Britain to convert portions of its theoretical sovereignty into real sovereignty (it is important to realise that 'real' sovereignty never exists in any absolute sense), then this is clearly advantageous to the interests of the British electorate, provided the increase in real sovereignty is handled properly by British governments.

This is an area in which British governments have considerably under-performed in the past, and one in which they have squandered what should have been powerful bargaining advantages. Ironically the calculation that often has to be made is how much real sovereignty in some areas of governance should be *traded* in order to secure a greater *overall* level of real sovereignty. It may be necessary to sacrifice a degree of sovereignty in order to create the efficient collective conditions in which the desired economic benefits which facilitate a greater level of overall sovereignty can be realised. Mrs Thatcher reluctantly and only temporarily recognised the advantage of this kind of tactic when signing up to qualified majority voting within the Single European

Act in order to make the EU effective as an aid to British economic power. If viewed from this kind of perspective, for example, EMU can be seen as an opportunity for gaining a degree of influence over the German economy that would not otherwise be possible (i.e. trading the loss of control over national exchange rates for wider control at another level). Exchange rate controls provide only short-term control advantages, while an influence upon the German economy, in return for EMU membership, is a long-term prospect.

The key to the understanding of the sovereignty issue is that the EU, like the rest of the world, is made up of states with different and often conflicting interests, and this means that increases in real sovereignty within the Union, or even the maintenance of existing levels of the same, often do not, and cannot, come for free. Other states want them too, and in order for everyone's goals to be realised as far as possible, there has to be a process of horsetrading in which, as with the Thatcher example mentioned above, trade-offs can occur between aspects of real sovereignty in one area, and those in another. Furthermore, because politics and economics are processes subject to continuous pressures and change, such trade-offs will need to be periodically reinforced or renegotiated. These processes are the continuous functions of inter-national political and economic activity, and in consequence never constitute an absolute in terms of real sovereignty that any state can achieve and hold on to forever. What is crucial about the EU is that it provides a means by which Britain's *overall* real sovereignty can be increased in a way that would not be possible outside it, even though in return for that increase, Britain has sometimes to surrender some aspects of its existing real sovereignty. For this to happen, Britain must have governments which first understand this argument and, secondly, which also have the political will to implement a strategy to this end by the deployment of diplomats and other civil servants with the appropriate negotiating skills.

Should the Eurosceptic press accept this fact, then the ground is laid for a change of perspective also on the relationship between further EU integration and Britain's security interests.

The question, therefore, *might* be seen as being one of 'how can the Eurosceptic press's understanding of the concepts of real and theoret-ical sovereignty and their relevance to the EU debate be increased?' Not to be too cynical, however, one might suspect that some, at least, of the relevant papers' editors *already* understand perfectly all of the above, and that they continue to construct agendas promoting theoretical sovereignty for circulation reasons or other commercial purposes. The question, then, becomes one entirely of whether the security argument on its own can be advanced in such a way as to make them change their editorial policies. If it can't, then the long-term consequence could be a quite unforgivable contribution to a future massive loss of life in Europe. In the calm, quite possibly no more than medium-term, 'security' of the present no one should be under any illusion about the kind of conflicts that modern weapons make possible, should a Europe without the *complete* peacekeeping framework of which the EU is a crucial part once more become destabilised by economic or political/ social traumas. In order for the EU to survive into the long-term future as part of such a framework, it needs, among other things, Britain to switch to a more promotive and supporting role, and that in turn requires an adequately informed and supportive UK electorate. The press's information role is vital in the last respect. Any future major wars on Britain's doorstep will be twice the hell on earth that Hitler was able to dream up. For the Jewish people in particular, one hell has been quite enough, and that is perhaps a lesson that much of the British press has yet to learn. It is only the great fools of history who, during times of peace, presume that there is any guarantee that the future will be as safe as their present.

A media perspective: the press and the 'grand narrative'

In terms of an ideal representation of Europe in the British press, and given the extreme importance for the British people of the issues relating to sovereignty and to future European security (i.e. freedom from war), the 'grand narrative' that we referred to in earlier chapters should have had (and should have) a much greater airing. Occasionally we encountered aspects of this overarching narrative, mostly in the pro-European papers and occasionally in the Eurosceptics. It was both too rare and almost exclusively located in the broadsheets. If political freedom, peace and prosperity stand importantly at one end of the grand European narrative, then social freedoms, privileges, and benefits stand as importantly at the other. If the Demos Report is to be believed, the social aspects of EU membership to Britain are, if anything, more important for promoting Europe as a benevolent force to the people than the political and economic issues. From the evidence of our data, neither was adequately represented in the European discourse overall. As we pointed out in Chapter 7, the ways in which the EU contributes to the well being of Britons in their daily lives via the Structural Funds are almost completely ignored in the press (as indeed they are elsewhere in the media). When in the second period of our study, the Blair government adopted the European Working Time Directive, it is significant that the importance of this European initiative, affecting as it will the lives of millions of Britons, was downplayed by all the Eurosceptic broadsheets, ignored by the *Mail* on the day and relegated to less than 100 words of text in the *Sun* and the *Mirror* in low status locations in the papers.

This inadequacy of representation of European issues is due among other factors to contemporary causes such as the political self-interest of both the major parties, whether in or out of office, the influence of the proprietors, low professional journalistic standards in some cases, lack of specialised knowledge, and very importantly, the commercial influence governing the saleability of newspapers. We also find the efforts of the Commission and European Parliament to promote positively the European cause within the United Kingdom to be decidedly lacklustre and in consequence to leave a lot to be desired.

The dominance and quality of Euroscepticism: insulting the public?

There are, as we have already noted at the beginning of this chapter, fundamental geographical, historical and linguistic reasons why all the 'European' discourse of the British press may be deemed to be fashioned by a basic instinct or feeling of separateness with regard to Europe. These instincts find their expression in varying measure in the discourse of the Eurosceptic and the Europhile press. If we add to this fundamental general scepticism some real, contemporary and important issues of an economic, political and cultural order which confront both sides, most of which have been referred to in our preceding chapters, it is wholly to be expected that in the overall discourse we should find voices representing a reasoned expression of doubt at the prospect of Britain's closer engagement with the EU. We are speaking here of a kind of scepticism which, as we have seen, is not limited to the self-proclaimed Eurosceptic titles such as *The Times*, *Telegraph*, *Mail*, *Express* (although the *Express* now appears to be in the process of 'changing its spots') and *Sun*, but which has voices across the whole range of the British press including the *Financial Times* and the *Guardian*.

This underlying general scepticism, it may well be argued, is an imperative in any discourse of this magnitude. When it is extended and translated into identifiable political stands for or against Europe, then the issue of the nature and quality of British press performance manifests itself.

Of the two camps, it is clear that the pro-European press is in a disquieting minority (for reasons we shall explain below) when compared with the anti-European titles. If we quantify the strength of the respective camps (somewhat crudely by circulation figures in the absence of other criteria), we can identify 76 per cent of the written press as being Eurosceptic and only 24 per cent as being pro-European.

The quality of this pro-European press, whilst adequate and indeed eloquent at times, is nevertheless restricted to the comparatively modest readership of the *Financial Times*, the *Guardian*, the *Independent*, the intermittent coverage of the *Mirror*, and to the Sunday companions of these papers.

We do not make the same claims of adequacy for the discourse of the identifiable Eurosceptic titles. Their quality ranges from the strongly informational, albeit within a limited number of issues, on one hand, to the most inadmissible distortion and xenophobia on the other. Overall the Eurosceptic press engages a potential readership of 21 million people. Although the tabloids are in large part responsible for the more extreme forms of distortion and xenophobic outbursts, they are by no means alone. As we have seen, *The Times* and the *Telegraph* are quite capable of including in their coverage of Europe representations of dubious origin and intent. But it is in the discourse of the Eurosceptic tabloids that the answer to the question that frames the title of this study is mostly located. It is here that we find a predominantly crude stereotyping of peoples, distortion of issues and omission of information which would be laughable were not the issues at stake so important for the future welfare and security of the citizens of this country. Again, we would point out that this kind of performance is characteristic of a group of tabloid papers which between them reach a potential readership of over 18 million people.

We have already, we hope, amply illustrated the characteristics of this particular brand of Euroscepticism. And so on the basis of these and other examples, not included in our study for want of space, and in the explanatory context of the socio-cultural factors mentioned in previous chapters, we conclude that the majority of the reading public is indeed insulted by the quality of the press performance with regard to European issues.

The nature of this insult is threefold. It operates first at the level of a presumption about the incapacity of readers to understand the issues in anything but a trivialised, personalised and simplified form (i.e. denuded of information). The second is the presumption that even if they could understand the issues represented in more complex ways, the readers do not desire to know. Thirdly, and in consequence of the first two, it operates at the level of disempowerment: the public is not given information of sufficient quality upon which to base opinions which seems to us to be an abuse of its fundamental democratic rights.

Whatever impact the tabloid discourse of Euroscepticism has upon the people, it is assertive and heavy with ideological force. We infer from this the intention at least to influence public opinion. In the light of what we have said about its characteristics, we consider this discourse, in large part, to be an insulting performance. The extent of the insult should of course always be tempered by the knowledge that readers no longer rely on newspapers as the primary sources of information. But the link between public opinion and the representations of the written press does exist, even if its precise nature is difficult to establish.

The existence of alternative sources of information, often more balanced and generally more informative, via radio and television is undeniable. Their availability and the current ready access to them, coupled with the widely accepted view that these alternatives are the preferred sources of information, are often cited as the reasons for discounting the effects of the perceived inadequacies of press performance on issues in the public interest such as Europe. There may be some considerable truth in this view. Public service broadcasting, despite a fashionable *fin-de-siècle* prognosis of its inevitable demise,[2] is still a central force for the dissemination of information. If despite the processes of social fragmentation and technological advance, PSB is still able to sustain itself as the major arena for public opinion formation, then concerns about the quality of press performance may well be exaggerated. If, however, the main terrestrial broadcasters in the UK continue to lose ground (as they themselves expect to do), in the face of more commercial, and less principled, competition, then the question of the quality of the performance of the written press – a matter of constant concern in media circles – will assume a new relevance and importance. In our view such a debate is due to be renewed with fresh vigour. We hope that this study may make a modest contribution to that end.

Notes

1. No doubt the Republic of Ireland, whilst it shares the experience of factors 1 and 3 with the United Kingdom, would view itself as having been occupied by a foreign power up to 1922.
2. We note with a certain wryness here the implications for our own ideological position.

SPEAKING *is media discourse*

For those readers who may be interested in trying their hand at the analysis of the kind that we have used here in order to evaluate the performance of the discourse of the press, we propose to offer in this appendix a memorisable summary of the principal socio-cultural components which constitute the variable discourse types of the media. There is, however, a risk attached to this strategy which we shall explain below.

Introduction

What follows is intended to help the non-specialist discourse analyst recall the essential socio-cultural features and associated theory which together help explain the production of media discourse. The essential components are summarised under eight headings and conveniently (from the point of view of memory) form the acronym SPEAKING. This device is not new and was first proposed by Hymes (1972), for a different purpose, and so we have been obliged to modify considerably the content of the components to make them relate more clearly to the concepts and socio-cultural issues which we have described in this chapter. The risk in the use of acronyms lies in the danger of over-simplification, conceptual overlap and wrong emphasis. We have tried to anticipate and overcome these pitfalls and on balance consider that the advantages – the availability to the non-specialist of an easy way to access media discourse types – outweigh the risks of possible confusion.

The use of the SPEAKING acronym then is helpful in several respects. It helps pull together the complex strands of socio-cultural factors which simultaneously act upon the production and use of media discourse, placing the latter within a wide explanatory context. In addition, its categories allow reference at least to the theoretical aspects of contemporary analytical studies in media discourse. Its use will reinforce the value of a close critical discourse analysis of the kind we have made use of in Chapters 3 to 5.

Using the SPEAKING acronym as a preliminary to discourse analysis

It is our purpose here first, to show how the SPEAKING acronym can be used to recall essential concepts in relation to the analysis of media discourse and second, to examine an example of media discourse in the light of the components suggested by the acronym. We hope that the reader will recognise some of the theoretical issues already outlined in previous sections of this book as well as the relevant contributory socio-cultural features already mentioned which appear under each heading.

We suggest that from the evidence available to us such as previous readings of the newspaper (previous discourse), references to external sources of information (socio-cultural factors and features of the production and consumption process itself) and from the content of the particular text/discourse, we can establish a useful preliminary profile of a discourse type as shown in Figure A.1.

In order to demonstrate the use of the SPEAKING acronym in its application as an initial step towards the analysis of media texts, we propose to look again at the *Sun* article on the subject of the unveiling in Amsterdam of the designs for the new Eurocurrency in June 1997. We quote here a fuller version of the text although it is not exactly in the same columned format as the original and omits the accompanying photos of the new coins, the old English penny and the designer of the new money.

Text A.1 (*Sun*, 17 June 1997)

STAND BY TO SPEND A CENT
(THE EUROCRATS HAVE JUST BANNED THE PENNY)

**Brits may soon be unable to spend a penny –
because Eurocrats plan to kill off our favourite coin
after more than 1,200 years of history.**

Brussels bosses intend to replace the penny – introduced by Anglo-Saxon King Offa around 750 AD – with a new Euro **CENT**.

But the cash Brussels hopes we will use immediately came under fire. Shocked coin experts predicted the new 'funny money' would be deeply unpopular.

John Whitmore, treasurer of the British Numismatic Trade Association said, 'The penny has been with the British people all those years and now EU-bosses want to get rid of it ... It seems that the rest of Europe, which mainly uses a form of cent, is putting the boot into Britain'.

The eight new coins unveiled at the EU summit in Amsterdam feature stars and maps of the 15 nation-bloc which in turn 'portray European unity'.

The other side of the coins, designed by Belgian ex-computer pro-grammer Luc Luycx, has been reserved for the national symbol, in Britain's case the Queen's head, if the pound is ever ditched. The coins are one and two Euros – both in white metal – 50 cents in gold and 10 cents in silver. The approximate worth of the cent will be a mere 0.7 of the present day penny depending on exchange rates.

Mr Whitmore branded the new-look coins as 'boring' and added: 'They have tried to please every European country but have resulted in a dull-looking coin'.

Tory MP Christopher Gill said: 'These coins look like slot machine tokens. We've had the penny and the pound for centuries – and we shouldn't be getting rid of them'. Fellow Tory Ian Duncan Smith added: 'They will sweep away centuries of history. I'm sure the British people don't want them'. The design of the coins was also immediately slammed by
(cont. p.190)

Setting: **The discourse context of event and 'lifeworld'**
(a) The communicable event (representations)
(b) The shared lifeworld (assumptions/ideology)?
This includes the assumed recall of the content of previous
discourse as demonstrated in Chapter 1

Participants: **The origin of the discourse and of the identity of the user/
consumer**
Owners? Known views?
Government agencies?
Advertisers?
News agencies?
Editors? Known views?
Journalists? Known views?
Readers/Users/Consumers? Identifiable group
membership?

Ends: **The perceived producer's intention behind the discourse?**
i.e. Persuade? (overt bias) Influence? (covert bias)
Inform? (balance)   (see below)

Acts: **Dominant internal discourse function?**
i.e. Social relations, Social identities, Representations?
Mixture of discourse types? (intertextuality?)

Key: **Social identities (a) and Social relations (b)?**
(a) the status of writer and reader?
i.e. specialist/authoritative, non-specialist/
non-authoritative
(b) the 'tone' of the discourse
i.e. formal/semi-formal/informal?
serious/humorous?
subjective/objective?
positive/negative?

Implementation: **The wider context?**
Technology, Finance, Legislation, Regulation?

Norms: **Discourse practice: the use of a particular discourse type
by consumers/users/readers**
(a) (in the mass written press)
for opinion formation, information, entertainment,
leisure?
(b) (in advertising)
for fantasy, consumerism, entertainment, information?
(c) (in the new niche, specialist media)
for opinion formation, information, entertainment,
leisure?

Genre: **The structure of the discourse type?**
Newspaper/magazine/other?
advertisement/article/editorial/letters/sport/competition/
obituary/horoscope?

Figure A.1 SPEAKING *is* media discourse

> representatives of the blind, who said they were so similar that they would
> be almost impossible for a partially sighted person to tell them apart.
> Jill Allen-Knight, spokeswoman for the National Federation of the Blind,
> said: 'These coins are so similar – they are just dreadful'.
> *Even though the coins were unveiled, there were fears at the summit that the*
> *currency union is doomed.*
> Britain and Germany ganged up to stop France cooking the books to
> qualify. But that may backfire on debt-ridden Germany.
> Tony Blair fought off a bid by Brussels to control Britain's borders
> and ports.

Using the SPEAKING acronym as the first step in our approach to
the analysis of the above text, we can make the following provisional
entries:

Setting: **The discourse context of the event and 'lifeworld'**

(a) The communicable event: the introduction of examples of the
    proposed, new Euro currency, Amsterdam, June 1997.
(b) The shared 'lifeworld' – the assumed shared cultural knowledge
    (ideology), first, generally, from past media discourse, not neces-
    sarily the *Sun*'s (indicated below by *), and second, thematically,
    from past discourse in the *Sun* (indicated by italics) and third, new
    events which may be incorporated into future discourse as ideology
    (indicated by +).

- A new single European currency will be introduced in 1999.*
- The pound sterling will disappear along with all other national
  coinage.*
- The pound and the penny have been in circulation for centuries.*
- The Conservative Party is the main source of political opposition to
  the Euro.*
- *The European Commission is an unelected bureaucracy.*
- *The European Commission is anti-British.*
- *France is an untrustworthy member of the EU.*
- *The economy of Germany is unsound.*
- *Further integration with Europe threatens to deprive Britain of control*
  over its frontiers.
- The new currency is unaesthetic in appeal, impractical for use and
  will be unpopular in Britain as well as in the rest of Europe.+
- The new currency is worth less than the British currency.+

Participants: **The originators of the discourse, and the end users**

- Owners: News International (Rupert Murdoch) Strongly opposed
  to the single currency.
- Editor: Stuart Higgins (resigned in 1998).
  Journalist: Keith Perry.

Ends: **Perceived intentional force of discourse**

Influence, persuade and inform (see below).

Acts: **Dominant internal discourse functions**
Identities, relations and representations (see below).

Key: **Social identities and social relations**
- Non-specialist, non-authoritative journalist and non-specialist reader.
- Informal relationship.

Implementation: **The wider context**
- Technology: mass production, circa 3.5 million copies produced daily.
- Finance: part of one of the largest multi-media corporations in the world – News International.
- Legislation: indirect – 46 acts affecting media activity including anti-monopoly laws and Official Secrets Act.
- Regulation: self-regulation by the Press Complaints Commission (PCC) plus external by British Standards Council (BSC).

Norms: **The use of the discourse**
- Mass media.
- Entertainment, information, opinion formation.

Genre: **The internal organisation of the discourse type**
- Newspaper article on topic of public interest.

As we have already suggested, initial, impressionistic entries against the components of the acronym help us place the discourse into an accessible framework of constitutive features which, depending on the perspective from which we wish to examine it, will facilitate informed commentary and analysis. We can be selective in the components we use, according to our needs. Thus, for the purposes of reminding ourselves of the initial conceptual requirements of critical discourse analysis, we can limit ourselves to the entries against Setting, Ends, Acts and Key as exemplified in the next section.

Structuring the analysis discursively

A discursive form of analysis would be structured on the information entered against the following:

Setting: **The status of parts of the discourse, the representations function, ideology and the lifeworld**
(*the social identities and social relations functions are dealt with under 'Acts and Key' below*)
It will be noted under this entry that we try to distinguish between three kinds of discourse formation in order to help us in the analysis. The first, indicated by an asterisk, designates past discourse(s) which are

deemed by reference to our own knowledge to have been generally expressed in a range of media, and not exclusively in the discourse of a particular media outlet (in this case the *Sun*). The second kind, indicated by italics, designates references to a frequently recalled past discourse traceable to a particular media outlet, again in this case the *Sun*, upon which the current discourse draws. Along with the past discourse of the first kind, the second may be said to constitute the dominant ideological content of the particular discourse under analysis. The third kind, indicated by the + sign, effectively constitutes 'new' information or opinion which, depending on the unfolding of future events, may or may not become integrated as 'given' or 'known' information into the on-going Euro-discourse of the newspaper. It should be noted that the conventions of using the asterisk, italics and the + sign for the purposes stated above hold only within the SPEAKING acronym as demonstrated above under Setting. Where they are used elsewhere in the book they may designate other things.

In terms then of the first kind of discourse, past discourse not necessarily attributable to the *Sun*, we can identify from memory the communicable events, together with their own set of ideological assumptions, as described above. Among others, these are the historical origins of the British currency, the probability of a new form of currency being introduced in 1999, the probability of the British currency disappearing sometime in the next century, and the reminder that the Eurosceptic element of the Conservative Party is the foremost opponent of the move towards a single currency. Although this first kind of discourse is of considerable interest, it is the second kind, the past, *distinguishing* discourse of the *Sun* which, by definition, is the focus of our attention here.

Thus for the second kind of discourse, the first noteworthy ideological intervention characteristic of the *Sun* is the use of the items 'Eurocrats' and 'Brussels bosses' to designate the executive of the European Commission. These items are the ideological shorthand which trades on a whole web of assumptions previously asserted in the Eurosceptic discourse which has appeared at regular intervals in the *Sun* as well as in other newspapers and been subsequently reified to the level of fact. This web of previous discourse includes such assumptions as: the European Commission isn't working because it's an inefficient bureaucracy ('Eurocrats'), the European Commissioners are unelected and therefore undemocratically appointed ('Brussels bosses') and the Commission is anti-British ('planning to kill off our favourite coin'). There are other ideological interventions towards the end of this extract which are consistent with the *Sun*'s previous discourse: the quarrelsome, disagreeable context of European Union politics (Britain and Germany ganged up on France), the taken-for-granted corruption of the French ('France cooking the books'), the shared knowledge of the failing German economy ('debt-ridden Germany') and the common knowledge regarding longstanding attempts by the European Commission to determine who enters and leaves British territory ('a bid by Brussels to control Britain's borders and ports').

Finally, we come to the new communicable events, those which hitherto may not be wholly shared, or shared at all between writer and reader but which, at some point in the future may be recalled in the Eurosceptic discourse. Among others we can identify events which overtly assert that the proposed new currency is unappealing in appearance and ill-conceived from the point of view of use by the visually disadvantaged. Most curious of all is the illogical suggestion that, because given the exchange value the cent is less than the penny ('a mere 0.7 of a present day penny'), it is somehow inferior in essence. These assertions, along with others of a similar kind in the article, may be deemed by writer, reader (and discourse analyst) to be 'new' in the sense that they have not appeared previously in the discourse. But they now qualify for reification in the future wherein they return covertly as part of the ideological underpinning of the discourse of Euroscepticism appearing in the *Sun*.

Ends: Perceived intentional force in the discourse of persuasion, influence, and informing (to be placed in a prioritised order)

Entries against this component invite us to make a judgement about the presence and force in the discourse of elements of overt persuasion, of covert influence and of informing (the latter indicated by the presence of a more even-handed discourse in the form of arguments for and against). We initially perceived the order of authorial intention as being one of influence (presence of high level of covert, ideological bias), persuasion (presence of a high level of overt bias) and informing (a low level of even-handedness in the discourse).

This provisionally perceived order of authorial intent of influence, persuasion and informing can be confirmed by subsequent reflection and elaboration by the examples entered below.

- The conspicuous presence of covert, ideological elements of a general kind (asterisked above under Setting), and of particular kind frequently stressed in the past by the *Sun* (in italics above under Setting).
- A high level of overt persuasion, particularly by the use of quotations (secondary discourse) such as 'Mr Whitmore branded the new-look coins as "boring"' and 'They have tried to please every European country but have resulted in a dull-looking coin'.
- An absence of any 'balancing' discourse offering any advantages which may, or are perceived to, flow from a common European currency.

Acts and Key: Social identities and social relations and their relationship with representations
('representations' is dealt with under Setting above)

The representations function of discourse has been already examined under the Setting component above. These two components of Acts and Key call for entries against them which draw upon Fairclough's

(1995) definition of the other two functions which underpin media discourse, (social) relations and (social) identities, firstly under Acts by commenting on the way in which they interact with representations, and secondly under Key by identifying their nature more precisely. We have already commented in Chapter 1 upon the manner in which these functions manifest themselves in the discourse of the *Sun*, but to complete the demonstration of the use of the acronym for the purpose of adopting a critical discourse analysis (CDA) approach, it is worth amplifying here.

Entries under Acts invite the analyst to examine the discourse impressionistically at first, and subsequently to comment on the *balance or relationship* between the discourse functions of representations on the one hand and (social) identities and (social) relations on the other. In this case, it could be argued that the expression of the two functions of social identities and social relations is particularly strong, suggesting that the ways in which the writer and reader identify themselves, and relate to each other in the discourse, *are at least as important as the representations function itself.*

Note for example how the representations function (the introduction of examples of the proposed Eurocurrency) is subordinated to the other two in the headline. The assumed, commonly held social identities of the writer and reader – humorous, non-specialists, sceptical – and the assumed social relationship of informality between them suggested by the slightly risqué allusion to spending a penny, which take precedence over the representation of the introduction of the Eurocurrency. Having assessed under Acts the relationship between the representations function and the other two functions of social identities and social relations, it remains to identify under Key the precise manifestations of the two latter functions. As we have already noted above, the projected identity of writer and reader is one of humorousness, non-specialist common sense and a strong element of scepticism. The reader is deemed to be 'a Brit' and is included in the discourse as one of the victims of the plot wherein 'Eurocrats plan to kill off *our* favourite coin', and also, included in a common sense of humour by seeing the funny side of being 'soon unable to spend a penny'. In the main discourse, items such as 'bosses', 'cash', 'funny money', 'branded', 'slammed', 'ganged up on', 'cooking the books' and 'backfire' reinforce the identity characterised by commonsensical plain speaking presumed to be mutual to writer and reader. With regard to the relations function, all the foregoing points made concerning the identities also contribute to making the assumed relationship between reader and writer to be one of informality and closeness.

Overall summary of the analysis

The results of the analysis undertaken with reference to the components of Setting, Ends, Acts and Key can be summarised as follows below.

The ideological force of this discourse is particularly strong and draws extensively upon the *Sun*'s past Eurosceptic discourse of the kind already identified above. The presence of strong elements of overt and covert bias suggests that the primary purpose of the discourse is to influence (high level of ideological assumptions) and to persuade (high level of overt bias) the reader concerning the non-acceptability of the new currency for the British. The presence of these two biases is in marked contrast to the absence of any 'balancing' discourse suggesting the possible advantages which might accrue from the introduction of the new currency. Throughout the discourse the expression of the discourse functions of identities and relations is particularly strong. Indeed, at times (i.e. in the headline) their expression appears to take priority over the representation of the event itself. The identity projected is one of a common sense of humour, non-specialist know-ledge, common sense, and extreme scepticism. The relation between reader and writer is characterised by informality and closeness.

The components entered under Setting, then, have allowed us to undertake a sufficiently detailed analysis of the discourse of the *Sun* for the purpose of locating this discourse and its ideology within an assumed lifeworld. Entries against other components of the acronym throw further light upon the nature of the discourse. However, it is important to note that the weight we place upon the conclusions that can be drawn from the information under each component varies according to the perspective from which we approach the analysis. Thus for critical discourse analysts the entries under Setting (communicable events, ideology and lifeworld), Acts and Key (underlying discourse functions of representations, identities, and relations) cover some of the essential concepts necessary for CDA. On the other hand, information entered under the other components is helpful in providing additional data which may be used for placing the discourse within a wider socio-cultural or statistical context, across the system as a whole, and in which the written press in particular can be compared.

Tony Blair's speech to the French National Assembly 24 March 1998

President, Prime Minister, Ministers, Deputies: I am delighted to be able to speak to the National Assembly today, and am most grateful to you, President Laurent Fabius, for inviting me to do so.

Britain and France are both countries of achievement, and ambition. Many things link our countries. Our deep sense of nationhood. Our pride in our history. Our military prowess. Our science and engineering. Our standing shoulder-to-shoulder in the great struggles of this century. Our political engagement on a global scale.

Our lawyers, police forces and even National Libraries are linked. Our film industries have co-produced 80 films. France leads the world in fashion – but with three Britons heading major French fashion houses. Some 1500 French and British assistants take part in the world's largest annual exchange of teachers.

France is the holiday destination for a third of everyone from Britain going to Europe. Five times as many holiday visits are made from Britain to France than the other way round. And spending by British tourists in France is three times the total spending of French visitors to Britain. So we've got some ground to make up.

But some 100,000 French people are believed to be living in Britain now. This is a different kind of cohabitation, and, like the other kind, also successful. More than trade and work, we exchange ideas and tastes, too. About fashion. Food. Design. Lifestyle. Culture. The other night I had the pleasure of watching Juliette Binoche at the theatre, in *Naked*. She was wonderful.

Between the people of our countries there is a genuine contact. It is real. It is rooted. And it matters. And today, France and Britain face the same challenges of profound economic, social and political change.

To some, the New Labour government in Britain exhibits what they call an ideological confusion. How can you say you are of the left but welcome business into government? How can you help the poor but say you are in favour of wealth and an absence of penal taxes on it? How can you introduce greater competition and yet say you are in favour of job security? How are you against too much power being vested in government but in favour of social action?

But to me, there is no confusion. There is, instead, an attempt to make realistic sense of the modern world. It is a world in which love of ideals is essential, but addiction to ideology can be fatal. It is a world in which people seek from their governments not dogma and doctrine, but a strong sense of national purpose, underpinned by clear values.

196

Above all, it is a world in which ordinary people see change happening at a pace and depth they find frightening. They seek security amidst the whirlwind. They try to retain some control over their lives as change hurls them this way and that.

Our task as modern governments, is to help them do it. But here is the dilemma. People know that change cannot be resisted. There is no comfort in isolation. It doesn't work. But neither do they want change to control them, to rule them. So: our task is to equip people for change, to shape its impact, to make sense of it, to embrace it in order that we make it work for us.

In case anyone should doubt the nature of change, just look around us. Global financial markets that can send currencies and shares soaring or falling. Mass media, music, art and communications that alter tastes, perceptions and national culture with stunning rapidity. New technology and competition transforming the world of work, bringing revolutions in jobs and industries. In turn, this breaks up traditional family and social structures, which are already feeling the effects of changes in social and moral thinking. Much of this is exhilarating. But its impact is enormous on the lives of our people.

What impresses me most is not the differences in the challenge this change poses for our countries. It is the similarities. And not just for countries like France and Great Britain that are at similar stages of economic development. But in Latin America, in Eastern Europe, in the Far East, even in parts of Africa. All of us struggle with these two questions:

- How do we equip ourselves for economic change?
- How do we impose some order in the face of social change?

In other words, how to provide security in a world of change? Our guide has to be our values. And here let me explain what I mean when I talk of a Third Way or New Labour. My conviction is that we have to be absolute in our adherence to our basic values, otherwise we have no compass to guide us through change. But we should be infinitely adaptable and imaginative in the means of applying those values. There are no ideological preconditions, no pre-determined veto on means. What counts is what works. If we don't take this attitude, change traps us, paralyses us and defeats us. But it is modernisation for a purpose. These values: solidarity, justice, freedom, tolerance and equal opportunity for all, the belief in a strong community and society as the necessary means of individual advancement. These are the values that drive and govern my political life.

But to fulfil those values now, today, we need new ways of working, and of recreating the bonds of community life. In each case, it will mean a changed role for government.

In economic terms, it has four consequences. First, we must maintain strong, prudent discipline over financial and monetary policy, within financial systems that are open and transparent. There is no right or left politics in economic management today. There is good and bad.

The situation in Asia has been an object lesson in why a lack of transparency and clarity leads to crisis. In Britain we have given the Bank of England independence in setting interest rates and we have dramatically reduced the budget deficit. The price is hard. Short-term interest rates have gone up; the spending squeeze has been unpopular. But long-term it must be right and will pay dividends.

Secondly, the role of government becomes less about regulation than about equipping people for economic change by focusing on education, skills, technology, high quality infrastructure and a Welfare State which promotes work and makes it pay. This is the third way: not *laissez-faire* nor state control and rigidity; but an active government role linked to improving the employability of the workforce.

Thirdly, we need specific measures to tackle the scourge of social exclusion. I mean that group of people cut off from society's mainstream, inhabiting a culture increasingly connected with crime, drugs, family instability, poor housing and education and long-term unemployment. Since taking office, we have launched the largest programme of work for the young and long-term unemployed Britain has ever seen. We have set up a specific unit – the Social Exclusion Unit – to coordinate action across government departments to meet this challenge. I believe in one nation, one Britain. There should be none shut out from its opportunities.

Fourthly, we need a new emphasis on entrepreneurship, small business creation and creating a climate in which our people are ready to take risks in becoming self-employed, in learning new ways of working, in recognising that starting your own business is a natural and sensible thing to do.

As proof of that, I am pleased to announce that Lionel Jospin and I have agreed that the British and French governments will work together closely on the specific issue of encouraging small businesses.

We are establishing a Franco-British Task Force, led on the UK side by David Simon, to examine specific ways in which public policy at national and, where appropriate, European levels would be made more positive towards the smaller business sector.

The Task Force will examine business start-ups and their early development. It will consider how we can get wider access for entrepreneurs to venture capital on the right terms. It will look at difficult questions such as regulatory structures, cost burdens and how an economy with a preponderance of small firms ensures an adequate supply of high quality labour to the business sector. We are asking the Task Force to report back by October 1998 and identify key areas for priority action.

None of this means that in Britain we reject the idea of basic fair terms of employment for people. The New Labour Government is introducing a minimum wage, trade union representation, and has signed the Social Chapter. What is more, I embrace with enthusiasm the notion that successful companies are those which value their workforce and regard them as partners in the enterprise.

But the partnership must show an understanding on both sides of the challenge the modern economy poses. The word 'flexible' has a loaded meaning in the French translation. But for me it means adaptable. In the world of change, business and employees need to be constantly open to new ideas and new opportunities; constantly adapting so that change can be properly faced. If our labour market or our economy becomes too rigid, if it is too hard for businesses to function effectively or too expensive for them to employ, the result is merely another form of injustice. In truth, the best job security today comes not simply from legal protection but from having skills, making the most of your talent and having an active employment and welfare service that enables you to move on and move up.

In the end, none of our nations can compete in the old way. There is no future as low wage, low skill sweatshop economies with the rewards going to the few, in the hope they trickle down eventually to the many.

Nor is there any hope in maintaining the old processes of mass production, of intervention and control. Rather we use the power of government to set a framework in which the potential and talent of our people is liberated, in which new businesses can be created and old ones adapted to survive. We called last week's Budget – 'new ambitions for Britain'. But it is ambition married to compassion. It is ambition for all.

The challenge is just as great when we analyse the state of our society. Ask any of our constituents what is their biggest worry, and large numbers will say: crime and the fear of crime. I remember in my constituency in the north of England, growing up there, when you could leave your door unlocked without any hint of fear, where elderly people were treated with respect. Yes, the young men fought as they always have. But there was not the sheer brutality and wickedness we see in our cities and even our towns today, crimes which leave numb our powers of comprehension.

For some, the objective is to get back to the old days. But it is an illusion, as indeed many of the best political lines are. In that north of England constituency, in those old days, there were 25 local mines. Everyone knew everyone. People worked together. At night in the club or pub they socialised together. Today, there are no mines left. The communities do not have that powerful glue to bind people together. But, of course, their standard of living is higher, they enjoy the good things of life in a way their grandparents never dreamt of. Women have the chance to work. That is good. There are different attitudes to sex, sexuality, to the moral world.

Yet amongst the material wealth and freedom, people search for stability. We need to respond to that quest. We need to fashion some order amongst the disintegration. People want a society free from prejudice but not from rules. In Britain now, we are toughening up our youth justice system; there are stronger penalties for certain crimes. We have banned guns. We are taking new measures against drugs. Parents are being held more responsible for the conduct of their children.

We are trying to tackle the underlying causes of crime; fighting social exclusion, creating jobs, improving the worst estates in some of our cities. But also – here again a third way – we are examining how to strengthen family life, attacking truancy and indiscipline at school and insisting that our welfare system is there to provide opportunity, not to be fleeced by fraud, abuse and people playing the system. The new contract between citizens and society is made up of rights, but also of responsibilities.

We should combine these measures with an absolute commitment to equality of treatment for all our citizens. We may be Conservative or Labour in our politics. But when it comes to race, we are all human beings. And we must never allow the evil of racism to disfigure our nations. That is one lesson Europe does not need to repeat.

In meeting both the economic and the social challenge we face, we need a new and changed concept of government itself.

Our people have almost lost confidence in the very institution of government. They believe it is bloated, inefficient, and designed to look after itself rather than to help them. It is only by reinventing the machinery of government that we can begin to reconnect the governed and those that govern them.

Government should not try to do everything itself, but work with private and voluntary sectors. The government should set the parameters and policy goals, but it does not always have to deliver the outcome itself.

Power should be decentralised. A project you in France started in 1982. The hardest thing of all for any government to do is to give power away. But we believe in subsidiarity not just for Brussels but for Whitehall and Westminster too. Power should be exercised as close as possible to the people whose lives it affects. We are passing legislation to devolve power to a Parliament in Scotland and an Assembly in Wales, and we will do the same in Northern Ireland where we continue to work for peace.

The citizen should have clear rights and they should be properly protected. That is why we are going to pass a Freedom of Information act. That is why we require information about the performance of schools, hospitals, and local government to be made public.

Yet it is these same fundamental changes which call for new ways of working and organising our society that impel us to cooperate ever more closely between nations. Just over half a century ago, Europe was at war. Then for 40 years or more, the Iron Curtain descended. Now we are members of the European Union, and clamouring to enter are the former East European communist dictatorships. It is on any basis a remarkable achievement.

Yet here too the challenge of change confronts us. Let me first clear away any remaining doubts about the new British Government's position. Britain's future lies in being full partners in Europe. At Amsterdam, we played a constructive part in bringing about a new European Treaty. Now, as EU President, we are launching the enlargement negotiations and doing our best to ensure the Euro starts successfully.

As for Britain joining the Euro, there must be sustainable economic convergence between our economies. That does not presently exist. I have never made any secret of my concerns at the economic risks in EMU unless the economic conditions are correct. It is a very big step, which implies huge changes in our economies. We have said that a single currency in a single market makes sense and already British business and the City of London are fully geared up to dealing in and using the Euro. We will be prepared – do not doubt that – and will make a decision based on clear and unambiguous economic facts.

But you do not have to be a Eurosceptic, in any shape or form, to appreciate the deep concern amongst our peoples as to how they make sense and relate to the new Europe. They worry about their national identity. They find, let us be frank, Brussels and the European institutions often remote and unsympathetic. They ask what Europe does for them. It comes back to their search for control and freedom over their own lives, when they see so much change around them.

I believe these concerns can be answered. I believe too that France and Britain can help, together, to answer them. But we have to explain to our people what our vision of Europe is.

I believe in a Europe of enlightened self-interest. Without chauvinism. It is the nation–state's rational response to the modern world. If globalisation of the world economy is a reality, if peace and security can only be guaranteed collectively, if the world is moving to larger blocs of trade and cooperation – and look at ASEAN or Latin America – if all this is so, then the EU is a practical necessity. I happen to share the European idealism. I am by instinct internationalist. But even if I weren't, I should be internationalist through realism. The forces of necessity, even of survival, are driving us to cooperation. In the United Nations, in Bosnia, no less than in international trade.

But we politicians must constantly explain, and justify, our vision. For me, the spirit of Europe's development is the idealism of practical people; high ideals pursued with new realism.

I have little doubt Europe will in time move closer still. But choosing where and how to move closer will determine whether our peoples accept these changes or rebel against them. There is a sense in which there is a third way in EU development also. We integrate where it makes sense to do so; if not, we celebrate the diversity which subsidiarity brings.

In economic union, in trade and the single market, in the conditions of competition, it makes complete sense for us to cooperate ever more closely. How can we tackle the environmental challenges, pollution and the degradation of our planet, except together? How can we defeat organised crime and the menace of drugs other than together. In all these areas, cooperation and integration over time is sensible and is clearly in our self-interest.

There is one other area in which France and Britain are particularly well qualified to cooperate: defence. In defence we can and should do more together.

We are both nations that are used to power. We are not frightened of it or ashamed of it. We both want to remain a power for good in the world. And we start off with great advantages. We both possess a minimum nuclear deterrent. We are both permanent members of the Security Council. We have without doubt the best equipped, most deployable, most effective military forces in Europe.

During the last government, defence contacts between the military of our own two countries did improve. We set up a joint nuclear commission for the first time. We are also working together to harmonise our doctrine and procedures for peacekeeping.

More than that, on the ground in Bosnia, our soldiers led the UN Force, delivering vital aid through three winters of war. On the ground, Britain and French forces enjoyed the closest possible cooperation, serving under each other's command. I would like this process of practical cooperation to advance much further and faster.

Now is the time for a new initiative on the military side. We are in the final stages of conducting a major defence review. You are in the middle of the complex process of professionalising and restructuring your armed forces. When our review is complete, I am asking the Defence Secretary and Chiefs of Staff to report to me urgently on the scope for future Anglo-French cooperation. How we can create a capacity to deploy forces rapidly on a joint basis in future crises, where both countries agree.

I know that some feel that being close with the United States is an inhibition on closer European cooperation. On the contrary, I believe it is essential that the isolationist voices in the United States are kept at bay and we encourage our American allies to be our partners in issues of world peace and security. Strong in Europe. Strong with the United States. That should be our goal.

So in some areas, we integrate more closely. In others, how we run our education and health systems, welfare state, personal taxes, matters affecting our culture and identity I say: be proud of our diversity and let subsidiarity rule. We don't want a Europe of conformity, a United States of Europe run by bureaucrats.

A word of warning here, perhaps. We have an economic framework for the EU. We now need a political framework that is dramatically more relevant, more in touch than the present one. I say this quite apart from the pressure of enlargement. The next step for Europe is to match its vision of its economic role with one for its political and social role.

This political vision for Europe is necessary now more than ever. There is a political deficit, which our people feel keenly. As we enlarge, there is the opportunity for us to reconsider the essential mechanisms of political accountability and control. We have had the courage to create the European Union. We must now have the courage to reform it.

For Europe to grow and prosper, Europe must be close to ordinary people's concerns. Europe must reflect the wider social and moral values we all share. The construction of Europe must not reflect a technical commitment to the market-place – but a political commitment to community. Europe must reflect the best of our regional and national traditions. It must be founded on our heritage of freedom, and of social concern. It must be confident. Its economy must be dynamic, innovative and open to the outside world.

I want to work with you to achieve this. The first vote I cast was in favour of Britain entering the Common Market. As I watch my children grow up now, I want them to live in a Europe in which they feel as at home in the glory of Paris, the beauty of Rome, the majesty of Vienna as they do in their own London, where they enjoy a Europe peaceful, secure and prosperous because men like Monnet and Schuman and, yes, Churchill had the vision to declare that the world they found was not going to be the world they would leave to future generations.

I believe that you, in France, share that vision with the British. So let us open up a new epoch in relations between Britain and France. Today I stand before you, conscious of the gap that separates me from the generation formed by the war. But pledging on my behalf, and on behalf of my country, that the friendship between Britain and France must be renewed.

That is my ambition: that France and Britain come closer together in a real entente, a deep entente, and in a genuine partnership with the other countries of Europe. Let us create together a new world on the old continent.

William Hague's speech to the INSEAD Business School, Fontainebleau 19 May 1998

Monsieur Borges, staff and students of INSEAD, thank you for inviting me to Fontainebleau.

I come here to address members of my generation – born in peace, enjoying unrivalled prosperity, secure in freedom, proud of our inheritance, and anxious to pass it on to our children. I want to talk to you about the potential for Europe and about the limits to European Union.

I cannot think of a better place to make this case. For you are the people with the youth and ambition and talent to go out and conquer the new world of opportunities. INSEAD may be a European Institution – but it has a global outlook. Such places are the future. Such people are the future.

The last time I was in INSEAD I was an MBA student. Living in France, studying in Fontainebleau, was one of the most rewarding years of my life. George Doriot, the founder of INSEAD, had a vision of a truly international business school where students from different cultures and different professional backgrounds could come together and learn not just from their teachers but from each other.

When I was a student here I was in a class with people from twenty-five different nations. This year's MBA class is made up of students of fifty different nationalities. French, British, American, Korean, Japanese, German, Argentinian, Italian and Indian to name just a few. A truly global community brought together here to learn about competing in global markets. A global community that has an interest in Europe.

I believe the nations of Europe have the potential to seize the great economic opportunities of the new century. And the European Union can be a force for peace, stability and prosperity in an uncertain world.

But I fear that the European Union is in danger; in danger of accepting without debate a political destination agreed forty years ago; in danger of proceeding with political integration not because it is right but because it is said to be inevitable; in danger of living in the past rather than facing up to the future.

There are European politicians who believe that the EU should continue down the path to closer integration. They believe there should be a common European foreign and defence policy. They believe that there should be a common EU criminal justice and immigration policy. They want tax and spending powers taken out of the hands of national exchequers and given to Brussels. And many of them believe our ultimate objective should be the creation of a single European state, and that this is an inevitable destiny.

I believe they are wrong. There is a limit to European political integration. We are near that limit now.

I intend to make three arguments. The first is economic.

The European policies that were a natural response to the problems of post-war reconstruction are not necessarily appropriate for the future. In place of the ideas of intervention and regulation we need to create a free and flexible Europe.

My second argument is strategic. The fall of the Berlin Wall has completely changed the challenge facing European states. Bringing prosperity and stability to newly free states is now the most urgent of Europe's tasks.

And the third argument is political. Push political integration too far and accountability and democracy become impossible to sustain.

On 1 January 1999 eleven Western European countries will take a momentous step. They will adopt a single currency between them and accept the authority of a single central bank.

But momentous though this step will be, it will create as many problems as it solves. And the most important is the danger that the single currency will lead to an increasingly centralised Europe.

I therefore believe that Europe should not press on towards an unacceptable degree of political union just to make the single currency succeed. I fear that a single currency could push us beyond the limits to Union.

A single thread running through these three arguments is that it is not the critics of the current direction of the European Union who are isolationist, out of date or even anti-European. Rather it is the EU's direction which is in danger of becoming isolationist. It is its post-war assumptions that are increasingly out of date. And it is the danger of integration and the abandonment of our continent's diversity and pluralism that is anti-European.

I shall argue that true internationalism is about the relationship between states rather than their integration into a single state.

I shall argue that the nation state is not an outmoded concept, but is the best vessel for true democracy.

I shall argue that the real pro-Europeans, the people who really want to see a peaceful prosperous cooperating Europe, are the opponents of further political union and the supporters of a confident outward looking Europe of nation states.

I shall argue, too, that the favourite observation of integrationists – that technology is shrinking the world and that nation states cannot operate on their own – is in fact a strong argument against an exclusive Western European grouping. 'Little Europe' is as unattractive a vision as 'Little England'. For my country that means that our friendship with English-speaking nations remains vital and should be strengthened, and our role as a bridge between those nations and the nations of Europe will be of increasing importance.

Our generation should always be grateful to the generation of Europeans and Americans who rebuilt Europe, who restored freedom, who fought the Cold War, who built stable democracy, who ensured prosperity, who replaced enmity between states with friendship.

But now it is our turn. Our turn to unite Europe after the Cold War. Our turn to defend freedom and stability now that the familiar landmarks of the post-war era have been removed. Our turn to advance prosperity when economic opportunities and challenges are presenting themselves. Our turn to defend democracy, community and nationhood in a time of uncertainty.

And I do not believe that we can succeed by simply taking the ideas of the post-war generation and applying them to new problems. We must not allow Europe's future to be driven by an obsession with Europe's past.

To understand where the European Union is presently heading, you have to understand where it has come from.

The twentieth century has been the bloodiest century in a long line of bloody centuries for Europe. Forty-five million Europeans, a majority of them civilians, lost their lives in two World Wars of unprecedented horror and suffering. The slaughter of the trenches, the firebombing of cities and the pure evil of the Holocaust left indelible scars on the millions more who survived.

At the heart of the conflicts lay a lethal rivalry between Germany and France that extended back past the Franco-Prussian War, Napoleon and even the wars of the French revolution.

The political leaders who emerged from the rubble to build a new, post-war Europe devoted themselves to the task of ensuring that future war in Western Europe became unthinkable. After what they had been through, who could say they were wrong?

The means of preventing future war devised by Jean Monnet, Altiero Spinelli, Robert Schuman and others was based on three ideas: economic, strategic and political.

The economic idea was that economic planning and coordination was essential to rebuild the war-devastated economies of Europe.

The strategic idea was that establishing a political community that would inextricably bind France and Germany together would prevent war in Western Europe and at the same time put them at the heart of a Western bloc capable of checking Soviet expansion.

The political idea was that democracy and freedom would thrive when nationalism was eradicated and nation states replaced with a supranational political structure and a new European identity.

These ideas came together with Monnet's extraordinary powers of persuasion, to provide the driving force for the remarkable experiment that has resulted in the European Union. These ideas and Monnet's gradualist method have remained constant as the community has changed.

The post-war history of Western Europe has seen some great successes. Europe has enjoyed the longest period of peace in its history, with the nations of Western Europe uniting together in the NATO alliance rather than fighting each other. War between France and Germany, once unavoidable, is now unthinkable. The once fragile democracies of Greece, Spain and Portugal are now as secure as any in the world. Across the Union, peace and stability has brought rich economic rewards. And the only battles are those fought over a good lunch at the European Council.

The EU should take its fair share of the credit for bringing these things about, as too should NATO, the United States and the nations of Western Europe themselves.

They are real achievements. I salute them. But the time has come to ask whether a fifty-year old solution devised to heal a war-torn continent should dictate what happens in Europe over the next fifty years. I believe that it should not. But I fear that it might.

The task for our generation is to persuade the European Union that it has to stop addressing the problems of the 1940s with solutions devised in the 1950s, and start facing up to the challenges of the new century.

The immediate economic problems after the war were how to rebuild industries, how to get international trade flowing again and how to construct welfare systems that protected populations from the kind of hardship Europe had suffered under in the 1930s and during the war.

To the post-war generation the success of corporatist and interventionist economics was barely contested. Europe's leaders wanted to use it to not only rebuild Europe's economies but also to ensure that those economies were intertwined in such a way as to make war between the countries concerned economically impossible.

They began with the materials most necessary for war: coal and steel. The 1951 Treaty founding the European Coal and Steel Community refers to the need to 'substitute for age-old rivalries the merging of their essential interest' and to the task of building 'a broader and deeper community among peoples long divided by bloody conflict'.

This was taken forward in The Treaty of Rome which created a European *Economic* Community. And the Single European Act was introduced for the ostensible economic reason of helping to create the Single Market. This economic drive has now reached its apotheosis in the most grandiose and far-reaching European project of all – economic and monetary union.

Interventionism was at the heart of Monnet's vision and has led the drive towards political integration throughout the EU's history. But for some reason the failure of interventionism in the West and the spectacular collapse of communism in the East does not seem to have dented the EU's faith in the power of the state.

There is still great confidence, for example, in the efficacy of government intervention and the ability to provide social protection through labour market regulations.

These are old economic solutions and they are not right for new economic circumstances. For we now live in a world of opportunities unimaginable even a generation ago.

Billions of dollars and pounds and yen flow freely from one country to another at the touch of a button, information flashes across the globe in microseconds and journeys that a hundred years ago took months – and only 40 years ago took days – now take hours.

Businesses are becoming truly international in their outlook. Take the example of McKinsey, the management consultants I joined after I left INSEAD. The firm was founded in America. But it now has 74 offices in 38 different countries in five continents. McKinsey, like so many other firms today, no longer calls one country home.

Some argue that the proper response to globalisation is to create ever bigger economic and political units. They point to some of the large multi-national mergers that have recently taken place. But we are in fact in the age of the small unit. An age of small businesses and increased self-employment, an age of small cable TV companies and the Internet, an age when it is almost as easy for anyone to do business across the world as it is to do business across the street, and an age in which the idea of a physical market confined to one part of the globe is out of date.

In the age of the global economy, only the open, nimble and lightly regulated will thrive.

The European Union is slowly starting to face up to some of the challenges of this new world economy.

I applaud the vigour with which the EU, and particularly Commissioner Leon Brittan, has pressed the case for freer trade in the World Trade talks. And I welcome the fact that the EU has at least started to talk about the problems of heavy regulation.

The current rhetoric suggests that the Union has begun to recognise that the economic solutions of the 1950s are no longer appropriate. But to date only the language has changed. We need to go much further.

There are now more than twenty million unemployed people in the EU. European economies have the highest levels of structural unemployment of any advanced economies in the world. Europe is being out-priced and out-competed. Our record at job creation is lamentable. More new jobs were created in the US in just two months last year than in all the countries of the European Union together in the last ten years. The reason is that Europe has social overheads that make it the most expensive place in the world to employ someone.

It is hardly surprising unemployment is relatively high here in France when it costs a French employer an extra 410 FF in non-wage social costs for every 1000 FF it pays out in wages to an employee: an astonishing 41 per cent on-cost. By comparison Japanese employers face social costs which add only 16 per cent to wage bills while British non-wage costs are even lower at 15 per cent.

High unemployment is a human tragedy and a political time-bomb for Europe. Nothing is more likely to foster extremism and xenophobia than an economic system which throws people out of work and leaves them blaming 'Europe'. The nations of Europe have the potential to defuse that time-bomb.

I believe the EU has the potential to achieve a great deal in the economic field – particularly in the four areas of competitiveness, the single market, lower taxation, and free trade.

I believe the EU should throw its weight behind the drive for greater competitiveness. European businesses will find it increasingly difficult to compete in global markets if they remain overburdened with social costs and inflexible employment laws. Instead of contributing to high unemployment by introducing statutory working weeks, the EU should be encouraging Member States to make their labour markets much more flexible.

I believe the EU should also recognise the case for lower taxes. The recent ECOFIN Council, chaired by the British Chancellor of the Exchequer, called for an end to 'harmful tax competition' – a euphemism for removing from national governments their power to set their own tax levels. Why? The EU should be encouraging tax competition between its member states so that across Europe tax rates can fall and the people can keep a greater share of their own income.

I believe the EU should make sure that the Single Market is properly completed. People think it has been completed. But state subsidies, unfair public procurement rules, and uneven enforcement of EU regulations mean that many small and medium sized companies still find it difficult to export in the Single Market.

And I believe the EU should build on its record of promoting freer trade by setting itself the ambitious goal of achieving global free trade by the year 2020.

The nations of Europe are uniquely placed to take this forward. Ties of history, culture and language have given us special relationships with all parts of the world. Britain has its relationship with the English-speaking world. There is also that between Spain and Latin America, France and Africa, the Netherlands and Indonesia, Portugal and Brazil. In other words, Europe has the best contacts in the world.

So I want to see the European Union take the lead in promoting global free trade through a new round of WTO talks.

I welcome the EU's New Transatlantic Marketplace initiative which aims to remove industrial tariffs by 2010, create a free trade area in services, further liberalise investment and remove the technical barriers to trade that can prove so frustrating to exporters. European businesses alone could benefit to the tune of a staggering £100 billion a year from this initiative.

But why limit our ambitions? I want to see the free trade initiative taken further. For example, why is the multi-billion dollar financial services industry excluded? Let's take up Newt Gingrich's offer of support and ensure the EU and NAFTA works together to create a transatlantic free trade area. And let's not stop there either. We should aim to abolish the very concept of a free trade area by making the whole world a giant free trade area.

This will be an immense challenge for the European Union. We can conquer world markets and make the next century a prosperous one for the peoples of Europe. It is a great prize and we must have the determination and the dedication to fight for it. And we will need exceptional political leadership if we are to win through.

Instead, I fear that the EU is channelling its energies in the wrong direction. I fear that European politicians have been concentrating on EMU at the expense of assisting and liberating Europe's businesses. It is time for new economic vision.

And just as the Union's economic policies, conceived in the 1950s, are showing their age, so too are its strategic assumptions.

Europe's peacemakers had hoped to unite in permanent peace a continent divided by war. But long before the Treaty of Rome was signed Europe was divided once again.

We had the tension of the Cold War, the Berlin Airlift, the Hungarian Uprising and the Prague Spring, Checkpoint Charlie and the Four Minute Warning.

The European Union played a crucial role in binding together the democracies of Western Europe in the face of Soviet tyranny. And in making war between Germany and France unthinkable, it has achieved what at times in history has seemed impossible.

But the landscape of Europe has now changed completely. For fifty years the ancient kingdoms of Central and Eastern Europe were frozen under the glacier of Communism. That glacier has now receded, and the first tentative shoots of democracy have spread and need to become deep-rooted. The Ice Age of the Cold War is finished.

The old problems of Franco-German war and the Soviet threat are now things of the past. Instead the new danger is that the drive for political union in Western Europe that effectively excludes the new democracies from its heart will perpetuate a divided Europe.

Eastward enlargement is spoken of so often and in such grandiose terms that we can become numb to what it really means. But the phrase 'historic duty' is, in this context, for once truly apposite.

In the first place, Western Europe has a straightforward moral obligation to the states which, at Yalta, were handed over to Communism. Second, integrating the markets of Central and Eastern Europe is a tremendous commercial opportunity for all Europe's businesses. And third, repeatedly spurning countries which have gone through such pain to qualify for membership will eventually have the effect of bolstering the most reactionary and anti-Western elements in them, which would feed off a perfectly understandable resentment against Brussels. This could jeopardise the stability of the whole continent.

So eastward enlargement is as much a question of hard-headed self-interest as of Western altruism.

The irony is that an institution which was conceived as a means of uniting Europe could divide our continent just as surely as the Iron Curtain.

On the surface of it, the EU appears to be preparing for enlargement. At Copenhagen in 1993 the EU leaders committed themselves to opening the doors to the new democracies of eastern and central Europe. Poland, the Czech Republic, Hungary, Slovenia and Estonia have been allowed to start the complicated negotiations to join. Five other countries have been offered the carrot of eventual membership.

In London earlier this year 25 European leaders gathered to congratulate themselves on the progress they have made. But, so far, the EU has confined itself to hollow statements of intent. No practical steps have been taken to prepare for enlargement. Indeed, the Amsterdam summit, billed as the summit for enlargement, resulted in a Treaty which takes Europe in precisely the opposite direction.

Because the Union cannot expand without first overhauling its policies and institutions. That means radical reform of the CAP, cutting out price distortion and providing properly for farmers. That means sorting out the Community budget and the structural funds.

Expanding the membership of the EU will lead some to call for extensions in the use of qualified majority voting. This call should be resisted. It is true that a wider membership means getting more countries to agree before a decision can be made. But the discipline of getting nation states to agree is a vital control on EU policy making and should not be relaxed.

When it comes to preparing the EU for enlargement we have seen a conspicuous failure of leadership. But that is as nothing compared to the potentially disastrous way in which the Commission looks like fixing the system against new members. The EU could all too easily make the peoples of central and eastern Europe into second-class citizens. This must be stopped. This must end.

Instead of forcing new countries to agree long transition periods before they can join, they should be admitted to the EU as soon as possible. And instead of forcing new members to sign up to economic and monetary union as a precondition of membership, let us give them the choice of whether or not they wish to join – the same choice that was given to Britain, Denmark and Sweden.

We have got to reform existing policies to make it easier for others to join. Otherwise they will remain a permanent obstacle to enlargement. Just try for a moment to imagine a common agricultural policy stretching from the reindeer herds of Finland to the citrus groves of Cyprus or a common social policy for Swedish and Slovakian workers. The truth from which we must not shy away is that applicant states must be allowed to retain control over certain areas if they are to participate in the Union.

And why is the Commission reluctant to face this truth? I hope it is not out of a concern that existing members might also want to control certain of their domestic policies – for it is precisely such flexibility that the Union needs if it is to be competitive in the coming century.

The new challenge that confronts our generation is to bring stability to the whole continent by firmly establishing democracy and prosperity in the countries of eastern and central Europe.

What those countries want to hear from us is not that their nationality is a thing of the past. The crowds that marched in Leipzig and Timisoara wanted two things: national independence and political freedom. Those are the values they associate with Europe. Let us not shut them out.

Deepening the Union is not just a distraction from widening. It is the opposite. Neither the rest of the world nor our own descendants will look kindly on us if, out of sheer introversion, we lose this opportunity finally to heal the division of our continent.

Nine years ago the political landscape of Europe was transformed overnight when the young people of Berlin tore down the ugly, concrete wall that divided their city in two.

Yet we still have not shown courage to match the courage of those young people. How much longer must our fellow Europeans wait?

Economic and political integration were just part of the post-war project. The founding fathers of the European Union had a third and even more ambitious goal. They wanted to eliminate what they saw as the root cause of modern war itself – nationalism. They wanted to replace the nation state as the prime source of loyalty for Europe's citizens – and they wanted to replace it with loyalty to a European ideal.

For those on the continent of Europe who had lived under Nazi tyranny, nationalism became understandably tainted by fascism, collaboration and war.

Britain's experience had been quite different. It was our national identity, so powerfully expressed in Winston Churchill's speeches, which had helped see us through the darkest days of the war. For us, patriotism was the focus of our resistance against Nazi tyranny.

We have never been as nervous of national feeling as our continental neighbours and, as a result, I believe we have never really understood, let alone shared, the fears and ambitions of European federalism.

The ultimate goal of the Monnet–Schuman project is to create a European state with its own loyalty, its own identity, its own government and its own citizens. And it has a momentum all of its own.

Over time, the institutions of the European Union have taken key elements of executive, judicial and legislative authority away from the national governments. Most fundamentally of all, the European Court has established the supremacy of European law over national law. The result is a steady erosion of power away from national governments and the ever closer political union envisaged by the Treaty of Rome.

As we enter the new century the original danger which confronted the founding fathers of the European Union has gone. By re-establishing democracy and prosperity across Western Europe, we have eliminated the threat of war. Prosperous, democratic states do not go to war with each other.

If anything, the threat comes from precisely the opposite: the artificial repression of nationality. The lesson of Yugoslavia and the Russian Federation is that it is dangerous to force disparate peoples into a common political unit unless they already feel a sense of national affinity.

I believe there are natural limits to political union beyond which stability and democratic accountability within the nations of the EU itself could be in jeopardy.

I have argued in a series of speeches this year that human beings are more than just economic animals and that not all relationships are simply about buying and selling. There are ties of family and of community and of nation which go beyond the shop counter.

National identity fulfils a basic human need to belong. As Sir Isaiah Berlin argued in his essay on nationalism, *The Bent Twig*: 'to be human, you must be able to feel at home somewhere with your own kind. People ... need to belong to a group where communication is instinctive and effortless'.

Nationalism is not easy to define. It may be shaped by language or by religion or by culture or by other factors. But not always. The Swiss have a strong sense of nationality, which is neither ethnically nor linguistically nor religiously homogenous.

Perhaps the best definition of a nation is this: a nation is a group of people who feel enough in common with one another to accept government from each other's hands. That is why democracy functions best within nations. The defining characteristic of national identity is that when we disagree with a law we do not disobey it, we try to get it repealed. When we dislike the complexion of our government, we do not attempt to secede from its jurisdiction but try to persuade our fellow countrymen to change it. France in this sense is a nation. So is Britain. Europe is not.

Another characteristic of the nation is that it cannot easily be dissolved or abolished. In the eighteenth century, the Polish state was carved up and eventually ceased to exist. The result was almost constant tension and occasional bloodshed. But although the Polish state has spent three quarters of the last two hundred years subsumed and submerged, the Polish national idea was strong enough to survive and allow the Polish nation to be reborn.

General de Gaulle said that 'the nation state and democracy are the same thing'. I believe that nations are essential for real democratic accountability. For democracy to function properly, there has to be a *demos* or people. People must feel their vote counts. That they can influence the decisions that affect them. That they can have their say. And those people must share a common national identity.

This should be borne in mind by those critics of the European Union who complain about the 'undemocratic' nature of its institutions and about the 'democratic deficit' at Strasbourg. And by those who believe that we can integrate more tightly as long as we produce a democratic constitution.

There is, certainly, a marked absence of democratic accountability in almost all that the European Union does. Unelected Commission officials and European Court judges wield enormous power.

The European Parliament has an important job to do. The Commission's management of the Community Budget and the detail of EC legislation need rigorous scrutiny. But the work of European Parliament should be to complement that of national governments and parliaments, not be a substitute for it.

213

The real answer to the democratic deficit is to increase the role of national governments – for they are the real focus of democratic accountability in the EU. The answer is not, as some argue, to increase vastly the powers of the European Parliament or elect a President.

For the European Union will never be a democracy. It may have many of the attributes of a democratic state. It already has an elected Parliament, its own flag and anthem, even its own citizenship. And we could easily add more.

But these are the symbols and trappings of nationality. They are no substitute for real national feeling. The nations of Europe have existed for hundreds of years. They are bound together by ties of tradition and allegiance. The EU cannot, in the space of a few decades, hope to manufacture a sense of nationhood comparable to that which has grown organically among its separate peoples.

Europe is not a nation, but a patchwork of nations. It is made up of many diverse peoples with different languages, different cultures and different political traditions. There is no single European consciousness.

Even trying to get the countries of the EU to agree a common policy on, for example, the recent crisis in Iraq, proved impossible. Different historical links with the Middle East meant different countries approached the issue from different perspectives and came to different conclusions.

Anyone who believes that one day Europe can become a single democratic state needs to answer this question posed by the British academic Noel Malcolm: can we ever imagine a time when a London housewife stays up late on the day of a European general election to watch the leader of the Euro-party they voted for, a Greek, say, make a speech to the people of Europe in Greek? Or, for that matter, the time when a Greek housewife stays up late to watch the latest general election results from London?

I do not believe such a sense of political community in Europe will exist in my lifetime. But I am certain of one thing: if we establish common political institutions without, or at least before, such a sense develops, we will drive our peoples further apart.

That may not stop Monnet's successors from trying. But they would run a grave risk of undoing goodwill painstakingly built up over fifty years of European cooperation.

The peoples of Europe would soon begin to feel that they no longer had a say in the political decisions that affected them. We are already seeing disturbing signs of the rise of extremism: the vote in Saxony-Anhalt last month, the recent by-election in France. People who feel their voice is no longer being heard look for ways to shout louder.

I have to tell you that there is a limit to European integration. We are near that limit now. Push political union beyond its limits and you jeopardise the very peace, stability and prosperity which Europe's post-war statesmen were so anxious to secure.

My fear is that the creation of a single currency will take European political union well beyond its acceptable limits.

I have already set out the economic risks of economic and monetary union in my speech to the Confederation of British Industry last November.

The effect of imposing a one size, fit all, single interest rate on a set of different economies with different cycles, structures and circumstances, could be disastrous.

The single currency is irreversible. One could find oneself trapped in the economic equivalent of a burning building with no exits. But I am also concerned about the effects of EMU on the working of our democracy and our institutions.

Some may wish it otherwise but voters today live their lives in nation states. Voters expect national governments to be accountable to them for the state of their economy: growth, employment, interest rates, mortgages and inflation. If a government is thought to have performed badly it can be changed by the ballot box. That is the essence of our democracy, and underpins its stability.

Under the single currency the one size, fit all interest rate may affect different countries differently. In some countries it might produce rising unemployment. But if it does the voter cannot change the government or the policy. Indeed the government cannot change the policy.

In Asia those countries that have had the most violent reactions to the financial crisis have been those countries that do not have the safety valve of democratic elections. How will the peoples of Europe react to a recession without the electoral means of changing the people responsible?

Of course you can make no direct comparison between the situation in Indonesia and developments in the EU, but as Professor Feldstein, Professor of Economics at Harvard, in a well-known essay subtitled 'Monnet was mistaken' argues, the shift to EMU and the political integration that would follow will lead to increased tension within Europe. Because the single currency will affect different countries in different ways, exacerbating recessionary tendencies in some, and inflationary tendencies in others, new disagreements will reflect incompatible expectations from one policy.

Countries that are concerned about unemployment more than inflation will be critical of the European Central Bank for not pursuing a more expansionary policy. On the other hand, if the German public sees inflation rise, it will become antagonistic towards EMU, and towards the countries that vote for inflationary monetary policy.

But with a single currency these governments would suffer the frustration of not being able to decide for themselves and of being forced to accept the common monetary policy. If governments are likely to feel frustrated how much more frustrated will the voters be?

Professor Feldstein writes: 'if EMU occurs and leads to (such) a political union in Europe, the world would be a very different and not necessarily safer place'. These words may seem alarmist to some, but coming as they do from such a distinguished source, they cannot be ignored.

These are what one might call the political risks of the economic consequences of EMU. But I am also concerned about the direct political consequences of EMU.

The British Prime Minister and his Chancellor of the Exchequer have attempted to argue that the introduction of the Euro has no constitutional implications whatsoever, and is a purely technical question. I find it difficult to believe they really believe this. The Euro has potentially huge political consequences.

Some continental European politicians are quite frank that the purpose of the single currency is political. A single currency was always seen as fundamental to the creation of European political union. Chancellor Kohl has said quite openly that 'if there is no monetary union, then there cannot be political union and vice versa'. The 1992 Maastricht Treaty that creates EMU calls explicitly for the evolution to a future political union. But even without that language, the shift to the single currency would be a dramatic and irreversible step towards that goal.

There are precious few, if any, examples in history of a successful monetary union not related to a single government. There is no sizeable country anywhere in the world that does not have its own currency so why should the introduction of the Euro be any different?

The current President of the Bundesbank, Hans Tietmeyer, has said 'A European currency will lead to member nations transferring their sovereignty over financial and wages policy as well as in monetary affairs. It is an illusion to think that states can hold on to their autonomy over taxation policies'.

Dr Tietmeyer's argument is entirely logical. In any economy, monetary policy on the one hand, and on the other hand tax and spending policy, that is fiscal policy, have to be closely coordinated. In order to make the single currency work I fear the European Union will be forced to intrude more and more into the spending and taxation decisions of individual states. Even if the EU does not actually raise the taxes or spend the money itself, it will increasingly control the decisions.

The powers to raise taxes from one's citizens and to spend the money on their behalf are defining features of a sovereign state. I believe that to delegate powers over taxation and spending to the EU would take us beyond the limits of political union towards the creation of what would in effect be a European state.

It would be to cross a line and abandon the independence of nation states with all the consequences for the future stability of Europe which I have set out today. The centre would have more power than the component parts. It would have neither legitimacy nor accountability since there can be no real accountability except in nation states.

That is why I fear the political consequences of the single currency. For this reason the British Conservative Party is against British membership of the single currency now, and, subject to a ballot of Party members, intends to oppose it at the next General Election.

Today I have set out a positive vision of an open and flexible European Union. But I know that not everyone will receive it in this spirit. For as the intellectual case for the direction upon which the EU is presently set has become weaker, so those who advance the case have become more defensive.

Let me rehearse some of the arguments that will be deployed against what I have said today.

Some will say that this speech is another example of the British causing trouble and being *non communautaire*. I say to them that when Britain joined the EEC we took on responsibilities and pooled some of our power. But we also gained certain rights, and one of them is to have as great a say as any over the future direction of the Union. That's what being *communautaire* means.

Some will say that this speech is too late, that European political integration is inevitable and that Britain must jump on board or miss the boat. I say to them that it is not inevitable that the EU will fail to respond to the new economic opportunities. It is not inevitable that the EU will miss the historic opportunity to unite our continent. It is not inevitable that the EU will push political integration beyond its natural limits. None of these things are inevitable if Europe's political leaders speak out now.

Some will say that this speech is alarmist, that no one wants to create a European superstate. I say to them that everything about the EU's origins and development to date suggests that this is precisely the direction Europe is heading in and unless someone speaks out we will find ourselves dragged into an unsustainable political union.

The EU has already helped to bring together countries torn apart by a world war. Just imagine what it could achieve by uniting a continent divided by a cold war.

The EU has already helped spread prosperity through Western Europe with the Single Market. Just imagine what it could achieve by completing that single market and liberating Europe's businesses from the dead hand of regulation and social costs.

The EU has already been a powerful force for free trade. Just imagine what it could achieve if it reached out across the Atlantic to build a new trading partnership with North America and set itself the goal of global free trade by the year 2020.

I believe the potential for the European Union is enormous, provided it has the courage and the imagination to recognise that it needs to change direction, accept the limits to political union and embrace the challenges of the new century.

Bibliography

References

Aldrich, R.J. (1998) 'British intelligence and the Anglo-American "special relationship" during the Cold War', *Review of International Studies*, 24:3, 331–51.

Allen, M. (1996) 'Cohesion and structural adjustment', in Wallace, H. and Wallace, W. (eds), *Policy-Making in the European Union*, Oxford: Oxford University Press.

Althusser, L. (1971) 'Ideology and ideological state apparatuses', in Althusser, L., *Lenin and Philosophy*, London: New Left Books.

Anderson, P.J. (1996) *The Global Politics of Power, Justice and Death*, London: Routledge.

Armstrong, H., Taylor, J. and Williams, A. (1995) 'Regional policy', in Artis, M.J. and Lee, N. (eds), *The Economics of the European Union*, Oxford: Oxford University Press.

Artis, M. (1995) 'European monetary union', in Artis, M.J. and Lee, N. (eds), *The Economics of the European Union*, Oxford: Oxford University Press.

Bakhtin, M. (1981) *The Dialogic Imagination*, Austin: University of Texas Press.

Bauman, Z. (1996) 'From pilgrim to tourist – or a short history of identity', in Hall, S. and du Gay, P., *Questions of Cultural Identity*, London: Sage.

Blainey, G. (1988) *The Causes of War*, New York: Free Press.

Bourdieu, P. (1977) *Outline of a Theory of Practice*, trans. Nice, R., Cambridge: Cambridge University Press.

Boyer, J.H. (1981) 'How editors view objectivity', *Journalism Quarterly*, 58:24–28, cited in McQuail, 1992.

Bretherton, C. and Ponton, G. (1996) *Global Politics*, Oxford: Blackwell.

Carey, C., Low, S. and Hansbro, J. (1997) *Adult Literacy in Britain*, London: The Stationery Office.

Dinan, D. (1994) *Ever Closer Union?*, London: Macmillan.

Dyson, K. (1994) *Elusive Union*, London: Longman.

El-Agraa, A.M. (1994) *The economies of the European Community* (4th edn), Hemel Hempstead: Harvester Wheatsheaf.

European Community (1996) *Europe at the Service of Regional Development* (2nd edn), Luxembourg: Office for Official Publications of the European Communities.

Fairclough, N. (1995) *Media Discourse*, London: Edward Arnold.

Featherstone, M. (1991) *Consumer Culture and Post-Modernism*, London: Sage.

Fiske, J. (1987) *Television Culture*, London: Routledge.

Foreign and Commonwealth Office (1998) *Europe Working for the People – UK Presidency: half-term report*, London: Foreign and Commonwealth Office.

Foucault, M. (1972) *The Archaeology of Knowledge*, trans. Sheridan-Smith, A., London: Tavistock.

Fowler, R. (1991) *Language in the News: Discourse and Ideology in the Press*, London: Routledge.

Garnham, N. (1997) 'Political economy and the practice of cultural studies'. in Ferguson, M. and Golding, P. (eds), *Cultural Studies in Question*, London: Sage.

Gavin, N. (ed.) (Forthcoming) *The Economy, Media and Public Knowledge*, London: Cassell.

Giddens, A. (1991) *Modernity and Self-Identity*, Cambridge: Polity.

Gramsci, A. (1971) *Prison Notebooks*, London: Lawrence and Wishart.

Grunberger, R. (1971) *A Social History of the Third Reich*, Harmondsworth: Penguin.

Habermas, J. (1989) *The Structural Transformation of the Public Sphere*, Cambridge: Polity.

Hall, S. (1996) 'Who needs cultural "identity"?', in Hall, S. and du Gay, P., *Questions of Cultural Identity*, London: Sage.

Hirst, P. and Thompson, G. (1996) *Globalization in Question*, Cambridge: Polity Press.

Hobsbawm, E. (1994) *Age of Extremes*, London: Michael Joseph.

Hymes, D. (1972) 'Models of the interaction of language and everyday life', in Gumpertz J.J. and Hymes, D. (eds), *Directions in Sociolinguistics*, New York: Holt, Reinhart and Winston.

Jamieson, B. (1993) *Britain Beyond Europe*, London: Duckworth.

Kellner, D. (1997) 'Overcoming the divide: cultural and political economy', in Ferguson, M. and Golding, P. (eds), *Cultural Studies in Question*, London: Sage.

Kennedy, P. (1993) *Preparing for the Twenty-First Century*, London: HarperCollins.

Leibfried, S. and Pierson, P. (1996) 'Social policy', in Wallace, H. and Wallace, W. (eds), *Policy-Making in the European Union*, Oxford: Oxford University Press.

Leonard, M. (1998) *Making Europe Popular: The Search for European Identity* (The Demos Report), London: Demos/Interbrand, Newell and Sorrell.

Lichtenberg, J. (1990) *Democracy and the Mass Media*, New York: Cambridge University Press.

Marquand, D. (1995) 'After Whig imperialism? Can there be a British identity?' *New Community*, 21(2).

McLeod, A. (Forthcoming) *Europe's Democratic Deficit: Legitimacy and the European Parliament*, Preston: University of Central Lancashire (PhD Thesis).

McQuail, D. (1992) *Media Performance: Mass Communication and the Public Interest*, London: Sage.

Mitrany, D. (1966) *A Working Peace System*, Chicago: Quadrangle.

Morley, D. (1997) 'Theoretical othodoxies: textualism, constructionism and the "new ethnography" in cultural studies', in Ferguson, M. and Golding, P. (eds), *Cultural Studies in Question*, London: Sage.

Nugent, N. (1993) *The Government and the Politics of the European Community*, London: Macmillan.

Park, W. and Wyn Rees, G. (1998) *Rethinking Security in Post-Cold War Europe*, London: Longman.

Peak, S. and Fisher, P. (1997) *The Media Guide*, London: Fourth Estate.

Purdy, D. and Devine, P. (1995) 'Social policy', in Artis, M.J. and Lee, N. (eds), *The Economics of the European Union*, Oxford: Oxford University Press.

SOFRES (1997) 10è Baromètre, *Télérama* No. 2455, 29 January 1997.

Swann, D. (1992) *The Single European Market and Beyond*, London: Routledge.

Tsoukalis, L. (1996) 'Economic and monetary union', in Wallace, H. and Wallce, W. (eds), *Policy-Making in the European Union*, Oxford: Oxford University Press.

Waltz, K.N. (1959) *Man, the State and War*, New York: Columbia University Press.

Weymouth, A. and Lamizet, B. (1996) *Markets and Myths: Forces for Change in the European Media*, London: Longman.

Wyllie, J.H. (1997) *European Security in the New Political Environment*, London: Longman.

Further reading

Chisholm, M. (1995) *Britain on the Edge of Europe*, London: Routledge.

Curran, J. and Gurevitch, M., (eds) (1991) *Mass Media and Society*, London: Edward Arnold.

Curran, J. and Seaton, J. (1998) *Power Without Responsibility*, London: Routledge.

Davis, N. (1996) *Europe: A History*, Oxford: Oxford University Press.

Fairclough, N. (1992) *Language and Power*, London: Longman.

Fairclough, N. (1994) 'Conversationalization of public discourse and the authority of the consumer', in Keat, R., Whiteley, N. and Abercrombie, N. (eds), *The authority of the Consumer*, London: Routledge.

Garnham, N. (1986) 'The media and the public sphere', in Golding, P. *et al.* (eds), *Communicating Politics*, Leicester: Leicester University Press.

Hall, S. (1977) 'Culture, the media and the ideological effect', in Curran, J. *et al.* (eds), *Mass Communication and Society*, London: Edward Arnold/Open University Press.

Halliday, M. (1978) *Language as Social Semiotic*, London: Edward Arnold.

Kennedy, P. (1998) *The Rise and Fall of the Great Powers*, London: Fontana.

Kress, G. (1989) 'History and language: towards a social account of language change', in *Journal of Pragmatics*, 13:445–66.

Kress, G. (1989) *Linguistic Processes in Sociocultural Practice*, Oxford: Oxford University Press.

Kress, G. and Hodge, R. (1979; 1994 revised edition) *Language as Ideology*, London: Routledge.

Kress, G. and Van Leeuwen, T. (1990) *Reading Images*, Victoria: Deakin University Press.

Postman, N. (1987) *Amusing Ourselves to Death: Public Discourse in the Age of Showbusiness*, London: Methuen.

Taylor, P. (1996) *The European Union in the 1990s*, Oxford: Oxford University Press.

Wilson, K. and Van der Dussen, J. (1995) *The History of the Idea of Europe*, London: Routledge/Open University Press.

Index

222